Bringing together a wealth of perspectives fro.   ., ч₁ cultures, *Dance On! Dancing through Life* is an essential contribution to our knowledge about intergenerational dance. Through in-depth case studies and the flow of conversation, it communicates the vital ways that dancing changes perceptions of what the body can do, regardless of age. Expert practitioners share their experiences and contemplate a future for dance that, freed from the prejudice of ageism, is open to the prodigious possibilities of dancing wise and dancing long.

—*Professor Carol Brown*, *Choreographer and Head of Dance, Faculty of Fine Arts and Music, University of Melbourne, Australia*

Dance On! Dancing through Life is a unique and much needed collection of perspectives on dance for all ages. With this book, the editors, Stephanie Burridge and Charlotte Svendler Nielsen, bring their broad experience, fruitful collaboration on previous editorial work, and passion for social justice in the field of dance to a fruition. The book adds to the literature relevant to dance practitioners, researchers and students of all ages and across diverse dance forms. I warmly recommend this valuable reading to anyone, also beyond the dance field.

—*Professor Eeva Anttila*, *Head of Dance Pedagogy, University of the Arts Helsinki, Finland*

DANCE ON!

Burridge and Svendler Nielsen bring together many perspectives from around the world on dancing experiences through life of senior artists and educators, whether as professionals working with community dance groups, in education or for recreation and well-being.

Broadening our understanding of the burgeoning sector of maturing dances and dancers, this book incorporates a range of theoretical approaches with an emphasis on cultural and experiential dimensions. It includes examples of how artists, community practitioners, teachers, policy makers and academics work to better understand, promote and create new ways of thinking and working in the field of dance performance, education and well-being. Each section of the book includes a mixture of chapters based on research and case narratives focusing on practitioners' experience, as well as conversations between world-renowned mature dance artists and choreographers. It features an eclectic mix of lived experiences, wisdom, deep knowledge and reflection.

The book is a valuable resource for students of performing arts, pedagogy, choreography, community dance practice, social and cultural studies, aesthetics, interdisciplinary arts, dance therapy and more. Artists working across generations and in communities can also find useful inspiration for their continued dance practice.

Stephanie Burridge lectures at LASALLE College of the Arts and Singapore Management University and is the Series Editor for Routledge Celebrating Dance in Asia and the Pacific.

Charlotte Svendler Nielsen is Associate Professor and Program Director at the Department of Nutrition, Exercise and Sports, University of Copenhagen, Denmark.

DANCE ON!

Dancing through Life

*Edited by Stephanie Burridge
and Charlotte Svendler Nielsen*

Routledge
Taylor & Francis Group

LONDON AND NEW YORK

Designed cover image: *MIST*
Dancer: Anca Frankenhaeuser
Choreographer: Stephanie Burridge

First published 2023
by Routledge
4 Park Square, Milton Park, Abingdon, Oxon OX14 4RN

and by Routledge
605 Third Avenue, New York, NY 10158

Routledge is an imprint of the Taylor & Francis Group, an informa business

British Library Cataloguing-in-Publication Data
A catalogue record for this book is available from the British Library

ISBN: 9781032310152 (hbk)
ISBN: 9781032310138 (pbk)
ISBN: 9781003307624 (ebk)

DOI: 10.4324/9781003307624

Typeset in Bembo
by Apex CoVantage, LLC

CONTENTS

ACKNOWLEDGEMENTS

Many of the authors in this volume are affiliated with the major international organisations Dance and the Child International (daCi) and the World Dance Alliance (WDA) that serve as primary voices for dance institutions, the industry and dance artists throughout the world by encouraging the exchange of ideas and the awareness of dance in all its forms. The editors would like to recognise the importance of these dance networks as enablers for research and connectivity.

We appreciate the outstanding contributions that the authors have made to this book, which is a vibrant account of dance across continents and countries. Finally, the editors would like to thank Routledge for its foresight in commissioning this volume and their understanding of the complexity of assembling such a rich and diverse collection of authors for the anthology.

AUTHOR BIOGRAPHIES

Conversations

Germaine Acogny founded her first dance studio in Dakar in 1968. She has created her own technique of modern African dance and is often called the "mother of contemporary African dance". Between 1977 and 1982, she was the artistic director of MUDRA AFRIQUE (Dakar), created by Maurice Béjart and the Senegalese president and poet Leopold Sedar Senghor. In 1980, she wrote her first book entitled *African Dance*. In 1985, with her husband Helmut Vogt, she set up in Toulouse, France, the "Studio-Ecole-Ballet-Théâtre du 3è Monde". She returned to the stage as a dancer and choreographer after several years in 1987, touring the award-winning solo *Ye'ou*. In 2004, Acogny and Vogt established "L'Ecole des Sables", a centre for traditional and contemporary African dance in Senegal. She continues to perform solo choreographies around the world and has received numerous awards in Africa and internationally for her choreography and contributions to dance.

'Funmi Adewole (PhD) is a performer, dramaturge and dance researcher. She started out as a media practitioner in Nigeria and moved into performance on relocating to Britain in 1994. For several years, she toured with physical theatre and African dance drama companies whilst working as an arts consultant and voluntarily as a dance advocate. As she has an international reputation as a facilitator and speaker and has participated in conferences and led workshops, labs and discussion groups in West Africa, South Africa, Europe, Canada and the United States. In 2019, she was awarded a lifetime achievement award for contributions to Dance of the African Diaspora in the UK by One Dance UK, the UK National body for dance. She holds a PhD in dance studies and is presently a senior lecturer on the dance programme at De Montfort University, Leicester, England.

Aida Amirkhanian is an American-Armenian choreographer and performer in dance theatre, as well as a yoga teacher. She was born in Tehran; her maternal grandfather was a survivor of the Armenian genocide, from Van. Aida graduated from the world-renowned École Mudra in Brussels, Belgium under the direction of legendary choreographer Maurice Béjart. She has performed internationally with École Mudra and Béjart's Ballet du XXème Siècle. Aida moved in 1982 to Australia, where she continued her multidisciplinary career working in collaboration with many dance and theatre companies including the Human Veins Dance Theatre, the Canberra Dance Theatre, the Jigsaw Theatre Company and Women on a Shoestring Theatre Company. Aida continues her artistic journey in Los Angeles, and she has been creating and performing new solo works as well as collaborating with various artists. In 2004, Aida was nominated for the Horton Dance Awards in Los Angeles as outstanding solo performer.

Artsvi Bakhchinyan (PhD) is a philologist; researcher in Armenian diaspora, film and choreography history; art journalist; writer and translator. Since 2009, he has worked at the Institute of History of National Academy of Sciences of the Republic of Armenia. He is the author, editor, and translator of some 20 books, including *The Armenians in World Dance Scene* (2016) and *Committed to the Most Beautiful Art: Conversations with Choreography Figures* (2018), as well as the full-fledged biography of eminent Armenian dancer and author Armen Ohanian (in Armenian, 2007, in English, 2022, with co-author: Vartan Matiossian). He lives in Yerevan, Armenia.

Stephanie Burridge (PhD) is a dancer, choreographer, writer and researcher. She worked with Antonio Vargas and Flamenco Sin Fronteras on *The Rites Project* (2018) and *We Dance Alone* for the Men's Dancing Project (2021) performance and film. (See full biography in Introduction.)

Elizabeth Cameron Dalman (OAM, PhD) was the founder and first artistic director of Australian Dance Theatre, a company founded in 1965 and is still in existence. She continues to teach, perform and promote contemporary dance. Among her many awards are 2015 Canberra Artist of the Year and induction into the Hall of Fame at the 2015 Australian National Dance Awards. Elizabeth established Mirramu Creative Arts Centre in 1990, and Mirramu Dance Company in 2002. She has created and directed more than 20 works for MDC for theatre and site-specific spaces. From 2016, Elizabeth toured globally with Michael Keegan-Dolan's award-winning *Swan Lake/Loch na hEala*.

Henry Danton was born in England on 30 March 1919. He served in the Armed Forces until the age of 21, when he became a dancer to pursue a career in Sadlers Wells (now The Royal Ballet), Ballet des Champs Elysees, Ballet de Paris and Australian National Ballet. It is interesting to note that Henry's initial training began with the Royal Academy of Dance; he won the Adeline Genée Competition in 1942, danced with The Royal Ballet in its pioneering years in the 1940s, was the original cast in Ashton's *Symphonic Variations*, and eventually lived in the United States and taught in Mississippi, handing down his Russian-influenced method of classical training. His long teaching career includes Ballet Arts in Carnegie Hall, NYC; Martha Graham School, Juilliard; and the founding of Ballet International de Venezuela and Ballet Clasico de Colombia. He continued to teach until he passed on 9 February 2022.

Alex Dea (PhD) is American-born Chinese and studied Western music, and received a PhD in ethnomusicology from Wesleyan University, Connecticut, USA, specialising in Javanese gamelan music. He learnt voice from Pandit Pran Nath, master Hindustani singer, and studied composition with avant-garde minimalist "Bad Boys" La Monte Young, Terry Riley and Robert Ashley. Alex was a member of Young's Theatre of Eternal Music, and was assistant for his masterpiece "The Well-Tuned Piano". Dedicated to full-time ethnography in Central Java Indonesia since 1992, he studied with many of the last performing masters of the pre-Independence. As ethnographer-performer documenting thousands of videos, he had permission to record in Yogyakarta Palace, and is the only non-Javanese to sing regularly in Surakarta Palace with the title K.R.A.T Candradiningrat. Composing inter-cultural music, he worked with Asia's dancers Didik Nini Thowok, Ramli Ibrahim, the late Ben Suharto and others.

Anca Frankenhaeuser performed, taught and choreographed with London Contemporary Dance Theatre for 15 years, touring both internationally and throughout the UK, whilst also graduating with a BA in contemporary dance from the University of Kent. In Australia since 1990, she has taught extensively in dance schools, colleges and tertiary institutions, as well as co-creating and performing independent work with like-minded dancers, actors, singers, musicians and visual artists, including both Patrick Harding-Irmer and Eileen Kramer. Performing Stephanie Burridge's *MIST* for Canberra Dance Theatre earned her an Australian Dance Award nomination for Best Female Dancer. In 2005 she graduated from NIDA with a Master of Dramatic Art, Movement Studies, and she presently works as deviser/director/choreographer/performer, as well as lecturer/tutor of movement for actors, contemporary dance and choreography.

Shirley Gibson is an inaugural member of the Mature Artists Dance Experience (MADE) performing group, is a member of the MADE Board and has performed in most of their productions and toured to Japan (2018) with the company. Her lifetime experience in dance includes directing her own amateur dance company for ten years and a term as vice-president of the Salamanca Arts Committee. She was rehearsal mistress for the Hobart Repertory Theatre, an Australian Ballroom Dancing Champion and instructor, plus teaching movement to people living with neurological conditions in MADE's Movers and Shakers Group. She has danced through 70-plus years.

Patrick Harding-Irmer graduated from Sydney University with BA, Dip. Ed. and in 1973 was invited by Robert Cohan to join London Contemporary Dance Theatre. He remained with that company as dancer, choreographer, teacher and on two occasions, acting artistic director until his return to Australia in 1990. With LCDT he performed extensively throughout the UK and internationally, including two Olympic Arts Festivals in Los Angeles and Seoul. In 1985, he graduated with a BA with honours in contemporary dance from the University of Kent, whilst also maintaining a full-time performing schedule. Since arriving back in Sydney, he has danced with Sydney Dance Company, The Australian Ballet, Opera Australia, The One Extra Dance Company, Dance North, Music Theatre Sydney, Canberra Dance Theatre and in numerous independent projects, including four with Eileen Kramer. Until recently, he has been performing with the Australian Dance Artists, who have been collaborating for many years with renowned sculptor and installation artist Ken Unsworth.

Michael Keegan-Dolan was the artistic director of Fabulous Beast Dance Theatre from 1997–2015. He founded Teaċ Daṁsa in 2016 and now lives in the Corca Dhuibhne Gaeltacht in the southwest of Ireland with his partner Rachel Poirier and their two children. *Swan Lake/Loch na hEala*, the first production he created for Teaċ Daṁsa has toured extensively both nationally and internationally. *MÁM*, his second production, premiered in the Dublin Theatre Festival in 2019 and continues to tour nationally and internationally. He is currently working on new projects and trying to master the Irish language.

Eileen Kramer is a dancer, choreographer, costume designer, artist and writer who was born in 1914 and grew up in Sydney, Australia. Initially she studied singing but seeing the Bodenwieser Ballet, she immediately recognised her main calling. She toured internationally with the company for a decade, also designing and making many of the costumes, until the company folded in 1959 with the death of Madame Bodenwieser. Eileen then left Australia to live, work and create in India, Europe and eventually the United States before returning to Sydney in 2013 in her 100th year. Always actively practising her diverse talents she has, since her return – amongst many other things – written two books and created four dance productions, including the costumes, of which two have become films in collaboration with Sue Healey.

Graeme Murphy (AO) has been at the forefront of Australian and international dance as a choreographer and director for over four decades.During his 31-year tenure as the artistic director of Sydney Dance Company, he created more than 50 works, including 30 full-length productions. Awards include an AO, Distinguished Service to the Performing Arts (2012), the Order of Australia (1982) for his Services to Dance, three honorary doctorates, a National Living Treasure (1999) by the National Trust of Australia, for Contributions to Cultural Exchange by the

Ministry of Culture the People's Republic of China (2008) and the Fred & Adele Astaire Award for Excellence in Choreography for Film *Mao's Last Dancer*. Choreographic credits include among many others *Nutcracker: The Story of Clara, Swan Lake*, and *Romeo & Juliet* (The Australian Ballet); *Water* (Shanghai Ballet); *Embodied* (Mikhail Baryshnikov) and The Torvill and Dean World Tour Company. Graeme directed and choreographed operas including *Turandot, Aida, Madama Butterfly* and *The Merry Widow* (Opera Australia), *Death in Venice* (Canadian Opera Company), *Samson et Dalila* (The Metropolitan Opera, New York) and the Andrew Lloyd Webber musical *Love Never Dies*.

Antonio Vargas is recognised as one of the world's leading flamenco dancers and choreographers. Ingenious, innovative and a perfectionist, he performs and teaches internationally, with works for theatre, cinema and television. Vargas won accolades for his performance as the gypsy father Rico in the Australian box-office hit movie *Strictly Ballroom*, directed by Baz Luhrmann and the winner of the Golden Globe Award and of the Cannes Film Festival Golden Camera Award for Young Directors. Maestro Antonio Vargas moved to Singapore in 2008 and continues to dance, create and cross borders with flamenco. He is joint artistic director of Flamenco Sin Fronteras that performs extensively in the community, in collaborative projects and theatre production pushing the boundaries of the art form in engaging, quality productions.

Janet Vernon (AM) studied at The Australian Ballet School and has danced with The Australian Ballet, Ballets Félix Blaska (France) and Sydney Dance Company. In 1976, she was appointed, along with Graeme Murphy, to the artistic helm of Sydney Dance Company, where they remained for 31 years. Graeme created roles for Janet including *Shéhérazade, Daphnis and Chloé, The Protecting Veil, Salome* and *The Trojans*, a collaboration with Opera Australia. Awards include: Dance Australia named her 'One of Australia's Five Best Female Dancers Ever'; Centenary Medal for services to society and dance; Lifetime Achievement, Australian Dance Awards (2006); Fred & Adele Astaire Award for Excellence in Choreography for Film *Mao's Last Dancer* (New York, 2011).

Ravenna Tucker Wagnon taught in Singapore before moving to Mississippi, where she is currently Professor of Dance at Belhaven University, teaching ballet, repertoire and Pilates. Other activities include guest teaching, private coaching, attending conferences, and as an evaluator for Jackson's USA International Ballet Competition. As a former principal dancer with The Royal Ballet and Birmingham Royal Ballet, she has danced the lead roles in major classical ballets. Wagnon is certified in the Royal Academy of Dance (RAD) and Pilates, and she holds a Masters degree of creative industries from Queensland University of Technology in Australia. Ravenna's career uncannily parallels Henry Danton's in these ways: she began her training with the RAD, won the Adeline Genée Competition in 1978, worked with The Royal Ballet throughout the

1980s under the coaching of Henry's peers, performed in Ashton's *Symphonic Variations* and now lives in Mississippi, also keenly interested in the Russian method of classical training.

Chapter authors

Ann Kipling Brown (PhD) is Professor Emerita in dance education in the Arts Education Program in the Faculty of Education at the University of Regina in Canada. She has worked extensively with children, youth and adults in dance teacher preparation, creative/modern dance, composition, and notation. Research, presentations, and publications focus on dance pedagogy and curriculum, the history and impact of the organisation "dance and the Child international" (daCi), the integration of motif and structured notation in dance programmes, the role of dance in the child's and adult's lived worlds and the learning and teaching of dance in intergenerational groups.

Szu-Ching Chang (PhD) is an associate professor in dance at National Taiwan University of Sport. She also serves as a board member of Dance Research Society, Taiwan and as the editor-in-chief of TDRJ No. 15. She holds a PhD in critical dance studies from the University of California, Riverside. Her book *Dancing Body, Discourse, Agency: The Min-Zu Dance Boom in 1950s-1960s Taiwan* was published in 2019. Her papers had been published in *Taiwan Dance Research Journal, Arts Review* and *Sports & Exercise Research* in Taiwan. She often presented papers at SDHS, CORD, WDA, CORPUS, APDF and other dance international conferences.

Pornrat Damrhung (PhD) is a professor in the Department of Dramatic Arts, Faculty of Arts, a research professor in the Division the Research and Innovation at Chulalongkorn University, and an Associate Member of The Royal Society of Thailand in the Academy of Arts. In 2018, she helped found the first Research Cluster at Chulalongkorn University in the humanities, centred on Innovation in the Arts & Culture, and runs the section on "Cultural Ecologies of Performance: Creativity, Research and Innovation". She recently completed a Senior Research Scholar grant (2016–2019) from the Thailand Research Fund to nourish young researchers and artist networks around Thailand.

Simrit Deol is a PhD student in the Faculty of Kinesiology, Sport, and Recreation at the University of Alberta. Her research interests are looking at the body, physical activity, and health from an intersectional lens, with a previous focus on immigrant girls. She has worked on the frontlines for various grassroots and non-profits such as Fit Kids Healthy Kids, Girl Forward, Rec and Read Mentorship Program and the Boys and Girls Club. She is currently working on her doctoral thesis that critically engages settler colonialism, post-feminism, and intersectionality within contemporary physical and digital cultures.

Tan Ngiap Heng (PhD) holds a doctorate in engineering and has been a full-time photographer since 1999. It is his love of dance and the performing arts that started his journey into photography. He has participated in solo and group exhibitions in Singapore and overseas. He started creating installations in 2014. He completed a Masters of Art (Fine Art) at LASALLE College of the Arts in 2018. He is now working on immersive installations which stimulate various senses. He is also interested in the histories of photography and dance, and his personal family. He is researching these topics and creating documentaries on them.

Gail Hewton is an award-winning dance artist and educator. She has more than 40 years of professional dance experience as an artist, educator, producer and community practitioner. Gail has been immersed in working with older people across a range of contexts and settings through her RIPE Dance practice since 2012. She has travelled nationally and internationally to research and develop expertise in this field becoming a leader, particularly in health and well-being aspects of dance for older people. Together with colleague Julie Chenery, she established Gold Moves Australia in 2018 to contribute to the field of dance for older people through training, mentoring and advocacy.

Francine Hills is a facilitator, dancer and PhD research student within the Creative Arts and Industries at the University of Auckland. Weaving falls prevention, dance for Parkinson's and community dance pedagogy and practice, Francine's research and teaching interests centre around questions of well-being as we dance through later life.

Allison Jeffrey (PhD) in sport sociology, University of Waikato) is a postdoctoral research fellow at the University of Alberta, Canada. She is currently a member of the Body, Movement Culture Research Group and working with Professor Pirkko Markula on a project that engages new materialist theory to broaden understandings of women's experiences of dance and ageing. Her research interests include new materialisms, posthumanism, well-being, embodiment and innovative methodologies.

Liz Lea is a nationally and internationally recognised dance artist, choreographer and producer. Over three decades, she has toured her work internationally and been commissioned in India, the UK, Australia, South Africa, Singapore, the United States and Kuwait. Liz was the 2017 ACT Artist of the Year and received a 2017 Australian Dance Award. She directs two Festivals – DANscienCE where dance and science meet and BOLD, celebrating the legacy of dance. She directs The Stellar Company, a not-for-profit arts organisation and recently launched the Chameleon Collective, Canberra's first inclusive dance company. Liz is represented by Karen Gallagher and Associates, UK.

Pirkko Markula (PhD) is a professor of socio-cultural studies of physical activity at the University of Alberta, Canada. She is also a contemporary dancer and choreographer. Recent publications include *Deleuze and the Physically Active Body* (Routledge, 2019); co-author, with Michael Silk, of *Qualitative Research for Physical Culture* (Routledge, 2011); co-editor, with Marianne Clark, of *The Evolving Feminine Ballet Body* (University of Alberta Press, 2018); and co-editor, with William Bridel and Jim Denison, of *Endurance running: A socio-cultural examination* (Routledge, 2016).

Jennifer Nikolai (PhD) is an associate professor, lecturer, performance studies scholar and dancer. Her research spans projects surrounding dance as we mature and art practice contexts including live and digital performance making, dance and mobile camera improvisation and screendance. Jennifer conducts research between Canada, her country of origin, and Aotearoa New Zealand, her country of residence. She lectures and supervises postgraduate research in the School of Sport and Recreation and in the School of Art and Design at AUT University, Auckland, NZ.

Melissa Quek is Head of the School of Dance & Theatre at LASALLE College of the Arts and is also Programme Leader for the Diploma in Dance. She is a choreographer, performer and educator whose choreographic interest lies in investigating the body-subject. Her works and creative process attempt to touch on questions of agency, materiality and perception to create a visceral experience for the audience. Melissa occasionally writes to make contemporary dance more accessible. These include articles such as a chapter on contemporary dance in Singapore for the book *Evolving Synergies: Celebrating Dance in Singapore*, dance reviews and various performance edu-packs.

Gerard M. Samuel (PhD) is an associate professor at University of Cape Town, Centre for Theatre, Dance and Performance Studies and Head of CTDPS Dance Section. He is the Convener: Post Graduate studies in Dance, Editor: South African Dance Journal, and Chair of *Confluences*, a biennial, international dance conference hosted by UCT. During the apartheid era, he performed with the NAPAC Ballet Company and The Playhouse Dance Company in Durban. His notable choreographies include *Prabhati* and *The Man I Love*. He received the Durban Theatre Awards in 2006 for *The Sound of Music*. Gerard produced *Place of Grace*, a dance film, in 2011 and is an advocate of disability arts in South Africa and in Copenhagen.

Urmimala Sarkar Munsi (PhD) is an associate professor at the School of Arts and Aesthetics, Jawaharlal Nehru University, New Delhi. Her specialisation is in critical dance studies, visual anthropology and ethnographic research. She is a dancer/choreographer trained at the Uday Shankar India Culture Centre. Her current work is on changing landscapes of dance in India, sex-trafficking and survival processes for survivors, and performance of local, global and national identity and citizenship in times of globalisation and crisis in democracy. Her most recent book, *Uday Shankar and his Transcultural Experimentations: Dancing Modernity*, has just been published by Palgrave (2022).

Helle Winther (PhD) is Associate Professor and PhD in dance and movement psychology at the Department of Nutrition, Exercise and Sports, University of Copenhagen. She is also a trained dance and body psychotherapist and educated in heartfulness. Her research and teaching focus on dance, movement psychology, dance movement therapy and the language of the body in leadership and professional practices. She has educated generations of university students and has worked with leaders, teachers, nurses and other professional fields for many years. Helle has published books and numerous research articles about her work.

Sonia York-Pryce (PhD, visual arts) is a dancer, and interdisciplinary artist. She trained extensively in ballet and contemporary dance in the UK. Her doctoral research examines how senior professional dancers, aged older than 40 and still performing, navigate the bias of ageing and discrimination, and the effects it has on their practice. She interviewed numerous dancers, based in Australia and internationally, including founder members of NDT3 and Berlin's Dance On Ensemble. Her aim is to demonstrate "how their practice rather than their age, defines them".

Case narrative writers

Jenny Barnett joined Fine Lines on Day 1, having been a keen member of The Elderberries, a mature dance company in Ipswich, UK. Creativity, learning and development have been at the heart of all her work: as a teacher of English and drama, in community theatre and arts projects, and running her own training and development consultancy. She has been an external evaluator of arts projects in the UK and has published books and materials relating to her professional life. Now 73, she is enthusiastically pursuing her own development in dance, music, writing and visual arts.

Jan Bolwell is a choreographer, performer, playwright and director of Crows Feet Dance Collective, Wellington's popular 40-strong dance company for mature women. In 2021, despite COVID-19, the collective staged and toured *Carmina Burana*. Jan spent many years as a dance educator in higher education, and currently is an adviser and moderator on the NZ Curriculum dance achievement standards at Te Kura, the New Zealand Correspondence School. Jan has written eight plays which have toured extensively throughout New Zealand. Her latest work, *Silent Spring Revisited*, is a solo about Rachel Carson, the great American writer and environmentalist.

Caren Cariño (PhD) is Hawai'ian-born and an educator at Nanyang Academy of Fine Arts, Singapore. She is Principal Lecturer and Acting Dean (School of Arts Management, Dance and Theatre); Vice Dean (Dance Programme); and Course Leader (BA [Hons] Performance Making). Her educational degrees include PhD (SEA Studies – Contemporary Dance), MFA (Drama and Theatre – Dance), and

BEd (Elementary Education – Dance). Trained in contemporary dance, she was a dance artist with the Ririe-Woodbury Dance Company, USA. Her research is centred on dance education, performance and cultural studies. She is dance advisor to Singapore's Ministry of Education, National Arts Council and People's Association.

Mary Davies collaborated with artists across Europe as a young dancer, devising and performing her work in site-specific and theatre spaces. For DanceEast, Davies was artistic director for dance performance companies EncoreEast (over 50s) and Dance Unlimited (trained movement practitioners). Commissions for large-scale projects devising movement for community groups and artists from all disciplines led Davies to the Royal School of Speech and Drama, where in 2021 she completed her Masters in movement directing and teaching for actors. As a postural stability instructor, her practice includes falls prevention techniques and offers a focus on rehabilitation methods.

Amy Dean is a Masters student, dance teacher and former artist with Cape Town City Ballet. Her dissertation is titled: "A South African perspective on dancers and career transitions". She has a BMus in dance (majors: classical ballet, contemporary dance and dance teaching methods), Certificate in Ballet Teaching (Royal Academy of Dance [RAD]), is an RAD-registered teacher and silver swan licensee and a member of International Golden Key Honors Society.

Paige Gordon has been in the Australian dance for more than 30 years. She has performed with Western Australian Ballet, Meryl Tankard Company and independents, and she created a project company (ACT, 1993–1998) which drew national interest. She was the artistic director of Buzz Dance Theatre (Western Australia, 1998–2003) touring nationally and internationally. She seeks to connect dance, community and place through vital partnerships and has led numerous dance-in-health programmes such as Tracksuit (2010), OnTrack (2015), Dance for Parkinson's Classes (2015), Lifespan Dance (2019) and in-hospital programmes. A report by the Chamber of Arts and Culture identified Paige's work as a "key resource" in Western Australia.

Lesley Graham is a freelance curriculum consultant and casual academic at University of Tasmania (UTAS). She has taught Dance at all levels of education and training including TAFE and lecturing in dance and education at UTAS and Queensland University of Technology, and has served as the Senior Project Officer Performing Arts, DOE, Tasmania. She mentors emerging artists, undertakes rehearsal direction and dramaturgy and teaches contemporary dance technique, choreography and ballet. She is chair of DRILL Performance, Hobart's youth dance company, and writes reviews for Dance Australia and Arts Hub. Lesley is a member of the National Advocates for Arts Education and the Ausdance Awards panel.

Angela Liong is a prolific dance-maker with a large body of works that shaped the distinctive dance profile of THE ARTS FISSION since the company's inception in 1994. She draws inspiration from literary classics and cultural sources, and she borrows form and methodology from other disciplines to create choreographic structures that engage with human expressions. She attended arts, science and climate change conferences in Norway and in 2008 was invited by Asia-Europe Foundation as advisor and facilitator in organising an exclusive workshop that involved a group of established artists and scientists from Europe and Asia. She is the recipient of the 2009 Cultural Medallion award.

Katrina Rank (PhD) is an artist with 24 years of professional dance practice. In 2013, she initiated Fine Lines, contemporary dance classes for experienced, mature dancers. Her recent work with Fine Lines includes *Mean Feat* (2015), *The Archivists* (2018), *The Right* (2019) and *Firebird* (2021). She has lead classes for people with Parkinson's disease and produced and directed the film *Stupendous* (2018). Katrina was the Caroline Plummer Fellow in 2017 and received the 2018 Australian Dance Award for services to dance education. Her 2019 work *The Right for Fine Lines Dance* was awarded the 2020 Australian Dance Award for Most Outstanding Achievement in Community Dance.

Barbara Snook (PhD) is a senior research fellow at the University of Auckland. Her research is in dance education and community dance. She is currently co-editing a Routledge publication, to be released in 2023, *Celebrating Dance in North East India: Reflections of dance along the Bramaputra* with Debarshi Nath and Ralph Buck. Barbara was the Caroline Plummer Fellow in Community Dance at the University of Otago in 2008. She is a successful author of dance textbooks widely used in Australia and New Zealand. She was the recipient of an Osmotherly Award for services toward the development of dance education in Queensland, Australia in 2007.

FIGURES

INTRODUCTION

Stephanie Burridge and Charlotte Svendler Nielsen

Dance is an embodied language passed on from body to body and is transmitted through energy in place, time and space. The encoded body exudes memories – dance languages learnt, choreographic phrases remembered from classes and performances, and the emotional engagement from the joy of participating, practising and performing and sharing with other artists, the audience and communities. The purpose of this book is to feature the extraordinary creative dance-making and practice of older dance artists, innovative community dance groups, students and recreational dancers who come together regularly and are inspired by committed teachers and exemplary pedagogy, and dance for well-being across several medical conditions and special needs sectors. The areas defined are professional dance practice, community dance practice and performance, pedagogy and recreational dance practice, dance for therapy and well-being and a special section titled "Conversations".

This volume will include content that broadens the understanding of this burgeoning sector by incorporating examples of artistic practice and a variety of theoretical approaches, along with an emphasis on cultural and experiential contexts. The anthology includes examples of how artists, community practitioners, teachers, policy makers and academics work to better understand, promote and create new ways of thinking and working in the fields of dance performance, education and well-being.

Defining the nomenclature for this sector might be problematic. Throughout the world, countries define their ageing populations with various terms and have generally struggled with an internationally agreed term. Variations include seniors, elders, the elderly, retirees, the adjective 'older' (dancers) and more. Terminology is important, as it shapes identity and public perception – words like 'elderly' or 'old' might imply some incapacity and frailty and certainly not account for the diversity of lifestyles, capabilities, desires and interests of the group. It also homogenises the many different stages of life that occur for this group over several decades.

DOI: 10.4324/9781003307624-1

In dance there is also some additional confusion. A senior dance artist might be referred to as someone who has an established professional career and moved up in the hierarchy of the company – ballet companies have clear stages of career rankings and titles for these such as a member of the corps de ballet or a soloist. Whilst some contemporary companies use the term 'senior artists' to acknowledge their more established dancers, it is not necessarily common practice. So when applying the term 'senior dancers' to a dancer over 60, a writer could be referring to a professional dancer who is continuing to make work and or perform.

This book features a section that we call "Conversations". These include exceptional international artists actively engaged in performance and choreography who share decades of wisdom and experience. It is interesting to note how they describe themselves – many consider themselves as just dancers, choreographers or dance artists and defy terminology that defines their age. Dance remains central to the continuum of their lives and identity.

Some of our writers, however, use the term 'senior' based on age. For instance, many community dance companies cite an age at which someone can join the group – often over 50 years of age. Many do not require prior experience and simply require participants to commit to a number of classes per week and rehearsals if they want to perform. Often, they employ highly regarded choreographers and it is up to the choreographer to create work that embraces the group of dancers and their skill level – few audition the dancers and for these choreographers, it is a two-way journey of discovery as they dig deep into their creativity and are inspired by the individuals within the group, their memories and responses to mostly task-based processes. Moving together, or alone in the studio, affirms a somatic connection between the mind, body and spirit. For some communities in the book, the need to remember cultural material and recreate it together is a driving force; for others, it is the chance to create and express feelings and emotions, to tell stories connecting past experiences to the present time and enjoy dancing together with the social interaction it brings.

The book recounts the work of several community groups that are exciting audiences with innovative, insightful productions.

A growing area in the dance industry offered by studios and dance companies are classes for 'older adults' – again often cited as for those over 50 years of age. Many in this group learnt dance as a child and are eager to take it up again – some classes feature a particular genre, whereas others embrace a more individual format encouraging creativity and free expression. Most of the community dance groups mentioned previously offer these classes to their members and other participants. Quality pedagogy is essential in addressing factors such as safety and appropriate codes of practice, as well as offering inspiring material that is fun and engaging. Chapters in the book look at best practice and pedagogy across different cultural forms of dance.

Dance therapy for 'older adults' has played an essential role in many people's lives. Across diverse medical conditions – or simply to join in a group, move and relax – dance exists in nursing homes and health and community centres, and its benefits are well established in enhancing physical mobility and coordination, and developing strength and flexibility, but often more importantly, enabling social interaction, hepatic and somatic experiences to support holistic well-being. The chapters and case narratives in the book recount examples and experiences of dance artists and facilitators working in this sector.

Added to these considerations an underlying factor in curating this volume over the past two years (2020–2022), has been the ever-present influence of the COVID-19 pandemic. Many individuals and projects have been affected deeply including the dancers having to take classes via Zoom, choreographic instructions relayed via apps and social media, performances cancelled, reduced capacity for shows and the drying up of income sources for teachers and facilitators. Some chapters and narratives tell of how these disruptions were accommodated whilst the loss of therapy time for some medical conditions, such as dementia, whereby social interaction is essential have consequences that are possibly unknown at this point.

Each section of the book includes chapters and case narratives. The chapter authors base their work on different theoretical perspectives approaching issues of senior dance practice through extensive research. Case narratives are situated within social and cultural, philosophical, educational and sociological frameworks and often represent a specific community perspective. Some recount special projects and activities, whilst others take a broader perspective; however, a common thread to all contributions of the book is that they explore change processes and transformations that come about in the lives of senior dancers. The anthology will be of interest to many subject areas, including performing arts, pedagogy, choreography, community dance practice, social and cultural studies, aesthetics, interdisciplinary arts, dance therapy and more. It will be an invaluable resource for artists working across generations and in communities, as well as health practitioners and those working in the well-being sector.

Documenting and giving voice to diversity through artistic expression underpins this story. Sadly, during the course of researching, writing, publishing and releasing this book, some of our artists have passed on – their legacy and spirit lives on to inform and inspire future generations. The book is an eclectic mix of lived experiences, wisdom, deep knowledge and reflection – it is necessarily a small sample of myriad excellent and essential projects and practices around the world.

More than 50 dance artists and writers contributed to this book and include Germaine Acogny, 'Funmi Adewole, Aida Amirkhanian, Artsvi Bakhchinyan, Jenny Barnett, Jan Bolwell, Stephanie Burridge, Caren Cariño, Elizabeth Cameron Dalman, Szu-Ching Chang, Pornrat Damrhung, Henry Danton (1919–2022), Mary Davies, Alex Dea, Amy Dean, Simrit Deol, Anca Frankenhaeuser, Shirley Gibson, Paige Gordon, Lesley Graham, Patrick Harding-Irmer, Gail Hewton, Francine Hills, Allison Jeffrey, Michael Keegan-Dolan, Ann Kipling Brown, Eileen Kramer, Liz Lea, Angela Liong, Pirkko Markula, Graeme Murphy, Jennifer Nikolai, Melissa Quek, Katrina Rank, S. Ngaliman, Gerard M. Samuel, Urmimala Sarkar Munsi, Rama Sas, Barbara Snook, Charlotte Svendler Nielsen, Tan Ngiap Heng, Bu Tarwa, Sonia York-Pryce, Antonio Vargas, Janet Vernon, Helmut Vogt, Ravenna Tucker Wagnon, Helle Winther, Bu Yudanegoro.

Stephanie Burridge (PhD) lectures at LASALLE College of the Arts and Singapore Management University and is a choreographer, performer and dance writer. She is Series Editor for Routledge anthologies *Celebrating Dance in Asia and the Pacific* and *Perspectives on Dance, Young People and Change* (2015, 2018, 2020), co-editor Charlotte Svendler Nielsen, and *Embodied Performativity in Southeast Asia: Multidisciplinary Corporealities* (2020). In 2021 she edited the *Routledge Companion for Dance in Asia and the Pacific: Platforms for Change* and co-authored Routledge *Choreographic Basics* with Jenny Roche. Her current choreographic focus and research is collaborating with senior artists.

Charlotte Svendler Nielsen (PhD) is Associate Professor in Educational Studies focusing on dance and Program Director at the Department of Nutrition, Exercise and Sports, University of Copenhagen, Denmark. She is co-editor with Stephanie Burridge of the Routledge series *Perspectives on Dance, Young People and Change* (2015, 2018, 2020). She is chair of the European Network of Observatories in the Field of Arts and Cultural Education (ENO) and has been a board member of Dance and the Child International (daCi) for many years. Her research focuses on dance education, arts integration and interculturality in an embodied perspective.

SECTION 1
Conversations

FIGURE 1.0   Dancer: Germaine Acogny

Source: Photograph by Thomas Dorn

DOI: 10.4324/9781003307624-2

1.1

A CONVERSATION ABOUT JUNCTIONS, MILESTONES AND THRESHOLDS

Germaine Acogny and 'Funmi Adewole with Helmut Vogt translating and contributing

Germaine Acogny is a legend in the dance world. I have followed her adventures in dance closely over the years. Our conversation took place over two meetings on Zoom in June 2022. Helmut, her husband and collaborator, happily translated when necessary, as Germaine is Francophone and I am Anglophone. Our conversation was one about junctions, milestones and thresholds. The reminiscences were a delight and a pause. Here are some paraphrased excerpts.

'Funmi Adewole

GERMAINE: When I was a young girl of about 9 years at school, in the playground, I would point out to other young girls the movement of the trees and show them how to dance like them. They would say I was crazy. But they enjoyed it and would come back and ask for more.

'FUNMI: Often when we speak about dance in the African continent (in the professional realm), we rarely tell stories like this about our creativity. We usually discuss dance on social and political levels. We do see children behaving like this, but we do not talk about it much.

GERMAINE: I was born in Benin and did not dance like the other little girls. I did not grow up in Senegal. I did not know the traditional dances (at the time), but I wanted to dance so I had to invent . . . . The confrontation with classical dance later, with other dances, that made me want to investigate my own dances. I created a grand plié with an undulating spine, and that became the grand plié of Acogny. When I returned to Senegal, I taught dance to middle class families. I had two children to bring up after my divorce. Gradually, I became a professional. I did not think of myself as an artist in the beginning. I thought of dance as "useful".

'FUNMI: What you say resonates with me – I came from another place and wanted to connect with people and the way was through creativity and invention. I feel

DOI: 10.4324/9781003307624-3

these stories of dance's usefulness in intercultural and work spaces are important . . . . My first experiences of dance were from television and the stage.
When I visited my grandmother in the village, I would join the festival, *Olojo*,
and follow the entourage to the King's palace, but my actual experience of
dancing came through television and the theatre. After university, I worked in
journalism and interviewed artists for the press in Nigeria. I came into professional performance when I got to England in the mid-1990s. I wanted to be
part of the discussions in those spaces. It was the topics that dance ignited that
lead me into dance as a profession.

GERMAINE: It is important that we work with the imagination [she demonstrates a
dance movement] and with the insights we gain from meditation – When you
can look at a plant and imagine that the flower, a head and the body is like the
roots. The dancer observes and transforms imagination into movement.

'FUNMI: I have not heard you discuss this aspect of the technique before. I have
always known imagery was important to the technique . . . . What risks have
you taken to bring your work into being?

GERMAINE: I was the director of Mudra Afrique, which was created by President
Senghor and Maurice Béjart. After five years, the school closed. It was a great
shock for me. About the same time, I met Helmut, who became my husband
and collaborator and I also moved to France. At 40 years old, I was starting
from point zero. I began thinking of establishing a school in Senegal. Helmut
help me in realising this dream . . . .

HELMUT: I should add, since we are talking about taking risks – Germaine sold her
small apartment and started with that money. I had some money from an
inheritance, and I helped fundraise. When Germaine did her first workshop
in Senegal, we were dancing outside under the sun. Susanne Linke, who was
present, wanted to create a work with the students of the workshop. But we
said no, we would rather start a dance company with them – and that was also
a risk, because the money we had was put aside for the building. However, it
is good that we took the risk because the resulting project was successful and
we toured. In America, we met foundations and we received a major grant.

'FUNMI: Would you say, both of you, that you had to take the risk and then the support came after . . . ?

GERMAINE: There was no guarantees. We took the risk first.

HELMUT: To start both the school and the company.

'FUNMI: The risk I took was to step in and save an organisation. It now no longer
exists – the Association of Dance of the African Diaspora (ADAD). It was the
main organisation for dancers of African descent in the UK in the 90s. One of
the committee members, Ama Wray (known as Sheron then), stepped in and
saved it when it was closing due to a lack of funds. But when she went on tour,
I took over the organisation. I worked for a year voluntarily to keep the organisation going, and it almost ran me into the ground. When Arts Council agreed
to fund when we made a collaboration with a more established organisation,

I ran it for another year (with pay) before going back on tour. I struggled for some years after that. It was a disorientating experience but a great education. I learnt about cultural policy, funding systems, education policy, how dance organisations network and survive. So that was my training school . . . . It seems that if you want to pioneer an idea, it requires taking a risk because other people might not have a reference point for what you are doing.

HELMUT: Yes, risk and sacrifices.

GERMAINE: Dance has given me much satisfaction in life. It has given much joy and pleasure. It has given me the possibility to confront life. One of the major joys for me has been to establish École des Sables. *Tchouraï*, a solo choreographed for me by Sophiatou Kossoko, was a difficult but special experience. Another was working with Olivier Dubois a French choreographer, who – 35 years after Béjart had planned to cast me as the chosen one in *Sacre du Printemps* – created a version for me. I was already 70 years old. I have received many awards and travelled the world. I am now in a position to have less responsibility in running the school.

'FUNMI: That is wonderful to hear. I realised the joy of dance when I was young and struggled with language. I was born in England. My family moved back to Nigeria and I could not speak the language (Yoruba). Dance gave me an opportunity to be part of a "discussion". My training was in literature and I was writing poetry, but the discussion that gripped me was in dance because I found dance – more than literature, more than drama – responded to the challenges facing Africa. I recently returned to performance. I stopped touring in 2005, which is a long time ago. I feel I have done things back to front. Other people go into the academia only when they stop performing. For over 30 years, dance has been a place where I have grappled with many issues. Dance has become for me a lifelong investigation.

GERMAINE: My work in choreography comes from my connection to life around me: nature, day-to-day activities, the state of the world. *Faagala* (2007) came out of my desire to do a piece about the genocide in Rwanda with the hope this will not never be repeated. I co-choreographed *Faagala* with the Japanese dancer and choreographer, Kota Yamasaki. I had a company of men, seven dancers who were strong artists who also loved their mothers. That was important. I wanted men who could access their feminine side, not [be] afraid to show it. I wanted them to be able to empathise with the violence meted out on women during the genocide.

'FUNMI: I am actually a dramaturge, an outside eye, not a choreographer. I support artists to articulate what they want to communicate. This is informed by my being a journalist and a storyteller. Communication is a driver for me. How do we communicate the stories of post-independent Africa? That is a driver for me.

HELMUT: We are happy to have been given the chance to meet twice online and talk.

'FUNMI: Yes, thank you.

GERMAINE: We hope to meet in person soon.

Germaine Acogny's statement is resonant; "My work in choreography comes from my connection to life around me. Nature, everyday life and day-to-day activities, the state of the world." It gives credence to the literal translation of choreography as the act of 'writing with dance'. The stories of choreography are stories of interventions, connections and interactions, on stage and with the wider world.

'Funmi Adewole

FIGURE 1.1A   Dancer Germaine Acogny in rehearsal

Source: Photograph by Antoine Tempé.

FIGURE 1.1B   Dancer: 'Funmi Adewole

Source: Photograph by Irven Lewis

1.2

A LIFE TRAVELLING IN DANCE

Aida Amirkhanian in conversation
with Artsvi Bakhchinyan

The artist Aida Amirkhanian and the dance history researcher Artsvi Bakhchinyan first met in 1998 in Yerevan, Armenia. He has followed her career with
interest and has interviewed her over the past few decades.

ARTSVI: Aida, first we met in 1998 in Yerevan. Are there some essential changes in
your artistic and personal character [since then]?

AIDA: I was very fortunate to have met you more than two decades ago in Yerevan
and know you as an incredibly knowledgeable, inspiring character that advo-
cated various performing art forms – and for that meeting, I am grateful. As
about what has changed, for one thing, I am 20 years older – and hopefully a
little wiser. I am calmer, and yet the life force is still flowing through my veins
with intensity, so I have learned a little about subtleties and nuances and maintaining my integrity and using my inner energies mindfully and generously.
That is a good thing.

ARTSVI: Your biography includes various countries and cultures – Armenian, Ira-
nian, European, Australian, American, Hindi . . . . How has each shaped you
as an artiste and person?

AIDA: I love travelling and seeing the world. I have lived in various countries in four
continents. I have been exposed to different cultures and traditions; I have co-
existed with these different cultures because at my core I had my own strong
culture. Being an Armenian in this world is not an easy task! Even though
I was born not in Armenia, the roots are deep. Experiencing all the other
cultures were adding different flavours to my own culture: some were very
different, some were similar, some were unpleasant, some were rich – but at
the very core I understood that humans are the same; no matter where you
go, they just react differently to different things and have different perspective
on various things in life.

DOI: 10.4324/9781003307624-4

ARTSVI: I am sure many ask you to tell about your years with Maurice Béjart – may I ask, too?

AIDA: My years at Mudra and later in the Ballet de XXème Siècle under the artistic direction of Béjart was "Magical" with a capital "M"! He was a genius, he was the creator, he was the destroyer of obstacles like Shiva. He was kind and very intense. He had tremendous love in his heart; his love was contagious and genuine. He suffered and felt pain for humanity. He had humour. He truly was a legend, one-of-a-kind a genius. As a 17-year-old, I was exposed to these qualities in a human being and that was so rich and unique. He wanted his interpreters to not just use their bodies, but their voice, their intelligence, their awareness. He wanted us to be alive and present and conscious from moment to moment in whatever we did.

ARTSVI: How do dance and yoga complement each other?

AIDA: Yoga is an internal journey, an internal expression, that doesn't need to be exhibited. Dance is an external expression though it has to start from deep inside, but it has to be expressed and exhibited. Over 30 plus years, I think I have found a way to find a bridge between the two, a bridge where I can cross deep inside from one to the other if needed.

ARTSVI: Twice during 1998, you presented contemporary dance in Yerevan – a rare guest on our stages. I always remember your words that in order to have exper- imental dance, one does not need to borrow dance technique, that should be developed on the national basis.

AIDA: That is right. I came to Armenia twice in 1998 and met the wonderful artists from Yerevan choreography college, from the mime studio and even a couple of street artists and musicians, and we decided to put a performance on. That was a rich experience. My second trip in 1998 was to collaborate with Maestro Aram Gharabekian [the music director of the National Chamber Orchestra of Armenia] on the Topophono musical and dance project by eminent Arme- nian composer Haroutiun Delalian. It was a very creative and unforgettable experience.

In our interview, I remember talking about not wanting to use the word "contemporary" dance; instead, I called it innovative or experimental dance. Most people in the dance world, when they think contemporary dance, they refer to the various American contemporary dance techniques – which is fine, but I think that each culture has to develop their own contemporary tech- niques based on their own cultural roots. Various cultures have developed that very successfully, and we can achieve that as well, especially as we already have such strong roots in dance and movement.

Our national culture is very rich – the movements in our traditional dances, not staged ones, the naz pars for example – but the true traditional dances from various regions are the base movements from which then the new vocabulary can develop, and this is what I call innovative, a true exploration in the heart of the movement and then an evolution of it, an expansion of it – [it is] very dif- ficult to explain in words because this is a true experience, not an intellectual activity. I believe one has to know the very root and the heart of one's own culture – in this case, the dances – and then proceed from there if the intention is to become innovative.

ARTSVI: In 2006, Gharabekian again invited you to choreograph and perform Shchedrin's *Carmen*, at the site of the ruins of Zvartnots cathedral. [How did you experience that?]

AIDA: Maestro Gharabekian called me up to ask me to participate in this project and I straight out rejected it, saying he should look for someone else, and here was his response: "When I stand in the ruins of Zvartnots I can't see anyone else but you. This seems to be your responsibility and no one else's." The trust he gave me was remarkable, and that level of trust made me take on this responsibility. It was an extremely challenging project, which we co-created. There was a moment during the performance [when] I had a powerful experience of belonging to that land, standing solid on my two legs, getting a glimpse of what it is like to feel so deeply and to dance with the music, the wind, the stars, the sweeping dust and everything and become one with it all. Zvartnots is a very powerful place and had tremendous energy if one is open to receive it. I was devastated when maestro Gharabekian left us in body and moved on to other dimensions.

ARTSVI: Unlike classical dance, contemporary dancers do not retire early – do you continue dancing, and what are your current projects?

AIDA: Please allow me to answer this question with a poem by the C13th Persian poet Rumi:[1]

> Dance when you are broken open
> Dance if you've torn the bandage off,
> Dance in the middle of fighting,
> Dance in your blood,
> Dance when you are perfectly free.

It does not really matter anymore if anyone sees me dance. When I am inspired and feel that from the depths of my being I have something to express which will serve other[s], then I will.

Sections of this 'Conversation' first appeared as an article in the *Armenian Mirror Spectator*, February 21, 2022, available at: https://mirrorspectator.com/2022/02/21/aida-amirkhanian-dance-is-in-her-blood/?fbclid=IwAR02M5ZPkIaLm5Rpmtb6yoX6LLL3e1FdC0p4DM1IHl_X9jB5AecilVmG52k

FIGURE 1.2   Aida Amirkhanian with the legendary choreographer Maurice Béjart

Source: Photograph from artist's personal collection

Note

1   www.poetryverse.com/rumi-poems/dance

1.3

DANCING IS SHAPE-SHIFTING

Elizabeth Cameron Dalman and
Michael Keegan-Dolan

A conversation between the artists with emphasis on Michael's award-winning production, *Swan Lake/Loch na hEala*, in which Elizabeth performed an actor/dancer role.

MICHAEL: The people you collaborate with are fundamental to the outcome, to the success. The dancers need to be self-confident, in that they are happy to make many mistakes, happy to try things together endlessly, willing to laugh or cry. They need strong legs and lungs and hearts. They need to be in love with their art and have some depth.

I believe that in the sacred process of making dances, theatre, songs and stories, your attention is crucial to the success of the work. Your undiluted attention can lift another up. The quality of your attention can bring something tiny and apparently insignificant into life, into reality. Your attention is like a prayer.

ELIZABETH: Attention to place is fundamental for me. Lifelong research in the Earth-centred spirituality of First Nation peoples of Australia developed my understanding of how place influences us all. Creative collaborations with people from Yolngu and Pitjantjatjara lands enriched my practice. Many of my choreographic works over the past 30-plus years have specifically addressed current issues of environmental damage, our place in the natural world and the urgent need for us all to take care of it. In creating these works here at Mirramu on the shores of Weereewa/Lake George in Ngunnawal and Ngambri country, it is as if the land and the lake speak through me. Stories, many mythic in nature, have emerged out of this place.

Living here has also connected me back to my own Celtic ancestry and mythic stories acknowledging the sacredness of our interconnectedness to the Earth and the Cosmos. So in 2016, it felt rather uncanny to find myself

DOI: 10.4324/9781003307624-5

working with you in the midlands of Ireland on *Swan Lake/Loch na hEala*, which relates so deeply to the land and stories, ancient and current, that came out of that place.

MICHAEL: It was my ancestors who guided me to the midlands and it was the midlands that made *Swan Lake/Loch na hEala* appear as a piece of theatre/dance performance.

The midlands, as well as being flat with poor soil, can be a sad place, as on occasion deprivation and emigration have brought about difficulties for the local community. I integrated a real story from the area into the narrative fabric of *Swan Lake*. I had read how Siegfried in *Swan Lake* suffered from dark moods and was uninterested in marriage. This made me think of the bachelor farmers in the midlands, some of whom live alone and in isolation. One such man was John Carty, who through mental illness and a sequence of unfortunate events ended up getting fatally shot by the police.

ELIZABETH: I found it intriguing the way you integrated the John Carty story and the contemporary issues of depression, gun violence and child sex abuse in the Church into the *Swan Lake* script.

It reminded me of when I created *Sundown* for Australian Dance Theatre in 1967. As a passionate anti-war activist, I felt emboldened to speak out through my art about the war in Vietnam. *Sundown* was my anti-war statement. As a starting point, I took Euripides' play, *The Women of Troy*. I contemporised the ancient script and added underground stories that were coming out of Vietnam at the time.

Why did you choose *Swan Lake* as your story?

MICHAEL: *Swan Lake* is a good story, and good stories need to be told. The way this story is presented within the genre of classical ballet can be very superficial. So, I felt in some way obliged to rectify this, for the sake of the story.

ELIZABETH: Working with you and subsequently touring the world for four years with the *Swan Lake/Loch na hEala* team – or "Tribe", as you called us – has been a highlight in my nearly seven-decade performing career.

I remember answering your audition notice for an actor of about 60 years old, someone preferably with long white hair, to play the role of Nancy (the mother figure). I was much older than the woman you were looking for, a dancer/choreographer/director and not an actor, and I lived on the other side of the world. But, I did have long white hair. Your acceptance gave me the opportunity to experience your amazing creative process.

MICHAEL: My process starts with an urge, like a whisper. It often seems to come from nowhere, but over time, through a process of insistence, like an itch that won't go away, it eventually becomes something, maybe a script or a series of written descriptions, feelings or ideas.

I try very hard not to impose on the idea and then not to impose on the group of artists assembled to bring the work into being through hours of improvisation. However, it's also good to use the metrics of form and of discipline to bookend this very free process of creativity.

ELIZABETH: Inspired by your text or movement ideas, we spent hours improvising for the development of *Swan Lake/Loch na hEala*. I also use improvisation in my creative process. I find such processes bring an organic authenticity to choreographies. They also link the performers together kinetically and engage them strongly in their commitment.

You and I have some other similarities in our dance and theatre training backgrounds. We both began in the classical ballet tradition, but each in our own way rebelled against the classical ballet forms and training, and the hierarchical group structure.

I immediately connected to the way you developed the group dynamics of the company. I have always chosen dancers in my companies not only for their dance and theatre skills but also for their generosity of spirit and commitment to the team. I always talk about how important the spirit of the company is, especially because I believe that how we relate together as a group is reflected in the performances that we present on stage.

Your challenges were always inspiring and pushed me to new levels. I know that you always wanted Nancy – who you created as a working-class widow from the Irish midlands – to smoke on stage. As an anti-smoker, I found this challenging. So in order not to disappoint you, I had to think creatively to portray her as the rather depressed, cynical, arthritic old woman, but without the cigarettes. I appreciated that you always wanted us to be honest with you, as you were with us.

MICHAEL: I believe that you need to get good at experiencing the sensation of honesty, sitting with and shouldering the sometimes-uncomfortable nature of the truth. But in order to do that, you have to practise it.

I also believe that energy is everything. A bird is a particular manifestation or expression of energy. A dancer is another. A real dancer is a master of the manipulation of the movement of energy. Energy makes shape. By changing shape, you can change the flow and nature or quality of energy. Dancing is the transitions or the action of energy changing. Changing shape in a rhythmical natural way is dancing. Dancing is literally shape-shifting. The work is to become conscious of this and develop the ability to see and hear and feel what is unfolding around you, in a true and real way.

ELIZABETH: In the 1960s, my mentor Eleo Pomare introduced me to the importance of energy flows through the body, from dance and dramatic points of view. The repetition of simple movements builds energy in the body, then gradually transforms movements into new movements and/or new rhythms.

Later in my career, I studied with Master Kajo Tsuboi from Japan. His practice of Mobius Kiryuho focusses on energy flows through the body. I have become much more conscious of energy as a vital element in my own work as a choreographer and a performer.

I think what kept *Swan Lake/Loch na hEala* so alive was your attention to energy and the fact that it was like a ritual. Every performance was fresh, and even after our hundredth one, it was like doing it for the first time.

MICHAEL: Rituals are dreamed into being by profound work and acts of imagination and experience. The "show" is a ritual, a sequence of actions, brought together in a specific order that can cause transformation in the actors and dancers who carry out the actions, and in the audience (in a different way) who give witness to those actions.

I always felt that what I was doing was ritual.

ELIZABETH: I remember our discussions about ritual. Your feedback enabled my character Nancy to set up the ritual space from the moment she walked on stage in the beginning, and to hold the ritual together throughout the entire show, even when she was not speaking. To be present in every moment demanded enormous concentration and constant use of the imagination.

As a senior performing artist, I understand the power of stillness and of holding presence on stage. So I harnessed that energy. Then in the last scene, when you let me dance with all the young dancers and the feathers, I was able to fly!

FIGURE 1.3 *Swan Lake/Loch na hEala*; choreographer: Michael Keegan-Dolan; dancer: Elizabeth Cameron Dalman

Source: Photograph by Luke Danniells

1.4

A CONVERSATION ABOUT LIFE IN DANCE

A crossing of two paths

Henry Danton and Ravenna Tucker Wagnon

One morning, early in January 2022, I drove two hours south of Jackson, Mississippi to the small town of Petal, to visit my friend Henry Danton, resting over the winter break from teaching his twice-weekly ballet classes. It was some time since I last saw him in person, and I looked forward to seeing him again. I saw how noticeably frailer he now was, though over the years that I had known him, I saw his incredible self-discipline and ability seemingly defying time and maintaining youthful inner strength, energy and sharp mind. As we visited, enjoying the time together, we picked up where we had last left off, it seemed. During our conversation, one cherished memory surfaced, his calling me up one night, out of the blue, to ask me to learn, and dance, the *Nutcracker* pas de deux.

Ravenna Tucker Wagnon

RAVENNA: You made me do the [*Nutcracker*] pas de deux, which was wonderful!

HENRY: That was incredible . . . at your age! It was in pointe shoes and you waltzed through it like [was] nothing!

RAVENNA: Well, I practised about six weeks beforehand to get myself back into shape.

HENRY: No, but I mean, at that time when you did that, you were just teaching; you were not supposed to be in condition, but you just got up and did it!

RAVENNA: That's right! [To him, that may be how it *seemed*!]

HENRY: I'm so glad because that is the authentic version as I taught it [he was taught it by Victor Gsovsky in 1946 and danced it with Lycette Darsonval of the Paris Opera Ballet, and later with Mia Slavenska of the Ballets Russes]. Choreographers will mess around with it!

RAVENNA: Well, there are many different versions of the *Nutcracker* [pas de deux].

[Here, we both somehow forget that this choreography was originally by Lev Ivanov, and we segue to Marius Petipa, considered by Henry a genius and

DOI: 10.4324/9781003307624-6

the masterful originator of classical ballet. Nonetheless, Henry had recently mentioned of his musing about Lev Ivanov, beginning to recognise Ivanov's extraordinary work as a choreographer on par with, or perhaps even surpassing, Petipa.]

HENRY: Yes . . . well . . . I have a special relationship with Petipa. He never made a mistake with the music. He never made a mistake in how to build from nothing up to a climax - ever – and his choreography was built that way. What they [choreographers in general today] do is they do everything "arse-backwards"! I have done an analysis, I took it [the choreography of the *Nutcracker* pas de deux] section by section to explain why it [a particular version of the choreography] is wrong. It's there [amongst his archives] . . . I have it.

RAVENNA: I think choreographers are entitled to choreograph what they would like. Everyone hears a piece of music differently.

HENRY: Yes, but start with a piece of music and do something original on it. Don't take a piece of music someone has already done something [to] . . . that's plagiarism.

RAVENNA: Well, it's not plagiarism if you create your own choreography.

HENRY: But they don't . . . they use the same steps! They use the same steps and put them in "arse-backwards" and change them. I will not accept that! The word "classic" means *to be learnt from*. Petipa turned out things which were perfect in every sense. Anyway, I know you must think that I'm completely crazy, but I do know what some of the classics - not all of them - are supposed to be, simply because I dug into it so deeply, you know, and I understand the relationship . . . the music, the choreography, and the narrative.

[Here the conversation digressed into multiple other topics, before meandering back to what follows.]

RAVENNA: Henry, what were those golden rules of classical ballets that you mentioned before [much earlier in the conversation]?

HENRY: The golden rules . . . the first one . . . it [the choreography] has to obey the music . . . the steps; it must be musical. [Secondly], it has to be technically correct . . . it must finish in a position from which the next step can be done without making a change . . . if you finish a step in plié and the next step should be started from a rélevé, it's wrong. One sequence of steps, enchaînement, whatever you like to call it, has to finish in the absolutely correct position in which the next step starts from, except there's an exception to that, and we've talked about that. Sometimes, we step arabesque with the right leg [followed by a temps levé, then chassé passé with the left leg, followed by] pas de bourrée [a pas de bourrée dessous with the right leg, into a pas de chat], and then to do it to the other side and you've got the left leg behind . . . .

[I get up to do the steps to try to feel what Henry is explaining.]

RAVENNA: So you step arabesque . . . .

[I step forward onto my right leg into first arabesque . . .]

HENRY: 1-2-3-4-5-6-1-pas de chat . . . yes, step [he indicates the stepping forward with his right hand into a first arabesque onto the right leg], jump – "2", plié, pas de bourrée, "1"–pas de chat . . . so your left leg is in the back the second time [to repeat the steps to the other side the second time]. You start with one [the first time], with the front leg, and the repeat starts from the back leg. So you're doing two possibilities . . . Understand? That's not just me . . . what's his name . . . ?

RAVENNA: Petipa?

HENRY: [Nikolai] Legat! Legat said that every step started from . . . [Henry points a finger at me to emphasise an important point] . . . this is not a golden rule . . . well, it is, actually . . . every step starts in fifth position croisé, always, even if you go to éffacé, you turn [he shows me and turns his torso to éffacé]. Every step starts in fifth croisé . . . this is not a golden rule [he decides!].

RAVENNA: Is there a rule where[by] you do a step three times and the fourth time is a different step?

HENRY: No, that's not a golden rule; that's an observation [how steps in an exercise for class can be put together to benefit the student's learning]. The next one [third golden rule] is that it has to say something: if I am a canary singing, it has to be clear that there's a canary singing!

RAVENNA: Where do you think ballet will go from here – today? What do you think about how the classics are done today?

HENRY: I think they have deviated from what they were originally, which is a pity because what they [were] was perfect! And you cannot change perfection.

RAVENNA: But dancers today are so perfect, technically. How are dancers today different from when you were a dancer in your generation?

HENRY: Well, take Margot [Fonteyn], for example. She never exceeded her physical possibilities. I mean, she never had a 180-degree leg [extension into the air]. She did everything within her possibility, which gave her a tremendous calm.

RAVENNA: She always looked completely calm, like she stepped out of her dressing room with her hair done and makeup perfect. She was perfect at all times. I must say, whenever I saw pictures of Margot, she would sometimes be in this extraordinary back bend and she would make it look so easy.

HENRY: Well, that's because she was a good dancer – because she was not striving to do something which was beyond her possibilities. You know she had very good taste. That's what dancers don't have anymore is *taste*.

RAVENNA: What is "taste"?

HENRY: Taste is knowing what looks good or sounds good, or doesn't look good or doesn't sound good – to the practised eye! You see, it depends who's looking at people, you know, people who are educated or they think that a split [high extension of the legs] here is fine! That's the trouble . . . the public are not educated.

RAVENNA: Do you think when characters are portrayed in ballets we get the same feeling as when you used to do it in your generation?

[Then, suspecting that my opinions might be biased, and perhaps to reassure myself, I asked Henry what he thought about how dancers today perform and interpret the classics.]

HENRY: Nobody is ever sure about anything – everything's an opinion. You should obey what you feel, what you remember; you remember something different, something better, and that's what you have to teach!

[Later, when our conversation is coming to a close . . .]

RAVENNA: I just admire you so much, that you keep going [his striving to maintain his fitness, and now to rehabilitate from several recent falls, which led to premature deterioration of his health near the end of his one hundred and second year]. I am so much younger than you . . . sometimes I get the feeling that I just want to give up [on studio training]!

HENRY: There's no alternative. I mean, I can get into bed and say I am going to die. I could do that! But I don't want to. I want to get well! I feel I've got something still to do.

RAVENNA: Yes . . . you do!

[He was planning to write several books, and for one in particular, on Vera Volkova, I helped him organise and label some photographs that captured the moments between the two of them, on a holiday, with his mother, by the sea in England in 1945 (Meinertz, 2007, p. 75). Henry recalled, "My mother saw it all . . . she tried to tell me . . . (that their affair could not last) . . . . But we were in love! . . . Vera was very alone. Nobody really knew her the way I did."]

HENRY: But I want to be in shape . . . but I'm getting there. Day by day, I'm getting there.

HENRY: [*As I hug him goodbye*] I haven't given you anything! [in return for several vegetarian dishes that I had cooked and brought to him].

RAVENNA: Henry! Don't you worry about that . . . just your friendship is great . . . just your friendship! You've given me so much!

FIGURE 1.4 Ravenna Tucker Wagnon with Henry Danton

Source: Artist's personal collection

Note

Slightly over a month later, on 9 February, Henry passed away peacefully at his home, just shy of his 103rd birthday. Ever devoted to his beloved art form, he had said, many times, jokingly, whenever we talked about musicality, "When I die, you'll find the 'upbeat' inscribed across my heart!". It was the secret, he said, the "breath" to begin to dance. Now, my friend, you are gone . . . quiet empty space remains, but I carry on and hear your words: "it will all work out . . . it always does".

Reference

Meinertz, A. (2007). *Vera Volkova a biography*. Hampshire: Dance Books Ltd.

1.5

THE LOVE AND KINDNESS OF TEACHERS

Reflecting on working with senior Javanese masters

Alex Dea conversing with Javanese senior dance artists Rama Sas, S. Ngaliman, Bu Yudanegoro and Bu Tarwa

> I am a composer/performer who fortuitously became an ethnographer, and I had the great fortune to have studied with and recorded the old Central Javanese performing arts masters of pre-Independence Indonesia.
>
> *Alex Dea*

Through the masters' teaching, performing, casual talking and laughing, I became aware of their spirit of kindness, unselfish energy, and strength through their embodied archives of old and new knowledge and understanding. It was not just technical information through lessons – of which there were plenty and without holding back anything – but it was a love and kindness which was most obvious, and which was an underlying ephemeral invisible transmission which sustains the Javanese performing arts.

I recorded over a thousand video and audio, whether formal or casual, during a critical transitional pre-industrial time in Java Indonesia. These amazing classical performing artists are on the level of a Balanchine, Margot Fonteyn or Bach, who would share their knowledge with anyone. Somehow, they opened to me, a beginner, and gave the love and kindness of their arts.

I will now introduce the Javanese masters who have been my most important teachers. Rama Sas (K.R.T. Sasminta Mardawa) was born in 1929, and was a principal dancer and master teacher at the Yogyakarta Palace. Being brother-in-law of Pujokusumo, a son of Sultan HB-8, he has created many major classical Javanese dances, including Bedhaya Amurwabumi, part of the repertoire of the sacred royalty arts. He founded his own dance institute, Yayasan Pamulangan Beksa Sasminta Mardawa, becoming one of the best places to learn and perform outside of the palace. S. Ngaliman (Condropangrawit) was born in 1919, and growing up in the famous Kemlayan living quarters of prominent performing artists of the Surakarta Palace, at a young age he became a music courtier. Due to talent and desire, he

DOI: 10.4324/9781003307624-7

became a dance master learning from many of the legendary dancers of the early 20th century. He was prolific in creating new dances, many which have become standard in the Javanese dance scene. These include Batik, Gambyong Pareanom, Manggolo Retno, Bondan Tani, Serimpi Retno Dumilah and Pamungkas. Bu Tarwa (Suyati Tarwa Sumosutargio) born in 1933, was taken into the Mangkune-garan Palace Surakarta at an early age of 11. She became one of the main dancers and is now the principal teacher, and she is proud to still be a palace courtier these 79 years. Bu Yudanegoro (B.R.Ay Yudanegoro) was born 1931 into the royal milieu of the Yogyakarta Palace. She learned dance from an early age, becoming a leading teacher, especially of the Bedhaya-Serimpi sacred repertoire, in the palace, at other universities, and the Siswa Among Beksan founded by her husband Yuda-negoro, son of Sultan HB-8. She was responsible for the reconstruction after more than 60-plus years of absence of the paramount sacred ritual Bedhaya Semang, culminating the Sultan's coronation anniversary. Here are some peeks into some of the many interactions I have had.

My search

I searched for the understanding of Javanese dance and music. Master Rama Sas said,

> I started dance at the Yogyakarta Palace. My teachers were all masters. Later, I rearranged (I did not compose!) some choreographies to abbreviate some of the repetitious sections. The older teachers objected greatly. However, dance should fit the times of the audience tastes. It's true! I am not "fanatik" [fanatically prejudiced].

By the time of Sas's passing in 1996, he was recognised as the top teacher of the palace style, attesting his modernising efforts. For me, he gently suggested, "You could study some dance. Not to be a dancer, but to understand how things work".

Indirectness, quiet power

In 1993, Rama Sas's group was invited to tour Brazil. Back then, especially for a non-governmental group, this was a big deal. His students were the best, and in their prime (around age 20s). During rehearsal, one of the dancers missed his cue. During the break, Rama Sas quietly announced "this is not the time to study", meaning you should have studied details at home. In an American rehearsal, the director or teacher would speak directly – and most likely, loudly. In Java, it is indirectly. Rama Sas did not point to the guilty student, but to the general group, and spoke softly. The velocity of his intent, while voice-quiet, pierced loudly to all of the students. There is a resolute and firm but soft, unhurried way of talking. This candour was evident also when Bu Yudanegoro, the principal palace dancer and teacher, said "When I was learning, the teacher would teach by example. We only had to be told once, not like the younger generation now".

Casual grace

Not all the masters were aristocrats or courtiers of the palaces. In my many vocal lessons at the humble village home of Pak Sastrotugiyo, one of the greatest singers of their world, we would pause for a tasty lunch – home-cooked noodles, thick sweet tea. Then, back to the serious work of making my singing sound Javanese, so no one would know it was a foreigner singing. He would go for hours, with me fading out before him. During one song, he light-heartedly said, "Think of your wife. This is a love song!". Suddenly, he waved and called his grandchildren, pointing to my video camera saying "Come over! Say hello to Mas Alex's friends in America! Don't be shy!" Through these informal interactions, I understood the nuances of their life and therefore, art.

This kind of disarming casual attitude – part of the invisible transmission – greatly expanded my understanding of composition and performance. When finally I undertook dance, it was with Bu Yudanegoro, the top dance mistress of the Yogyakarta Palace. Here was a Margot Fonteyn patiently showing me the steps. I was awkward and asked if I could video my lessons. She laughed "Oh sure. Whatever you want. This is your lesson. I'll do whatever you want." I wondered why she was so patient with a raw beginner like me. She was already over 70 years of age, but still spry and full of cheerful talk.

> I don't know why I am a dancer. It's something I liked since I was a small child. My father was an important palace musician. We were aristocrats, proud to be of royal lineage. Actually, when young, you do not think about that. You just follow your parents, the elders.

She revealed:

> I was encouraged to dance, but only the royal pieces. Back then, the golèk dance was considered too coquettish, not fit for a refined dignified woman. Father forbade my learning it, but I liked it, so snuck out to secretly learn it.

Serious matters

All of my masters expressed this casual calm and grace, even regarding serious matters. Bu Yudanegoro had the important (and spiritually dangerous) task of rearranging the reconstruction of the sacred ritual dance Bedhaya Semang.

> This dance is sacred, maybe the most sacred. The dance is about the mythical Queen of the South Sea's conjugal meetings with the Sultan. Sajèn [ritual food] must be carefully and precisely set to the gamelan instruments every rehearsal. We give a moment of silent prayer before starting the dance lessons. It is dangerous.

Even so, she could lightly say "When working after a year, we presented the result to the Sultan; he said it was too long. It should be cut in half . . . to two and half hours! So said, I did it."

Unselfishness and diligence

Teaching is a sacrament, as clearly evident with the Javanese masters from whom I studied. Teaching is also a kindness. In Java, this is to the supreme degree. It seems that kindness is one thing – and so is love – exemplified by knowledge givers. Even after S. Ngaliman, premier Surakarta Palace dancer/teacher, suffered a serious stroke, he agreed to work with me to create a video of his Pamungkas dance. He could not walk, but through gesture and rhythm tapping, he directed his youngest son, who knew the dance.

Another was Bu Tarwa (Suyati Tarwo Sumosutargio) of the Mangkunegaran Palace. Due to her high diligence to art, even after she could hardly walk alone, she would sit at the side of the gamelan orchestra and teach with gestures while the students were dancing (not facing her!). She said "I entered the service of the palace at age 11 and now, at over 80, I will never stop being a dancer and palace courtier."

Intangibility

From these many interactions, I learned something intangible which I call indirectness, stillness, and meditation. Rono Suripto, dance master of the Mangkunegaran Palace, said "Even simply sitting cross-legged to play gamelan music, 'sila' is the same word and position of sitting in meditation." Gamelan is a kind of meditation. The effect of the bronze gongs, the sinuous pathways of dance, are like blood or the soul of water. Meditation looks like nothing is moving, but there is abundance of activity. This aesthetic applies equally to dance. Due to the masters' generous life energy, I lucked into getting some of that invisible transmission – a bit of their ethos came into and greatly helped my composing and performing, especially with inter-cultural collaborations.

The future is here

While large changes to the transmission of performing arts are clear, it is not – as feared over 20 years ago, at the passing of Rama Sas – of "some catastrophic loss of tradition". The current-generation teachers have their own way. Some examples are the get-togethers of over 60 dancers commemorating the 35-day birthday of the late dance master Rama Sas in Jogja, informally reviewing and renewing the classical repertoire. Another one is at the Mangkunegaran Palace with the Pakarti informal practice led by a master musician and expert dancer. The dancers are of all ages, from beginners to students from the masters' heyday. The leaders are students of the masters; they now have become masters themselves. These events are all volunteered. They are announced through mobile phone social networks. It seems that in this way, a new expression of love and kindness is continued.

Note

This writing is partially based on and mingled with the video "The Love and Kindness of Teachers", presented in 2021 at the International Council for Traditional Music PASEA. and PGVIM Princess Galyani Vadhana Institute of Music Bangkok: https://youtu.be/sSrXtY4ILlo. A shorter version in 2022 was presented at World Dance Alliance Global Summit: https://youtu.be/9zgdXDzO1ic.

1.6

A LIFE IN DANCE

Collaborating and working together

Anca Frankenhaeuser and Patrick Harding-Irmer
with Eileen Kramer

Eileen has choreographed and performed with Patrick and Anca on several occasions since her return to Australia. They have also been involved in films created by Eileen Kramer and Sue Healey including *Lady of the Horizon* (2020) and *The God Tree* (2021). This Conversation via telephone took place in Sydney in September 2021 during the COVID-19 lockdowns that restricted live performances. There was plenty of laughter interspersed throughout this discussion among Eileen Kramer (107), Patrick Harding-Irmer (76) and Anca Frankenhaeuser (74).

ANCA: I've been thinking back a bit, and we have known you for almost six and a half years now.

Remember when we first met? At the Hughenden Hotel in Woollahra. Maggie (Haertsch) and Shane (Carroll) had asked a few of us to come and meet you because you wanted to do a project.

EILEEN: That's right. It was in the hotel and she treated us to high tea. I was very impressed with "high tea".

ANCA: So that was the beginning of *The Early Ones* that you had done in America and wanted to recreate here. Shane brought us and Julia (Cotton) to that tea party to discuss it all, and I suppose you were going to see whether you thought we'd be suitable. [It was first performed in Australia on March 13, 2015 at the Independent Theatre, Sydney.]

EILEEN: I would never have questioned whether you were suitable. What I would have questioned was did your dance style and mine go together. I thought they did. Did you?

PATRICK: Well, yes, I think you felt that we had a compatible kind of aesthetic to interpret your ideas.

EILEEN: Yes, contemporary dancers. We were called modern dancers. Ours was before contemporary became a word.

DOI: 10.4324/9781003307624-8

ANCA: And then we went to Bundanon and had that wonderful time there exploring and rehearsing.

EILEEN: In *The Early Ones*, you adapted yourselves to all the different things that were happening. Patrick came out of the sea, crawled up onto the land and then stood up and made strange primitive sort of movements. And I remember all these people crawled out of the sea and started moving around the stage and it looked as though they hardly knew what they were doing, and you bumped into another dancer. I loved that bit, bumping into him – you both backed away from each other, absolute strangers, innocent people who didn't even know what a war meant. And I wished they'd go on fighting a bit. That was a very effective little moment.

PATRICK: Yes, it is little accidents like that that make things work.

EILEEN: Well, that's the training. You have had your training. The only people I ever worked with was at Bodenwieser Ballet [1939–1959, considered the first modern dance company in Australia] and then after Madame [Bodenwieser] died, I went eventually to Lewisburg, West Virginia and I joined a dance company there, too.

ANCA: Can we go back to talk about the productions. We've done four productions with you and . . .

EILEEN: *The Early Ones* was first, then was it *The Buddha's Wife*?

ANCA: That's right. Those two were actually recreations of what you had done in America. What made you want to do them again?

EILEEN: Well, *The Early Ones* in America was called quite a fancy sort of name. It was called *Songheart of the Dreamtime*, and somebody who typed it up for me didn't like *Songheart* so she wrote *Heartsong*. I don't know what *Songheart* means but I like the sound of it.

But that was the result of I'd been back to Australia on a visit and while I was there, I read about Aboriginal myths or stories. So *Songheart of the Dreamtime* had three Aboriginal stories. First, they came out of the sea and they would develop as human beings. Then they got to the point when they thought of settlement. And in the settlement, because they had a home, they had children. So, we had three children in it, in America. And then finally they made the big march across the country to find a suitable place to start their home.

They [choreographic sections] all had something to do with Aboriginal myths.

Then there was *Isis and Osiris*, and you became *The Lady of the Horizon*.

ANCA: Yes, that was the one after *A Buddha's Wife*.

EILEEN: And what's the fourth one?

ANCA: Then we had *The God Tree* project.

EILEEN: By the way, it's just finished. The book and the story and the dance work are finished. And you're in that, too, of course

ANCA: So *The God Tree* was a completely new project, wasn't it? That was not a recreation of anything from before.

EILEEN: A new project. I don't know how I started that. Well, I already associated it with you and Patrick.

ANCA: Did you see the tree first? Was that where your inspiration came from? Seeing the actual tree [a very big old Moreton Bay fig tree]?

EILEEN: But you know that big tree. They have big thick branches. From those branches other little branches come out that get rooted in the ground, so when you go in it is hard to find the central trunk. The little branches are called aerial roots, and you were one of the aerial roots. Those aerial roots were my favourites.

ANCA: You actually were very particular about how we should do things. You remember?

EILEEN: I wanted to turn you into Bodenwieser dancers!

ANCA: That's right. But, did you succeed? That is the question.

EILEEN: Well, it is my favourite part of the film we made, so I must have succeeded

ANCA: Must have, and to get the camera to pan around, with us standing still, worked really well, too.

EILEEN: Well that was to do with the cameraman, and Sue Healey became the editor of the film.

ANCA: Yes, she is so good at that.

PATRICK: What also looked incredibly impressive was your masks within that tree environment.

EILEEN: Yes, but what meaning had they?

PATRICK: They were just so fascinating, and the juxtaposition of the strength of the tree and the aerial roots with the ethereal quality of the mask faces . . .

EILEEN: Were you scared of them?

PATRICK: Was I scared of them? I think I was scared of the women behind them!

ANCA: It had a lovely mysterious feel to it.

EILEEN: Yes, that's the part I've seen. And I have seen you and Julia and Shane in a pose that I loved, and I think that is in the edited version, too. And your costumes – I made them, and they are my favourite costumes. It did make you all look like aerial roots. I had aerial roots hanging down from your headbands, but they were soft ones. That part of it, in my opinion, was quite successful. First of all, you're seen hanging from the branch by one arm up, hanging onto the big branch and then you escape and turn around.

The film is finished, the music is finished and the dance is finished.

ANCA: And it goes together with the book. Rather than a live performance, it is a book and a film, so that is interesting.

EILEEN: In the film of *The Lady of the Horizon*, I imagined the character in a very close shot standing up looking down on a village, and that's not what you did. You walked across the horizon; you walked along a ridge so all you could see is you walking on this big ridge of land.

ANCA: Well, it's not so easy to find a village with a ridge, is it . . . ?

EILEEN: The Lady of the Horizon was a goddess or a famous character in Egyptian stories.

ANCA: That came from Isis and Osiris.

EILEEN: Yes, that's right. I came across some photos of that with quite a lot of the masks. I don't know what prompted me to make those masks, but I did.

ANCA: They are wonderful.

PATRICK: And it was shot in so many different locations. We were in the sand dunes in Cronulla and up on the grassy slopes of Vaucluse, in Centennial Park at the Labyrinth.

ANCA: And on Cockatoo Island. We went out by ferry.

EILEEN: That's right. We saw that big window. Sue was there. She couldn't resist it. I was the only one around at that moment, so she got me to walk past that window.

ANCA: And that worked really well, too.

PATRICK: A beautiful shot!

ANCA: I remember a funny thing from the rehearsals of *The Lady of the Horizon*. You told us that you'd heard somebody rapping, that you wanted a rapper, I think it was for the Underworld, so you did some for us. which was very funny.

PATRICK: Very good you were. too, even using proper street speak, as well.

EILEEN: Oh yes. [in rap speak:] I went down the street and I saw a guy rapping and I said I gotta be a rapper myself.

EILEEN: I don't look like a rapper, do I?

PATRICK: Sometimes you are wrapped though Eileen – wrapped in your beautiful finery.

EILEEN: Yes, well, I must say, I feel blessed with all those good friends, and I find this the best time of my life. I've been here such a long time.

ANCA: Well, we are very lucky to be part of your group of friends.

PATRICK: We are fortunate to have you in our lives.

EILEEN: Well, we are all lucky. And all I can say is "press on"! So are you ready for this new dance film?

ANCA and PATRICK: We're ready. Let's do it!

FIGURE 1.6   *The Godtree* (2021); choreographer: Eileen Kramer; dancers: Patrick
Harding–Irmer and Anca Frankenhaeuser

Source: Photograph from artist's personal collection

1.7

THE JOY OF LIFE EXPERIENCE IN CONTEMPORARY DANCE

Graeme Murphy and Janet Vernon in conversation with Shirley Gibson

Founding member of the MADE Ensemble Shirley Gibson, chats with Graeme Murphy and Janet Vernon chat about the joy of life experience in contemporary dance. MADE (also see Chapter 2.2) creates and presents contemporary dance theatre performed by dancers that tells stories of lives lived, dreams sought, experiences shared and challenges overcome. This conversation relates to Graeme's choreography for the company; specifically, *The Frock* (2018).

SHIRLEY: You have completed some wonderful collaborations with MADE. I was so nervous contacting the internationally renowned choreographer. Do you remember how our journey began?

GRAEME: When you called, I didn't really hesitate. When a time became available, Janet and I just jumped at the opportunity, because what is life without new experiences? We'd never had the opportunity to work with an ensemble who knew each other very well after ten years of working together, who have runs on the board performing, but are also open to new adventures – which is what thrilled me. We were so ready for this experience. I mean, sometimes you get dancers who are very precious if they're taken outside their comfort zone. You all live outside your comfort zone, I'm sure.

SHIRLEY: I wondered how you would feel about working with our group – people of less athleticism but perhaps more experience?

GRAEME: MADE offers me something that no other company I've worked with does. You're a troupe of mature artists, and a troupe of very adventurous women for your age. I think you're completely courageous because some of the things I've asked you to do, I don't think I would get the same response if I was working with professional dancers or actors or singers. You bring such a unique slant to everything you do with a courageous energy. I think sometimes it's hard for you, feeling uncomfortable. But I'm not asking you to be technical ballerinas;

DOI: 10.4324/9781003307624-9

I'm asking you to be involved in the creation, to bring your wisdom and age to the work, and what you know about the world and living. You relish your wrinkles, and you delight in your dreams. And you take us somewhere that maybe we would not have the courage to go.

SHIRLEY: I'm interested in knowing if you found new creative expression and what kind of goal you had in mind.

JANET: Initially, when we started working with you, we were very careful in how we structured rehearsals. We wanted to make the work a dance theatre piece, and that took you out of your comfort zone a little bit. But you went with the flow very easily. And technically, you just wanted to learn more and more. You could give us all the emotion. I mean, God – Graeme and I cried through rehearsals so often, you just gave so much to us.

SHIRLEY: You both worked around the technical side extremely well. We are not professional dancers and some of us have never learned dance before, so thankfully you accommodated what we physically could and couldn't do. Also, Graeme, you were very cheeky and often made us laugh. And could I also say you were very considerate about arthritis!

GRAEME: I think I'm considerate because it is just around the corner for me too – arthritis!

I think professional dancers would probably faint if I actually asked them to do some of the things I've asked you all to do.

Your experience is better than technique. It is better than refined artistry. It is a lifetime of experience that when you all move, even when moving can be difficult, it reminds us of where you've been, what you've been through and what you've experienced. And in a work, that is what we're trying to achieve – that layering of emotions. It's interesting, because I am usually surrounded by people who are eternally 17, 18, 20. There is a sort of 'frozen in time' thing because every time I work with other companies, there is yet another new group of young dancers.

With elite younger dancers, the biggest problem is to find physical challenges for them. But they often don't have enough life experience to express something meaningful. I have to tell them what it feels like; it has to be broken up.

It was lovely to meet with MADE and think "these people are my age". It was a beautiful adventure for me which I approached so differently. The inspiration was within you all, and I could just pull out your world experiences and try to put that in movement; and also try to find words to express some of your stories – using the spoken word method/genre was a new experience for me.

An audience is looking beyond just the steps – an audience needs to see the thought process, feel the weight of someone's experiences, to see the suffering, to see the joy; and when I work with MADE, that comes out of your eyes and bodies.

SHIRLEY: We certainly grow when working with you – there are definitely challenges. People are saying "I can't do that" at the beginning, and then realising afterwards that "yes, I have done it!" There's a lot of research now around being physically active as we approach 60s, 70s and 80s – it is important, but also the creative side of thinking – it changes the pathways in the brain, which helps with mental health as well.

GRAEME: Janet and I started pushing with rhythmic, complex things that were actually hard and needed to be effective, but I also wanted to engage the brain power that dance is so good for – dance is used in so many therapies for real reasons. It was incredibly enriching for me.

As a choreographer, I treat people as individuals and look to what I can extract from within their DNA and their psyche. *The Frock* encapsulates what I feel, too. As my body decays, I go into studios and still have to demonstrate for beautiful young dancers. I feel that mentally, I am doing the step as well as they are, and sometimes much better. That is a really interesting way of thinking, because I think dance is 10% physical and the rest is mental control. I want to get across that internal storytelling matters – whether they are MADE dancers or mega-athletes from the Australian Ballet – it is what you say that gets it across, because dancers often just register the movement, and if you don't give them a reason, it just remains as movement.

I love that dance doesn't need words to touch people, I love the *directness* of it and I think we have to keep using that journey from the eye, into the brain, into the heart – keep people mentally engaged, but also keep them emotionally engaged. Help them see themselves up on stage; invite them to dance with you. What audiences look forward to is a "layering". I think that is what I love about MADE. MADE has done some very obscure and fascinating works, but the concept of a 60-minute storytelling work that really tapped into an emotional journey was a different adventure. MADE is a beautiful manifestation of that in a very tangible way – I just loved the experience.

SHIRLEY: Talking about storytelling, you also had a challenge creating the script for *The Frock*.

GRAEME: That was a new experience because I'm the enemy of the spoken word. Dance is that mute art form, you know, "Shut up and dance. We don't want to know anything about what you're thinking – just get your leg up higher!" And this was interesting. I suddenly realised that I needed to find a way where words and dance can sit comfortably together – and after 50 years of making dance, to find new ways of doing things is really satisfying.

I am forever grateful to MADE because you taught me how to write characters which pushed me into new areas. I had spurned the written word – dance is a silent art form – my quote was "dance is truth, mute but absolute". And I had to rethink that because words and poetry were beautiful for me to use in *The Frock*.

I was once asked if dance is a disposable art form. I see it as ephemeral. That's what I love – I love the ephemeral aesthetic – that's what makes it more precious. It only lives while it is in a dancer's brain and as long as that person and audiences remembers it.

If you honestly believe that what you're doing is right, you have an air of confidence about what you do. MADE shouts confidence and it is right. It feels fabulous to work with you all. You are stunning. You're wonderful. And I'm very happy you found us.

SHIRLEY: And we are also very happy we found you. What a wonderful journey we're on together, and we want to thank you both for your generosity, joy of dance and the two beautiful works that you've created with us. May there be many more in MADE's repertoire. What gems you are!

GRAEME and JANET: We embrace challenges. We are now doing as we have always done – follow passion, encourage talent, be creatively opportunistic and continue to believe in Australian artists and their importance globally.

FIGURE 1.7 Janet Vernon, Shirley Gibson and Graeme Murphy in rehearsal

Source: Photograph by Sandi Sissel

1.8

A SENSE OF PLACE AND CREATING TOGETHER

Antonio Vargas and Stephanie Burridge

> Stephanie and Antonio have worked together on a couple of shows and a film: *The Rites Project* (2018), a flamenco version of *The Rite of Spring*, and *We Dance Alone – Men Dancing Project* (2021). They are both long-term residents of Singapore and are married to Singaporeans.

STEPHANIE: Let's talk about how we first started working together in Singapore. I loved your company's work, Flamenco Sin Fronteras [FSF] and imagined a flamenco version of Stravinsky's *Rite of Spring*. I remember the idea shocked you a bit – what can you remember?

ANTONIO: It was funny – the thought of me dancing some contemporary, as I am not trained in that, with the flamenco . . . actually it was a bit intimidating! [working with another professional contemporary dancer in the show]. Stravinsky's *Rite of Spring* . . . the music is extreme . . . like the flamenco style, so I could visualise it working. It is concentrated power, but there is a connection through the timing.

STEPHANIE: I incorporated sections that were very familiar in flamenco – like the dance with the performers sitting on chairs and beating the walking canes on the ground. Also, the fiery section with the manton [big shawl]. I called it the *Rites Project* so that I could also incorporate the idea of migration, and human rights.

ANTONIO: I really liked the way it also incorporated another love of mine . . . cooking. You asked me to make paella during the show (we shared it with the audience at the end) and I enjoyed making percussion sounds with all the pots and pans! That was fun!

STEPHANIE: What about feeling the music? I admit to some frustration with flamenco dancers that are always counting the beats while contemporary dancers take a more instinctive approach to "feeling the music".

DOI: 10.4324/9781003307624-10

ANTONIO: All good dancers should sense it [the music] . . . visualise it as a whole and look ahead in the music. It should flow although the rhythms are very distinctive . . . you can feel it. I find some flamenco today too busy . . . like a competition to see how fast their footwork can be. Dance should look for the innuendos . . . I must find meaning in the dance – not just in the moment.

STEPHANIE: Yes . . . I feel the music intuitively. I approach the music in an instinctive way . . . but I must listen to it countless times to get to the point that I am very clear about it when we begin rehearsing.

STEPHANIE: You have danced in both choreographies we worked on with FSF. What did you want to experience in this journey?

ANTONIO: It was very enjoyable to collaborate together. To try something new – there was no pressure, as I was not trying to emulate what I had done before. You had a lot of clarity about what we were doing.

I have always wanted to explore and try new things. Hence, I called the company in Singapore Flamenco Sin Fronteras [Flamenco without Borders]. I do not need boundaries – I wanted to open up the space to many possibilities. For example, we have worked with Kathak dancers, and musicians from many backgrounds. I was born in Morocco and grew up in Casablanca, where many cultures come together. I have worked with gypsies in my companies and dancers with different world views – it all coheres on stage through the powerful emotion of flamenco.

STEPHANIE: With *Men Dancing*, we started channelling Nijinsky and Martha Graham in a couple of solo sections for you. I remember explaining the Graham contractions from the floor to you – your curiosity in wanting to do it correctly was amazing.

ANTONIO: I think Nijinsky was incredible performing *L'Après-midi d'un faune (Afternoon of the Faun)* – the details of the hands and parallel positions had such clarity. I watched several versions and was fascinated by how the body expressed the story.

STEPHANIE: We also experimented with some of the movements that came from the floor – like the Martha Graham pleadings. It was interesting to recall some of the earlier contemporary works.

ANTONIO: Yes, I loved Kurt Jooss' *The Green Table* (1932). It was so original, so exciting and such groundbreaking choreography.

[At this point, we digress to talk about many choreographers and dancers who have inspired us, from Mats Ek and Pina Bausch to Alexander Ekman, Mikhail Baryshnikov and more.]

STEPHANIE: We journey along together when we create transiting between your passion and knowledge of flamenco and my contemporary choreography. What do you think pulls the choreography together? The sensibility and philosophy of flamenco and contemporary are poles apart in many ways.

ANTONIO: It is all movement – it has meaning and connects. I also found connections to the contemporary style from my practice of Qi Gong that I do daily – it is very grounded.

STEPHANIE: For me, it is the authenticity and authority of the movement that comes across – it has a direct connection to the audience. It is also transformative and exciting to watch.

As time passes, we manage our dancing and choreography differently – with your ongoing injuries and my weakness and balance issues from MS [multiple sclerosis]. In an odd way, I find these become advantages – you value time, what you can do and the inventiveness that comes from what you can no longer do. Even the language we use shifts using more metaphors, stories and emotions rather than demonstrating so much. How do you feel about this?

ANTONIO: I always think of it as . . . "a perfect vase that has got a crack . . . yet it is still perfect!". I do not feel the need to perform . . . if it is something interesting and has meaning, I can. For flamenco, if I can't give it my maximum, I almost feel guilty [to the form] . . . But I am very happy in the background.

[Antonio is always involved on stage in his productions playing music – the cajón, castanets, palmas or guitar.]

For *Men Dancing* my bunions were so bad that I had trouble getting my boots on for the footwork sections [laughs!]

When I choreograph, I still demonstrate fully. I want to give the passion and emotion as part of the choreography – the dancers must find meaning in it.

STEPHANIE: I find myself sitting to demonstrate much more now – apart from choreography that evolves from the floor, where I am very comfortable with no balance issues! I tend to work with experienced, or mature, dancers that can visualise the intention and want to contribute their own story to the concept. I am more involved in framing and shaping the dynamics, giving nuance and storytelling to inspire creation rather than making up too many steps!

On a personal level, I think we have much in common that connects us and is also realised through working together in dance. We both have Australian connections, have lived in Singapore for over a decade and are married to Singaporeans. Any thoughts?

ANTONIO: It was destiny [coming to Singapore], a place to settle after touring the world for almost five decades with brief stops along the way. Time does take its toll eventually – we have to listen to our bodies. Now I like to collaborate. I live in the moment . . . creativity comes from living your life!

STEPHANIE: Totally . . . collaboration, friendship and creating together is really special after a long career in dance. There is still much to do . . . and a lot to say. So, our journeys continue!

FIGURE 1.8 *The Rites Project* (2018); choreographer: Stephanie Burridge; dancer: Antonio Vargas

Source: Photograph by Flamenco Sin Fronteras

SECTION 2
Professional dance practice

FIGURE 2.0 Dancer: Sonia York-Pryce

Source: Photograph by Barry Pryce

DOI: 10.4324/9781003307624-11

2.1

TOO OLD TO DANCE! SAYS WHO?

Senior professional dancers defying ageism

Sonia York-Pryce

Introduction

Advanced age on stage, once a taboo concept, is slowly becoming a reality despite the established aesthetics within Western dance culture that demands perfection, youth, and athleticism. The ostracism or 'killing off' of dancers aged over 40 is changing, with an increasing acknowledgement of their lifetime of embodied dance experience. This much-needed inclusivity sees a renewed interest in the craft of this older demographic and an appreciation from senior audiences who welcome the representation. My research has gathered the voices of senior dance practitioners to understand their determination to continue performing and to navigate the inherent biases in the field.

Context

> I don't care if no one ever wants to watch me dance again. I am going to dance because I love to dance . . . . I am not happy unless I can dance, so I plan to do it until I die.
>
> *(Pat Catterson, email to the author, September 2015)*

In 2013, I interviewed Canadian contemporary dancer Louise Lecavalier, then aged in her 50s, who was performing at the Adelaide Festival. In the 1980s, she had been affectionately known as the 'punk princess' of contemporary dance while part of the Canadian company La La La Human Steps, so I was intrigued to see what assets ageing had bestowed upon her. It was at that meeting that I wondered how many other senior professional dancers were still performing and, if so, why they were not more visible on our stages or screen. This prompted my doctoral research (York-Pryce, 2020), which investigated ageism and how the bias experienced by dancers aged over 40 impacted their practice in today's ballet and contemporary

DOI: 10.4324/9781003307624-12

dance culture. As Kathleen White states, this ideology is perpetuated by Western dance culture by "favour[ing] the young body" (1999, p. 61). In Western society 'old age' of over 65 as discussed in the United Nations, "World Population Ageing 2019 – Highlights", the 'old age dependency ratio' (the OADR), is a far cry from dancers over 40 who are 'old' but appear biologically youthful with fitness and agility that contrasts with their actual chronological age (United Nations, 2019, p. 11). I began gathering the voices of mature dancers in Australia and internationally to understand how they navigated the bias and 'danced on'. As dance is a non-verbal art form, this emphasised for me the importance for dancer's voices to be heard – and so, their opinions, strategies, and histories became my primary research. I am interested in understanding how they have managed to "age productively and healthily" (Bal et al., 2021, p. 24) through specific individual fitness programmes. These dancers are redefining what the older dancing body can achieve and feel, far from "fading into the background as they age" (Meagher, 2014, p. 137). By conducting interviews directly, I was able to appreciate how these dancers achieved their desired goals whilst retaining their autonomy within a prejudiced Western dance culture (York-Pryce, 2020). Their responses highlighted how the body, identity, and agency feature foremost as they fight to continue performing amidst a background of predetermined aesthetics and discrimination.

The position of senior professional dancers has been well researched by scholars (e.g., Schwaiger, 2012; Lansley & Early, 2011), whilst freelance dancers have also undertaken self-representational research (e.g., Martin, 2017; Edward, 2018). Dance scholar Elizabeth Schwaiger (2012, p. 139) addresses the unwritten bylaws of the dance world whereby set aesthetics rule supreme but acknowledges senior professional dancers as "drivers of change". She sees them as positive examples of ageing, showing that the older body can perform past 40 and still have much to express (Schwaiger, 2012, p. 141). Retiring quietly and conforming to the "dance-by-date" set down by Western dance culture is not for all, with many dancers in the research believing they have much more to experience (Edward & Newell, 2013, p. 15). Indeed, Mark Edward states, "The idea of a professional dancer continuing to dance above and beyond a certain age in Western culture is somehow deemed a social faux pas" (Edward, 2011, p. 22). American dancer Pat Catterson has no intention of retiring even though her ageing body has its issues; she is passionate about performing and takes classes daily despite some believing she should stop.

> I would prefer not to be seen as that old dancer, but just as a dancer who happens to be older. I would rather be seen as a good dancer rather than one who does pretty well for an old person.
>
> *(Catterson, email to the author, September 2015)*

The duality of the dance and the dancer, career and identity, are intertwined; one cannot exist without the other (Wainwright & Turner, 2003, p. 270). The body is a finely tuned instrument, and as such, it is "a tool . . . as both subject and object" (Aalten, 2004, p. 269). Dancers who wish to continue performing but are no longer within a company suffer exclusion; they become invisible.

In everyday society, we respect history and longevity, but these elements are not typically valued within Western dance culture – particularly in classical ballet, where dancers may graduate to play the character roles of 'ageing adults' as they age, or stop performing to coach, teach, or move away from dance altogether. Ross Philip of the Australian Dance Artists discusses the limited expectations of a 'senior' dancer in a ballet company, believing it is not the choice for all: "There are many senior dancers, playing kings, evil characters, queens, ladies in waiting . . . do you call that dancing? With Modern/Contemporary Dance, as a mature dancer you form your own company or go solo" (Philip, email to the author, August 2014). The narrative surrounding chronological ageing considers the 'old' body as culturally defamed and devalued, whereby decline is not welcomed. This cultural 'problem' is not shared in the world of dance in the East, where respect and recognition for older dancers is culturally the norm, such as in Japan's traditions of Butoh and Noh. In Spain and Argentina, ageing performers bring greater significance and importance to the styles of flamenco and tango, respectively, due to years of refining these techniques. Yet, this differs significantly within the field of Western dance culture; as observed by Japanese dance scholar Nanako Nakajima, "the ageing body challenges the system of dance and the politics of aesthetics in dance" (Nakajima, 2017, p. 22).

The senior professional dancer goes against the myth that ageing indicates decline, but the ageist 'expiry-date' has still been culturally slow to be addressed. French sociologist Pierre Bourdieu's theoretical schema concerning "the body as habitus and physical capital" gives a parallel understanding to ageing and how it is monitored within Western dance culture (Bourdieu, 1990, p. 56). His notion of the body is a lens that can be used to understand the practice and subjectivity of senior professional dancers. Feminist Julia Twigg (2007) considers how identity is interwoven with the body and its appearance; for the dancer, it is central, it is their physical capital, and it is "policed" (p. 297). This enforced aesthetic ensures the shortening of a career. Former ballerina Leanne Benjamin was often reminded of this aspect but not disgruntled by the British press, which nicknamed her "Benjamin Button" when she reached her 40s (The reference refers to Scott Fitzgerald's "the Curious Case of Benjamin Button (1922), a short story about a man who goes backwards from aging to childhood). Leanne Benjamin looked much younger than her chronological age, and found the label amusing and not at all negative. In spite of great reviews, she sometimes sensed they placed greater importance on her age rather than her performing ability. Benjamin was not unrealistic; she knew her capabilities and she was happy to be dancing well despite being a mature dancer. She experienced nothing but positive responses from audiences and that maintained her passion to keep performing. (Benjamin, email to the author, September 2014).

Twigg states (2010, p. 1), "ageing represent[s] a disruption of its cultural field", which is reflected by body-centric attitudes within Western dance culture; only when changes of attitude are initiated will equality be brought about. This 'disruption' needs to be contested to prevent older dancers feeling they are some sort of 'curiosity'; instead, the context should be to promote diversity and acknowledge their lived dance experience. By making provision to programme senior dancers, visibility is restored, and cultural capital could be championed. As Swedish dancer Rafi Sady states, "I think that they will not judge us for [our] age, they will judge us for what we present" (email to the author, March 2017).

Sociologists Steven P. Wainwright and Bryan S. Turner (Wainwright & Turner, 2006, p. 247) maintain ballet in particular "is a cruel business"; no sooner has a dancer progressed to soloist or prima in a company than age, injury, or disillusionment appear, and a career can end prematurely. Many dancers in the research have stressed that diversity and inclusion appear more achievable in the independent sector, but the dance industry needs to 'make room' and acceptance to provide performances for senior dancers. Prominent companies such as The Forsythe Company and Pina Bausch's Tanztheater Wuppertal have always championed diversity, but this is not the standard.

Aesthetic boundaries in dance culture dominate; it is a body-based profession supporting the objectification of youth, which continues to proliferate the stigma of an ageing body. Twigg emphasises, "the body is a key dimension in ageing" and is at the centre of scrutiny in the field of dance (Twigg, 2010, p. 17). Positive cultural representation and a widening of boundaries is needed to provide balance to an unequal dance environment, as in society. These dancers need to belong, not to be detached from their place of creativity and subjectivity. After all, an aged demographic would welcome representation, highlighting the positives with hyper visible, embodied, and physically active performers on our stages. As Swedish dance scholar Efva Lilja (2006, p. 22) suggests, "almost no one questions how old people feel seeing only younger people on stage. What would happen if we altered the perspective?" She describes introducing older performers into performances for more even representation. For example, Pina Bausch restructured her seminal work *Kontakthof* in 2010 by replacing her dancers with a cast over the age of 60. Bausch placed the subjectivity of ageing centre stage, giving an invisible demographic prominence and identity, a platform to be seen and for the audience to see representation through diversity. Again, Lilja (2006, p. 94) agrees with Bausch's restaging, saying "I can see beauty in the body on which time and life have set their stamp. I can see an expressiveness that is markedly different from that of the young person's body, since it has a different story to tell". By highlighting these qualities embodied in these older performers, the theme of *Kontakthof* was reshaped and emboldened. It was a provocation to address how ageing can be perceived positively through dance.

Feminist Michelle Meagher (2014, p. 103) discusses ageing as 'cultural exile' and my experience is that many dancers over the age of 35 feel this 'exiling' is an ageist phenomenon that needs to be challenged. For many, their craft gains greater depth as they mature, and they sense they have not yet reached the pinnacle of their careers. The United States has long welcomed senior dance artists – such as Merce Cunningham, Martha Graham, Eiko and Komo, Gus Solomons Jnr, Mikhail Baryshnikov, and Carmen de Lavallade – whilst in Australia, the process of acceptance has taken much longer to gain momentum. As *New York Times* dance critic Gia Kourlas states (2017), "The bravest thing a dancer can do is grow old".

Two companies

As is known, so many dancers are forced to retire early, depriving them of further-ing a career and audiences of the opportunity to see what can be achieved through maturing. Martha Graham's aphorism "a dancer dies twice" (Graham, 1991, p. 238) was understood by many of the dancers I interviewed, and some pushed hard to 'stay alive' by elongating their careers. Choreographer Jiři Kylián, former artistic director of Nederlands Dans Theater, was an early advocate for senior professional dancers. Kylián mourned the losses from his company due to their 'use-by date'; he recognised that these dancers' careers were ending just as they were 'growing up'. Kylián set a precedent against ageism, and neglect by creating Nederlands Dans Theater 3 (NDT3, 1991–2006). Seeing the untapped and undervalued potential of older dancers, he seized the opportunity to right the wrongs, realising "it is a little history of dance that is inside them" (Sulcas, 1998, p. 59). Kylián appreciated their expertise and understood how these assets could shine and embellish the choreog-raphy, understanding that as in society, dance should mirror life. "This company is a gesture towards the dancers. It tells them they do not have to give up, that there are ways of physical expression, endless possibilities that can go on until you die" (Sulcas, 1998, p. 58). Gérard Lemaître (1936–2016), a founding member of NDT3, realised that Kylián had given them 'a life' in a context that was unprecedented. He explained,

> [Kylián] took me out of NDT1 in that time and he took me back for NDT3 . . . he save[d] our life, and that became the love story with Jiři with Sabine with all those people, because we love to dance – we have so much experience, so much to say in the dance world still . . . we have a chance also, to work with the best choreographers.
>
> *(Lemaître, interview with the author, January 2015)*

Lemaître confirmed that ageing brings different qualities to a performance – the embodiment of lived experience provides an embellished difference – but he was realistic of their expectations, stating "but you know when we are 20, we cannot [do] what we do at 40, and when you are 40 you cannot do what you did at 20 . . . but we have something" (Lemaître, interview with the author, Janu-ary 2015). NDT3 proved that there is no doubt that senior professional dancers bring great virtues to their performances, a maturity that has been shaped by a lifetime of performing.

Dance On Ensemble (2015–)

In 2015, dance and age was again endorsed by the creation of a new mature dance company, Dance On Ensemble, (DOE), an initiative of Diehl+Ritter in Berlin. Executive and Artistic Director Madeline Ritter and former dancer Riccarda Herre were inspired by the success of NDT3 to create this new company. They, too, understood the injustice of curtailing dancers' careers and created the ensemble for dancers over 40, with the aim of producing new work with "today's most interesting choreographers and theatre makers". Ritter and artistic director and ensemble member Christopher Roman state their aim is "to show how dance as an art form benefits from the charisma, confidence, and expressiveness that arise from lived experience" (Ritter & Roman, 2018, p. 80). Ritter and Herre concentrate on giving dancers a presence in a culture that dismisses ageing, aiming to highlight diversity to the current dance world. Ritter explains, "it became apparent that at the core is really the dancer . . . and the invisibility" (Ritter, interview with the author, May 2018). The project is supported and funded by Germany's federal government. Ritter was surprised by the number of dancers who responded to the initial call-out:

> I think 230 or so people from all over the world appl[ied] and then 15 we invited for a three-day workshop to work with the artists; Rabih Mroué was there to see them. So, this was the selection process.
>
> *(Ritter, interview with the author, May 2018)*

Six exemplar dancers were chosen, and the journey of this second ground-breaking European mature dance company began. Ritter was adamant that DOE would create a robust dance dialogue promoting the lived danced experience of its performers, proving that there can be a supported career in dance after 40. DOE member Amancio Gonzalez reveals:

> I am lucky enough to be working in a company of dancers of the same age range, with a salary every month, with choreographers coming to choreograph specially for us, as mature dancers . . . . How much easier can I have it?
>
> *(Gonzalez, email to author, July 2016)*

DOE proves that older dancers can have a recognised and valued place in a company that is concentrating on their embodied riches, corporeal knowledge, and artistic excellence, showing the Western dance culture and beyond that change is welcomed. Following NDT3's example, eminent choreographers have needed no encouraging to create new works for this company. In the post–COVID-19 world, DOE is performing all over Europe, with feedback from audiences confirming that seeing 'age' represented on stage is an innovative and positive experience, whilst the dancers show that ageing is not holding them back.

Ageism and the mature dancer

The responses to the survey I distributed for my doctoral exegesis *Ageism and the Mature Dancer* (York-Pryce, 2020) revealed many things, but specifically dancers' love of performing and their unquestionable passion to stay in the spotlight. Many were realistic about what could be achieved, whilst some discussed a change of focus in their process, bringing mindfulness to the forefront, a different mindset when compared to their praxis as young dancers. The 'thinking body' was a prominent concept, as described by American dance artist Susan Sentler:

> I do feel my dancing and overall moving is more thoughtful, more detailed, perhaps more transparent. Also, I believe 'pushing' as well as the specific 'boundaries' are different for me now. Frankly, as I age, my interest in performance has shifted . . . . I believe the older, experienced body can yield an artistry that is far beyond the virtuoso of younger dancers. I only wish there were more opportunities for mature performers.
>
> *(Sentler, email to the author, September 2017)*

Amancio Gonzalez also felt maturing brought a different sensibility to his practice:

> I think what made me be where I am is my regularity in my daily training. I still push the boundaries, as always but I know better my limits now, so, I work, not more carefully but with a better understanding of my body.
>
> *(Gonzalez, email to the author, July 2016)*

Many felt they concentrated on the 'less is more' concept, instead of focussing on speed and flexibility, seeing life experience bring added skills and resonance to their performance. Some were adamant that ageing was not going to slow them down, as demonstrated by Brisbane-based dance artist Brian Lucas:

> I think my dancing now is more efficient, I know how to achieve what I want to achieve without having to throw everything at it. I think there is a level of control, there is a level of safety, but I'm still very interested in pushing myself.
>
> *(Lucas, interview with the author, March 2016)*

Sydney-based dance artist Annalouise Paul mirrors Lucas' thoughts, explaining her change in praxis from a contemporary to Flamenco dancer has made her push harder.

> I do push the boundaries for myself as a flamenco dancer . . . in fact I feel as a flamenco dancer . . . that is my practice every day. Because I am older, it has become my daily practice, and therefore, because of that I can push further and because of that I feel that this is where my creative practice is generating from more these days.
>
> *(Paul, interview with the author, September 2015)*

Some were more accepting of the changes that ageing brought to their physicality. Others were realistic of what could be achieved or adapted after surgeries such as hip and knee replacements. Patrick Harding-Irmer of the Australian Dance Artists explains,

> Fitness is an issue, so as physical strength diminishes, and flexibility decreases one must only do things one is able to do. No more jumps, no more throwing

the legs up! I have two hip replacements, which, however, have enabled me to do the things I want to do now without pain!

(Harding-Irmer, email to the author, June 2014)

British dance artist Ann Dickie describes those surgeries may have slowed her down a little, but she is still hungry to perform.

Even with physical limitations (both hips replaced) I still try to push myself beyond what I think capable without compromising my safety. This means I need to know myself and my body pretty well, hopefully an asset of being older.

(Dickie, email to the author, August 2014)

As dancers age, their bodies start to experience decline at a faster rate; like athletes, keeping such elevated levels of speed, virtuosity, flexibility, and endurance becomes a battle for those over 35. However, this does not mean that they are any less an artist; as is proved by many older dancers, their lived dance experience and a keen sense of reality is foremost. Swedish dancer Charlotta Öfverholm, a staunch advocate for older dancers and director of the 'Age on Stage' festivals, believes she could be the only dancer still performing after hip and ankle reconstructions. Öfverholm defies convention, a performer who continues to take risks; age is not present, but prowess is. She has no intention of retiring but recent reviews mention her ageing. This is a new ageist experience for her:

[the reviewer] talks about my age, and this is interesting, that they start to write that in the reviews. He said it in a very positive way, but this has never happened to me before. You know, ". . . despite her age, she . . ." so I think maybe with me because I am still so highly physical, that's why they talk about my age. He said, "I have no idea how old she is . . .. but when she dances, she is forever young".

(Öfverholm, interview with the author, October 2015)

DOE's Amancio Gonzalez was aghast when a critic discussed his appearance as opposed to his performance:

After one of the last shows . . . a critic wrote about me mentioning my grey hair . . . I found [it] strange that she should talk about that, instead of commenting about the dancing, good or bad!

(Gonzalez, email to the author, July 2016)

These dancers are not only working with 'rebuilt' bodies but their strength and hunger to continue performing is also palpable. That said, many believed they were now dancing without pain though a minority felt their bodies were 'a mess', but the power and joy of performing held firm.

Simone de Beauvoir spoke of "the degeneration caused by senescence . . . the deterioration is inevitable" (1977, p. 336), but this could not be farther from the truth when we acknowledge role models for ageing and the continued creativity paradigm such as Australians Eileen Kramer and Elizabeth Cameron Dalman. Indeed, these dance elders show "that the last age is a liberation" (de Beauvoir, 1977, p. 543). Kramer, the centenarian and former Bodenwieser dancer, maintains a practice that continues to be inspired by her training, whilst Elizabeth continues to inspire in her 80s:

> What I love so much about my discovery of modern dance and the philosophies behind the whole Movement is that modern dance encouraged us to push the boundaries of our natural bodies, but at the same time, to respect our bodies.
>
> *(Dalman, interview with the author, August 2017)*

Surprisingly, she discusses her reticence returning to the stage as a much older performer but confirms the importance for the aged demographic to see themselves positively represented.

> In some respects, makes me cringe a little bit. When I was 60, I got special reviews here in Sydney while performing in *Four Generations*: "Elizabeth Dalman now 60 is *hmmm* amazing!". I know that I get noticed now when I am performing because I am this older woman dancing. For me, instead of getting angry about the age question and the fact that perhaps I am only noticed because of my age, I try to rise above it. Dancing with the body I have now, I know that I am reaching out to and connecting with people in the audience, particularly people 60 years and older.
>
> *(Dalman, interview with the author, August 2017)*

Aesthetics

The oversight in Western dance culture of many mature performers does a disservice to the industry; as pointed out by dancer Fergus Early,

> An art form which denies the participation of its most experienced exponents is subjecting itself to a kind of lobotomy: the artist whose practice has grown and developed over many years has a voice that needs to be heard and a dance that needs to be danced.
>
> *(Early, 2013, p. 72)*

One way to overcome ageist programming is to move to the independent sector, where expectations are more fluid, and where there is greater diversity and inclusion. To dance on requires determination and the independent sector allows for freelancers to have a presence, but programming can still be an issue. That said, many dancers were frustrated by the dance sector providing few opportunities. British Dancer Susie Crow states,

> I think there is a growing awareness of the potential of mature dancers, although hitherto it has largely been in the community dance sector rather than the professional environment. Not sure that the establishment knows yet where to place mature professionals. There isn't exactly a repertoire for older ballet dancers; it requires having work made or making work to suit; this is more likely to happen in the independent sector, so it feels a bit like starting out from the beginning all over again.
>
> *(Crow, email to the author, November 2014)*

Interestingly, Ann Dickie believes there is an audience appreciation for seeing 'age' represented on the stage and feels space for diversity in the dance world should be supported.

> I am not sure who my audience is and in spite of what marketing departments claim, there certainly is a growing audience and interest in the work of mature dancers. In my experience, the audience is made up of a variety of ages. I think there is definitely an interest from and appreciation of mature dancers among younger people. I have frequently received feedback that an older dancer is more interesting to watch and identify with as they bring life experience to their work. Their tapestry has more colours.
>
> *(Dickie, email to the author, August 2014)*

In no way do I wish to disparage the wonders and importance of young dancers; indeed, their presence is essential to the art form. But allowing for dancers over 40 to feel as if they could share the same stage with their younger peers would be a positive move that would enrich and diversify Western dance culture. There must be a change in the field to stop discarding them due to the embedded "hierarchical structures" (Adair, 1992, pp. 88–89) that govern a dancers' retirement date. My empirical research has revealed many dancers' determination to remain visible and retain their identity and uncovers their unparalleled determination to keep performing.

Senior professional dancers 'disrupt' the conventional demands expected in the field; their resistance becomes corporeal politics, as suggested by dance artist Mark Edward, "Dancers over 40 are still worthy of having their physicality seen and should not exit the stage quietly and in the dark!" (Edward, email to the author, November 2014). Western dance culture from the grassroots upwards needs to address ageism, to remove the stigma ageing brings and to make dance ageless.

Indeed, as these 'grown-ups' of the dance world demonstrate, ageing may be seen differently through these bodies that have lived. They bring a maturity to their performance and present a demographic that has been sidelined as Western dance culture demands set aesthetics.

Conclusion

As discussed here, there has been a slow but noticeable realisation that diversity is necessary to make Western dance culture more inclusive and resistant to stereotypes. As dance scholar Randy Martin (2004, p, 47) suggests, "if performance not only produces images of life, but acts as the very mirror through which we reflect life, then it is possible to study not only certain depictions of the world, but how the world is depicted". To see older people in society mirrored on our stages would enable visibility for these disenfranchised dancers. Not only are these dancers 'acting their age', but they are also demonstrating that they should be visible, that their lived danced knowledge and artistry be celebrated on our stages. Louise Lecavalier sees no end to performing; indeed, believing there is still much to discover, she explains,

> Watching someone older dancing has no interest in itself, it can only have interest if this person makes us question, discover or simply dream in a new way. So generally, we are not so attentive to people getting older unless they still innovate and push us to review our thoughts or habits.
>
> *(Lecavalier, email to the author, August 2013)*

For the culture of dance to become ageless, senior professional dancers must become part of our visual culture, performing on stage or on film, in a danced dialogue that is inclusive and that welcomes their lived experience of dance. At NDT3's final performance, Kylián's farewell speech stressed, "Dance isn't just about performing as many pirouettes and fouettés as possible and jumping as high as we can; it is about something else. It is about experience, about sharing one's life experience and feelings with the public" (Kylián et al., 2014).

In Kylián's company NDT3, he dared to show solidarity by recognising the need to value and extend careers; today, Berlin's Dance On Ensemble and a cohort of older dancers nationally and internationally are defying the industry's norm. These dancers are 'staying on stage', spearheading a change of attitude, bringing about a metamorphosis concerning ageing within Western dance culture. These dancers are challenging this ageist attitude, and in return, their embodied artistry should be celebrated and recognised as positive attributes for dance and society. Dancing into the twilight may sound trite, but for these elders 'dance' is a calling; it is an art form that digs deep into the psyche; it is part of their very soul. Who are we to stop them? Dance on!

References

Aalten, A. (2004). 'The moment when it all comes together'. Embodied experiences in ballet. *European Journal of Women's Studies, 11*(3), 263–276. doi:10.1177/1350506804044462

Adair, C. (1992). *Women + dance: Sylphs + sirens*. London: MacMillan.

Bal, F. A., Honné, H., van Oosten, E., & Swinnen, A. (2021). *The art of resilience: Professional artists' experiences of continuing creative practices in place*. Maastricht: Jan van Eyck Akademie.

Bourdieu, P. (1990). *The logic of practice [Le sens pratique]*. Cambridge: Polity Press.

De Beauvoir, S. (1977). *Old age* (P. O'Brian, Trans.). Harmondsworth: Penguin Books.

Early, F. (2013). The beauty of reality: Older professional dancers. In D. Amans (Ed.), *Age and dancing: Older people and community dance practice* (pp. 64–72). London: Bloomsbury Academic.

Edward, M. (2011, Winter). More hip op than hip hop. *Animated Magazine*. Retrieved from www.communitydance.org.uk/DB/animated-library/more-hip-op-than-hip-hop.html?ed=14075

Edward, M. (2018). *Mesearch and the performing body*. Cham: Palgrave Pivot.

Edward, M., & Newell, H. (2013). Dying swans and dragged up dames: A photographic exploration of the ageing dancer. In *Animated* (pp. 14–16). Leicester: Community Dance UK. Retrieved from https://www.communitydance.org.uk/DB/animated-library/dying-swans-and-dragged-up-dames?ed=31348

Graham, M. (1991). *Blood memory, an autobiography*. New York: Doubleday.

The International Organisation for the Transition of Professional Dancers (IOTPD). (n.d.). Retrieved from www.iotpd.org/

Kourlas, G. (2017, December 19). Dancing down the years: Dancers of retirement age reflect on why they're still dancing. "Why not now?" *The New York Times*. Retrieved from www.nytimes.com/2017/12/19/arts/dance/dancing-down-the-years.html

Kylián, J., Lampert, F., & Staverman, D. (Eds.). (2014). *One of a kind: The Kylián project*. Rotterdam: Codarts. Retrieved from www.codarts.nl/wp-content/uploads/2015/11/2.-Onderzoeksverslag_Boek-Jiri-Kylian.pdf

Lansley, J., & Early, F. (2011). *The wise body: Conversations with experienced dancers*. Bristol: Intellect.

Lilja, E. (2006). *Movement as the memory of the body: New choreographic work for the stage*. (F. Perry, Trans.). Stockholm: University College of Dance, Committee for Artistic Research and Development.

Martin, R. (2004). Dance and its others: Theory, state, nation, and socialism. In A. Lepecki (Ed.), *Of the presence of the body: Essays on dance and performance theory* (pp. 47–63). Middleton, CT: Wesleyan University Press.

Martin, S. (2017). *Dancing age(ing)*. Bielefeld: transcript Verlag.

Meagher, M. (2014). Against the invisibility of old age: Cindy Sherman, Suzy Lake, and Martha Wilson. *Feminist Studies*, *40*(1), 101–143. Retrieved from www.jstor.org/stable/10.15767/feministstudies.40.1.101

Nakajima, N. (2017). Overview. In N. Nakajima & G. Brandstetter (Eds.), *The aging body in dance: A cross-cultural perspective* (pp. 11–27). London and New York: Routledge.

Ritter, M., & Roman, C. (2018). *Dance on 1. Edition 2014–2018*. Retrieved from https://dance-on.net/en/wp-content/uploads/sites/3/2021/03/DO-Publ-final.pdf

Schwaiger, E. (2012). *Ageing, gender, embodiment and dance, finding a balance*. Basingstoke: Palgrave Macmillan.

Sulcas, R. (1998). Bodies of knowledge. *Dance Magazine, 72*(5), 58–61.

Twigg, J. (2007). Clothing, age and the body: A critical review. *Ageing & Society, 27*(2), 285–305. doi:10.1017/S0144686X06005794

Twigg, J. (2010). How does *Vogue* negotiate age? Fashion, the body and the older woman. *Fashion Theory, 14*(4), 471–490. doi:10.2752/175174110X12792058833898

United Nations, Department of Economic and Social Affairs, Population Division. (2019). *World population ageing 2019: Highlights* (ST/ESA/SER.A/430). New York: Department of Economic and Social Affairs, Population Division, United Nations.

Wainwright, S. P., & Turner, B. S. (2003). Ageing and the dancing body. In C. A. Faircloth (Ed.), *Aging bodies: Images and everyday experience* (pp. 259–292). Walnut Creek, CA: Altamira Press.

Wainwright, S. P., & Turner, B. S. (2006). Just crumbling to bits? An exploration of the body, ageing, injury and career in classical ballet dancers. *Sociology, 40*(2), 237–255. doi:10.1177/0038038506062031

White, K. D. (1999). *Mirrors and dance culture: Modes response to the dancer's self image* [Master's thesis, San Jose State University]. SJSU Scholar Works. http://scholarworks.sjsu.edu/etd_theses

York-Pryce, S. (2020). *Ageism and the mature dancer* [Unpublished Doctor of Visual Arts dissertation]. Griffith University, Brisbane. https://doi.org/10.25904/1912/3928

2.2

CREATING IN THE LIMINAL SPACE

Connecting pathways of embodied experience

Stephanie Burridge

Navigating a creative path that connects heritage, physical and emotional resonance is an existential journey for senior dance makers. This chapter examines some of the enabling factors that are catalysts for this process, including choreographic methods, pedagogy and performance options incorporated by dance makers working across generations and specifically with senior artists. Part of this equation is presentation and performance. This involves the role of curators, producers and managers, along with collaborators such as filmmakers who initiate platforms, showcases and festivals to facilitate the sharing and performance of new choreographic collaborations. This chapter includes three case examples of projects about creating and performing within the frame of 'senior dance' – the term adopted to indicate performers and choreographers over 55 years of age – with two of the projects being intergenerational. The author was the choreographer and creative director on all three projects. The chapter is based on autoethnographic reflections on the intentions, processes and outcomes of the projects.

Introduction

The term 'liminal space' considers the spaces in between (Van Gennep, 1960; Turner, 1970). In an anthropological context, Victor Turner followed on from the work of French ethnographer Arnold Van Gennep's early studies of rites of passage to extend the theoretical framework applying this term when studying ritual practices among the Ndembu of Zambia. He examined what occurred between two states of being, the liminal stage, in their rite of passage to adulthood. Transition – uncertainty, but also expectations of new beginnings – is inherent in this term. In dance, this term has also been adopted by dance and theatre theorists to denote spaces in between as sites for invention and imagining. Movement specialist Mary Overlie (2016), for instance, uses this term to take in multiple perspectives through

DOI: 10.4324/9781003307624-13

her Six Viewpoints of Space, Shape, Time, Story, Emotion and Movement that operate in a relational matrix.

> One of the most significant features of the Six Viewpoints is the shifted role of the artist . . . [who] participates by "witnessing, and interacting, . . . working under the supposition that structure could be discerned rather than imposed".
>
> *(Overlie 2016, p. 189)*

This model is liminal in that the creative process is non-linear and essentially a 'limbo' space.

There are numerous examples of the usage of the term 'liminality', as John McKenzie notes in relation to its frequent adoption by university performance studies programmes: "As object, exemplar and emblem, liminality has served as a paradigm of the paradigm" (2001, p. 37).

Moving away from the original connection to the anthropological notion of a rite of passage, in this chapter, the term 'liminal' is also used as a metaphor and denotes the spaces between the present self with embodied memories, traces of cultural immersion, deep notions of genre and performative practice, and new creative impulses that synergise in new dance choreography or present configurations of past work. A plurality of meanings emerge that extend beyond the physical culturally contextualised body to explorations of mind/body connections; somatic and visceral experiences expressed through movement and gesture. These interweave to create new narratives, movement vocabularies and imaginative journeys that constitute liminality – a space between two points that connect past and present possibilities. They are emboldened with a threshold, or sense of anticipation, as new configurations emerge from the transition from the known to new beginnings.

The wisdom, creative expression and embodied artistry of senior artists is the basis for creative collaborations that enable such dance possibilities. In this context, the liminal space involves the gap between the lived body of memories and current realities and concerns. The physical body is negotiating the space between its capabilities and what it was once able to do, while the mind and spirit are open and free to explore new directions. This tension is absorbing to work with as the balance between mind and body, the visceral and somatic, coerce to enable new expression and a powerful presence encompassing grace and wisdom expressed through a depth of experience and interpretation. The growing worldwide recognition of this trait has led to a new wave of interest and performance platforms opening up for senior professional artists who are engaging audiences.

Centralising the body as a 'site of perception' and embodied experience (Richard Shusterman, 2013) enables shared traces, relics or artefacts to exist in moments of time. The ephemeral nature of dance often means that heritage can be lost and memories become blurred as the dance moves on through time and generations. But it is often the rich, collective memories of dancers working through their recollections of space, time and energy that will reveal the essence of expression – albeit with some new tangents and configurations. Affecting a process that enables embodied expression to thrive is essential when collaborating and creating with senior dance artists.

In the stages of research, workshopping and improvising to explore new material, the duality of working through embodiment in an unstructured, liminal creative space intersected to make 'magic' in the studio as personalities are coming into play and the concepts converged.

Defining the context of the liminal space in creative practice

Adding to the points already made, liminal spaces also occur across generations, between memories and present realities, past processes and current trends, for example, the pre- and post-digital decades. These spaces not only reflect heritage and linear time gaps but also a sense of place. Artists moving from their cultural roots and migrating to another country create diasporas where recreations, reiterations and preservations of cultural material occur alongside new influences and sources of inspiration. These interconnected spaces enable a mesh of embodied pasts with a new contemporary relevance – these complex spaces in between are often zones of exploration, risk taking and affirmation.

At the time of writing, the restrictive atmosphere of COVID-19 has markedly skewed the direction of our lives in countless ways from coping with loss, travel bans, the closing of studios and performance spaces, and much more. For some artists, new creative opportunities through exploring online platforms and sharing sites for performances, research, conferences, dialogues and discussion have been welcome; for others, there has not only been the lack of work, livelihoods and income, but an inertia that disenfranchises them from moving forward. This limbo state of flux was debilitating and stressful for many practitioners.

A sense of place, cultural memories and embodied ways of thinking and moving emerged as artists and audiences engaged with each project during this time. While restrictive in many respects as past ways of working had to be let go, options emerged and new directions were embraced. Charting and recording these variations are central to comprehending the impact of art as it crosses borders – geographical, cultural, social and educational, among others. The liminal space existing between the collaborators, the artists and the audience, the facilitator and the participants, become illuminated zones of experience incorporating action and reflection. In these shifting contexts, everyone is challenged to respond through their own epistemic knowledge via immersion: sensing, listening, experiencing, touching and viewing.

Creating in the liminal space – three case examples

This section recounts the intention, research, methods, choreographic processes and performance outcomes involved in making three dance works. As each responded to the changing conditions of the COVID-19 pandemic, these components were in flux throughout.

Belvedere Ballroom

This project Belvedere Ballroom, https://vimeo.com/madecompany (Tasmania, Australia), was conceived and choreographed with Tasmanian-based Mature Artists Dance Experience (MADE) for the 2021 'Ten Days on the Island Festival' in Tasmania. The work explores the nostalgia and reminiscences of people's stories emanating from the 1940s in the early days of Hobart and the ballroom dance hall era during World War II. The underbelly juxtaposes the fun of young people gathering for ballroom dancing during the bleak times when many of the young men were on the battlefields and the world was being torn apart. MADE creates and presents contemporary dance theatre performed by dancers over 50. The company cultivates a creative space for mature adults who are or want to be active through movement and dance engaging creatively through stories of lived experience. The work was a deeply personal one for me, as it was largely based on my mother's experience of going to the Belvedere Ballroom to dance, meet friends and – as time went on – frequently to mourn to loss of loved ones. Mavis Burridge (1923–2020) contributed many memories and notes that were shared during rehearsals and triggered conversations and movement ideas. She wrote of the context:

> As time went on we had a nice group of good friends and we kept together at the dances. Sadly, the numbers disappeared from 1940 when they [the young men] all joined the various [armed] forces. We saw them briefly when they were on leave and life for many changed forever . . . .
>
> *(personal correspondence, 2020)*

The choreographic process began with a workshop session with the group. Many of the ideas were presented with opportunities to develop scenarios and characters through improvisation and responding to stimuli and a general discussion about the period and the memories it evoked. There were also video recordings sent back and forth of choreography in a couple of pre-set routines. As the piece evolved around a site, the Belvedere Ballroom, there was a treasure trove of opportunities to revive, relive and work through memories. Hence, the research aspect of this work responded to the notion of liminality in the sense of researching material through family members, local societies, various articles, photographs and memorabilia that catalysed resonance with current concerns. The historical aspect was achieved in the production through incorporating poetry by a local writer who had also worked through memory and research to create poems about her family members during WWII, along with the projection of slides and the use of authentic vintage costume pieces.

After returning to Singapore, where I am based, the plan was to return to make the work with the dancers; however, COVID-19 travel restrictions curtailed this plan, and we went ahead rehearsing via Zoom. This necessitated a more precise planning of rehearsals and the material the dancers needed to work through to understand their roles. Although originally planned as a dance theatre work for which company members would develop a character that they maintained throughout, the 'long-distance' process did not allow for as much 'play' and experimentations as would have occurred in a face-to-face situation. Specific tasks were set such as learning a song in Auslan (a form of sign language for the hearing impaired used in Australia), and outlines of ideas for several sections became quite structured so that the group could take ownership and proceed. Part of the original plan was to conclude the work with a 10-minute or so community dance section led by a couple of company dancers with ballroom dance training; this worked very well and required little input from me. Hence, the physical separation between us enabled a deep sense of trust and gave the performers confidence to move ahead.

FIGURE 2.2A *Belvedere Ballroom* (2021), MADE Dance Company performing Auslan; choreographer: Stephanie Burridge

Source: Photograph from MADE company collection

This project was heavily supported by an excellent rehearsal director, costume designer and production crews under the umbrella of the festival for which it was commissioned. The space between memory and present realities underpinned this work and had great clarity for the performers. The audience members included people in their 90s who had danced at the Belvedere in their youth and many family groups across generations such that grandparents were able to relive some nostalgia and share it with the younger generations.

Bubbles

A bubble refers to a good or fortunate situation that is isolated from reality or unlikely to last. Children blow bubbles and their laughter is infectious bringing joy and fantasy. Travel bubbles are essentially an exclusive partnership between countries that have demonstrated considerable success in combatting the COVID-19 pandemic within their respective borders. The film entitled *Bubbles*, https://youtu.be/hawW_KpoGOw (Singapore), is the visual outcome of an intergenerational, multidisciplinary intensive creative partnership between Australia and Singapore within a digital residency. It juxtaposes the feelings of longing through isolation, and laughter, as the creative concept fluctuates between fantasy and imagination and present realities of artists working in different countries and family disconnection. Many moods are explored within this frame from fear, anxiety, claustrophobia, hope, serenity and joy.

FIGURE 2.2B   *Bubbles* (2021); dancer: Anca Frankenhaeuser

Source: Photograph from choreographer's personal collection

The music composed by Dr Robert Casteels was the starting point for this project and the unifying component as we worked between Australia and Singapore. Rather than too much Zoom conferencing, we set up a template based on time and place. Each dancer working with the creative concepts moved through a series of tasks in a grid based on a time component, an emotion and a specific stie – such as a corner or open space. These snippets were filmed and shared between all collaborators. *Bubbles* progressed by online research and experimentation between artists in Australia and Singapore. This rich journey led to a multi-media and modular performance through movement on synthetised music via video projection. It proposed a reflection about borderless artistic creation and human resilience despite the damaging COVID-19 crisis. Table 2.1 is the example of the grid followed by dancer Anca Frankenhaeuser in Australia.

TABLE 2.1 Creative Process Grid

Time in music	Space	Theme/Emotion	Body/Motivation
1.	• on stair case	• isolation	• stuck/steps • immediate • up/down
2.	• confined space	• scared	• cramped • foetal • rocking
3.	• water	• floating free	• swim, soak • water on the face
4.	• sand	• slips through fingers	• timers • time lost
5.	• grass	• running	• escape • free
6.	• corners	• hiding • ducking • out of sight	• sudden • sneaking looks
7.	• wind	• tossing • blown about	• fall and recover
8.	• stars	• dreams • looking up	• reaching • picking stars
9.	• bubbles	• blowing	• literal, but in various situations
10.	• tall building • roof top	• strong • optimistic • powerful	• held • strong moments
11.	• pounding the floor	• frustration	• can be stomping, • wringing
12.	• curling	• sadness	• slow, low • introspective
13.	• skip, hop, run	• happiness • joy • free	• phrase • repetition • fast

Time in music	Space	Theme/Emotion	Body/Motivation
14.	• wide and open	• free • dancing	• waltz • phrase of dance
15.	• gathering space	• trying to surround space • like catching a bubble	• curved pathways • shapes
16.	• percussive • cutting	• anger • pacing the room • silent screams	• sharp • angular

Similarly, Singapore dancer Yarra Ileto worked through the same grid and time frame making her own responses to the same tasks. Finally, they were immersed through the creative input of filmmaker Clare Chong. In this process, there were many instances of liminality, including spatial, physical and time lags in the passing of information back and forth. Ultimately, however, the separation of geographical and emotional space connected only through time, enabled many diverse possibilities that eventually flowed through the final film.

We Dance Alone – Men Dancing Project

I was the creative director and choreographer for this project, https://vimeo.com/manage/videos/598577461/privacy (Singapore). The artists include two Singaporeans (Kailin Yong and Zhuo Zihao), two Australian/Singaporeans (Stephanie Burridge and Antonio Vargas) and an Australian (Patrick Harding-Irmer). Antonio is 80-plus and Patrick mid-70s. Antonio is a flamenco dancer, Patrick and Zihao are contemporary dancers – between them, we were searching for connections and shared experiences to overcome separation through COVID-19 and how dance connects but also divides us.

The project aligned the reality of the current COVID-19 time when Patrick in Australia is unable to join us in the studio. Despite many Zoom and WhatsApp exchanges, swapping of images, ideas and video clips, we were apart not only physically but also emotionally and spiritually. In our imaginations, we 'tangoed' together with the stylistic rhythms composed by Kailin that were redolent with deeper metaphors of joy and loneliness. We used four chairs and always kept the spare chair for Patrick – *We Dance Alone* was always choreographed with the hope that he would make it to Singapore to perform and share with us. Kailin's music, our WhatsApp chats, Zoom meetings, online studio showings and final performance/livestreaming kept us together over the time of this project. Patrick filmed material in Sydney and Zihao uploaded it onto our group Facebook page. We also made a final film of *We Dance Alone* (see photo in Conversations section of the book).

The intention is based on memory – of events, feelings, places and times. These interweave and foreground in various configurations like a collage. Individual stories interact with meeting points that come together – more like people finding themselves in the same bar than friends appointing a time to meeting up. In the storyboard for this choreography, there is an underpinning sense of loneliness, nostalgia mixed with joy and happiness remembering past fun times combined with optimism moving forward. The atmosphere is like events occurring in a movie – they are scenes that are part of the lived experiences of the artists. It forms an 'emotional narrative' of the four protagonists rather than a sequential story within a structured timeline. This is very important and an innovation in the piece that lends itself to a film process whereby segments can be cut, repeated or segued in different ways.

The dancers came from diverse genres as previously stated – flamenco and contemporary. The process was severely affected by the pandemic such that the live performance aspect was severely curtailed and creating a film became the focus. The extraordinary talents of composer Kailin Yong united the work as he incorporated the structures of flamenco rhythms into a soundscape that moved from this onto more open music that echoed Asian sounds, giving a sense of place and space in the music for improvisations and variation.

Within the music and film strands that anchored the choreography, each man created a deeply personal solo that resonated with their life and experiences that they wanted to explore. The solos were integrated with acting segments that drew the dancers together for brief moments. Through discussions, we established that each artist practised tai chi, or chi gong, so the films of each in their own space or city (Sydney and Singapore) untied everyone, and the audience, in the same place. The tranquillity of this form looped as the audience entered the studio for showings of the work and was a peaceful respite from the restrictions of the pandemic in limiting audience numbers and social interaction. Towards the end of the work, there is a lively group section that I choreographed to tango music to represent the title of the work, *We Dance Alone*.

The performance sections created in collaboration with Antonio gave the strongest sense of physical liminality in any of the projects described thus far. Vargas is a world-renowned flamenco dance artist, and as he mentioned, he was once known to be among those with the fastest footwork in the world. In our project, there was a degree of frustration in not being able to replicate the dance sequences in the same way, though not only accumulated injuries but working with an older body. Flamenco dance is firmly rooted in expression but also particular musical genres that dictate rhythm sequences for the dancers. Composer Kailin incorporated many of these forms in his score that almost impelled the dancer to work within existing frames of the genre and push forward with the traditional interpretation of these. The speed of the footwork might have been curtailed to some extent, but the embodied passion, deep musicality and commitment to sustaining the rhythms were an essential component that underpinned the choreography. In stark contrast to the contemporary choreography of the other projects – and indeed, performer Zihao in this piece – there was a concern with adhering to the authenticity of the form. Working through injuries attained over a lifetime as a professional performer became part of this scenario, rather than adopting adaptation and compromise thus linking past and present in a exciting presence.

Connecting threads

There were many connections between these three projects: my own role as creative director and choreographer, cast members of dancers spanning decades from 55 years of age and above, while *We Dance Alone* and *Bubbles* included two younger performers in an intergenerational approach. All occurred during the COVID-19 pandemic and were adjusted to conditions imposed by both Australia and Singapore. This not only precluded international travel, but it also curtailed public performances, workshops and allied events normally associated with such projects. Mask wearing during a public performance of 30% theatre capacity in Singapore was a unique experience along with using online apps for fielding audience questions at a post-show dialogue. Zoom rehearsals, meetings and multiple internet programmes and sharing platforms were incorporated throughout.

A liminal space for creativity across geographical space and time was a given and underpinned what was possible for each project. While *Belvedere Ballroom* was able to proceed in a more traditional setting of in-studio rehearsals with a rehearsal director responding to my Zoom instructions, it had creative limitations. Simply getting to know the performers through being in the studio together, working through tasks in rehearsal and the many shared social chats through coffee breaks and the like limited spontaneity and the momentum that is achieved through a group building on ideas together as a work progresses. Looking into the small Zoom frame and following the dancers' questions about each part the process became more responsive to their needs via information and learning material that I had pre-recorded.

While the process of working with the MADE company was not ideal from a choreographic perspective, it resulted in a performance that was well staged and resonated with the audience. This was due to a clear intention from the outset with themes and topics that the dancers could relate to, along with my own embodied history and memories of growing up in Hobart, where the show was set.

Of the three projects, *Bubbles* was designed to be a film from the outset. At the time of the collaboration, the world was well into the pandemic and many artists were already adapting to making work via digital means and experimenting with this new form. Incorporating a task-based grid formular as a process was an experiment for all the artists and worked well across the geographical divide. The music was the unifying factor and the system enabled individual responses and a surreal concept to emerge with the overlaying metaphor of 'bubbles'.

We Dance Alone confronted us with dilemmas as the pandemic evolved. Designed as a cultural exchange performance project between Australia and Singapore, it was created with live performance in mind. As it moved along, constant adaptation of the original concept was required eventually moving towards making a film when the realisation of public live performance diminished. As such, the dance segments became more of a documentation than a dance film as such. There were limited special effects and cuts in the film (unlike *Bubbles*) and the project did not achieve the goal of two extraordinary senior dance artists from two different genres coming together on stage to rebound from each other, reflect and devise dance together.

In this sense, we are still in the liminal phase, as the original concept was not fully realised.

Concluding remarks

For senior dance artists, a lifetime of dance making, creating, performing, teaching, mentoring and reflecting broadens the spectrum of possibilities incalculably opening the possibility for rich material and dense creative imaginings to emerge.

Embodiment and liminality coexist in the process of dancemaking for senior artists. An open process of collaboration underpins these points connected through space and time. By allowing these two components to breathe across individual resonance of where each dancer's capabilities exist, authentic responses are affected. Presence, wisdom and honest interpretation makes a compelling performance that engages audiences through shared memory connections and emotions. This factor depends on the intention and choreographic concept but could be one of the 'givens' of performances by senior dancers. In these projects, and in many others I have observed over the years, collaboration could be another 'given' for senior dance. Two of the case examples in this chapter depended equally on working with a composer, while another involved a local artist. Sharing across concepts and themes with collaborators is a rich creative experience and adds another layer to the production.

To exist in a liminal space, the dancer becomes extremely vulnerable. This vulnerability has its own magnetism and is compelling. Senior dancers pay attention to the wisdom of the moment. They know how to make something work, even if it is a simple thing. A hand movement, a facial expression or complete stillness – the focus of the moment comes with incredible care as a lifetime of dance responds to a moment in time.

References

Gennep, A. V. (1960). *The rites of passage.* Chicago: University of Chicago Press.
McKenzie, J. (2001). *Perform or else: From discipline to performance.* London and New York: Routledge.
Overlie, M. (2016). *Standing in space: The six viewpoints theory & practice.* Billings, MT: Fallon Press.
Shusterman, R. (2013). Body and the arts: The need for somaesthetics. *SAGE Journals, 59,* 7–20. doi:10.1177/0392192112469159
Turner, V. W. (1970). *The forest of symbols: Aspects of Ndembu ritual.* Ithaca, NY: Cornell University Press.

Weblinks to choreography

We Dance Alone Men Dancing Project https://vimeo.com/manage/videos/598577461/privacy
Bubbles https://youtu.be/hawW_KpoGOw
Belvedere Ballroom https://vimeo.com/madecompany

2.3

'OPEN CULTURE' AS PRACTISED BY THREE SINGAPOREAN DANCE PIONEERS

Melissa Quek and Tan Ngiap Heng

In this chapter, we discuss the development and propagation of the practices of three Singaporean dance pioneers, Santha Bhaskar (1939–February 2022), Goh Lay Kuan (b. 1939) and Som Said (b. 1951). All three are winners of the Singapore cultural medallion (the highest honour for the arts in Singapore) and have influenced a generation of artists. Filmed interviews were conducted with the three dance pioneers, as well as with Goh Soo Nee, Goh Soo Khim and Dr Francis Yeoh, who have been contemporaries and collaborators of the three artists. From these interviews, we realised that their interactions and friendships affected their approach to dance and performance-making, as well as their collective relevance to contemporary dance in the city-state of Singapore.

Underpinning this research is the proposition of foregrounding their work as examples of Singaporean arts activist, theatre director and playwright Kuo Pao Kun's concept of 'Open Culture' (Kuo, 2005, pp. 248–257) whereby lines of difference are positively engaged. This approach to culture is rooted in traditions but remains dynamic and porous; allowing for selective additions from surrounding influences contrasts with the idea of a multicultural co-existence that has been the predominant focus of public policy in Singapore. These dance pioneers' development and motivation are critiqued by situating their work against the backdrop of migratory flows that shaped their lives, as well as the policy of building a national identity to which their practices contributed.

The arguments are developed by articulating a historical overview of the complexities that each choreographer faced when trying to challenge a fixed sense of cultural identity, while at the same time exploring forms of intercultural practice that allowed for fluid performance expression. The research takes an exemplary work by each of them and analyses its context and creative process. It offers key examples that, in the larger history of dance in Singapore, can evidence the extent to which conversations about 'open culture' may have taken centre stage in artistic practice.

DOI: 10.4324/9781003307624-14

A multicultural context

In his paper "Multiculturalism in Singapore", the Third Chief Justice of Singapore Chan Sek Keong noted that the multiculturalism that developed in Singapore from 1819 – when it became a British colony – was due to the legacy of an "Imperial power" that "ensured that each community preserved its own culture and respected the cultures of other communities" (Chan, 2013, p. 84). This respect often comes in the form of ensuring that the culture of the four main ethnic groups – Chinese, Indian, Malay and 'other' – are represented in all cultural activities. This labelling creates boundaries between the groups while glossing over the cultural distinctions that exist within these broad groupings. So, for instance, Bharatha Natyam, which originates in Tamil Nadu; Kathak, from Varanasi; and Mohiniyattam, from Kerala would all be classified as Indian dance, while a Peacock dance of the Dai people and Zapin would be referred to as a Chinese dance and a Malay dance, respectively. Multiculturalism in Singapore was therefore not of an integrationist bent but reflected Slovenian cultural theorist Slavoj Žižek's multiculturalism, whereby the culture and identity of the 'other' are conceived as an "authentic" closed community (Žižek, 1997, p. 44). While this did not grow within the same colonial context of global positioning to which Žižek refers, aspects of this remain in how any culture other than one's professed culture is seen as 'other' and is rarefied through the act of respecting its particularities. This respect for the cultural 'other' came to be regarded as a political necessity and a 'cornerstone' of nation-building efforts (Chan, 2013, p. 85). In a similar fashion, as the legacies of Santha Bhaskar, Goh Lay Kuan and Som Said have been tied to the nation-building efforts by policymakers, the repeated rhetoric in publicity material and by the media around their practices – and current funding categorisation under the label 'traditional dance' – often restrict them within the labels of Indian dance, ballet or modern dance, and Malay dance, respectively.

Singapore-based Malaysian educator, writer and dramaturg Charlene Rajendran outlines the implications that this top-down multicultural policy has in cultural practices. She states that "Chinese, Malay and Indian cultures are widely performed as if these constructs remain unitary, and unchanged by social integration or proximity" (Rajendran, 2016, p. 444). As stated previously, funding over the years for dance in Singapore and the dance scene itself has been – to a great extent – separated along ethnic lines, disciplinary boundaries and the binary traditional-contemporary divide, causing many dance groups to focus on developing their practice within potentially limited and narrow categories of culture and form.

In the 1950s and 1960s, however, the multicultural environment of Singapore and the fact that it lacked readily available formal dance training meant that the relatively small number of dance practitioners chose to develop their dancing by learning new dance forms from each other. We have found limited records of professional dance practices and training before the 1950s in Singapore. From our interview with the sisters Goh Soo Nee and Goh Soo Khim, we found that before the 1950s, ballet was taught by the wives of British colonialists. Maudrene Yap was the first Chinese woman to complete the Royal Academy of Dance course for teachers and in 1950 was the first local to start a dance school. Some other early proponents of traditional dance forms include The Singapore Indian Fine Arts Society, which was formed in 1949. Mr K.P. Bhaskar came to Singapore in 1952 and was known as the first classical Indian dance teacher. His wife Santha Bhaskar joined him in 1955 and they established the Bhaskar's Academy of Dance. They tried unsuccessfully to introduce Bharata Natyam classes in 1951 but were able to have classes in 1964 when they had their own premises. Malay cultural groups such as Sriwana (1955) and Perkumpulan Seni (1956) were formed to promote the Malay language and culture amongst Malay youth and rose to prominence in the Malay dance scene. Chinese dance became part of the cultural activities in the 1950s through community groups within trade unions, clan associations and Chinese schools. The development of these dance forms mostly progressed separately until Singapore became a self-governing state in 1959 and there was a need for social cohesion and nation-building activities. The Ministry of Culture organised a series of free open-air concerts called Aneka Ragam Ra'ayat, or 'People's Cultural Concerts' where dancers from these various groups met and performed on the same stage. This continued in other events such as National Day parades and National Day rallies.

The National Dance Company and Som Said's innovation in Malay dance

Perhaps the epitome of the cross-cultural nature of dance in Singapore was the Singapore National Dance and Theatre Company (later referred to as the Singapore National Dance Company or National Dance Company). The relevance of this company lies in that its work acknowledged the reality of the interweaving nature of the cultural interactions, as opposed to advocating for cultural purity or formal orthodoxy. The National Dance Company was led by artistic director Francis Yeoh and served as Singapore's cultural ambassador in international events. For example, the Company represented Singapore in the inaugural performance in 1972 at the Adelaide Festival of Arts, where it showcased the "rich multicultural heritage of a new nation" (Yeoh, 2019, p. 4). Before the company disbanded in 1985, when Francis Yeoh emigrated to the United Kingdom, in a press release issued that year about their performances at Victoria Theatre, the Ministry of Community Development wrote that the company's aim was to "pioneer in introducing composite dances reflecting the multicultural character of Singapore" (National Archive, quoted in Yeoh, 2019, p. 4). Although this aim may seem product-driven and focused on audience perception of a representation of Singaporean identity, the making of the works developed an intercultural process of choreography that did not end with the closing of the company.

The company consisted of a team of performers who would "showcase the cultural diversity of Singapore" (Yeoh, 2019, p. 1), so they were dancers from different ethnic backgrounds and professions who specialised in their own dance styles, but when in the company also learnt the dances of their colleagues. In his reminiscences as founding artistic director of the company, Yeoh notes that his mission was to preserve the "traditional ethnic dance styles" while also embracing the "crossing of multi-faceted influences" that were present in the company (Yeoh, 2019, p. 3). This was not only an artistic intention but an organisational principle, as it was the policy of the company to include works in the repertoire that were a fusion of many dance genres, thus laying a foundation of intercultural exposure for the members.

Som Said was an original member from 1970 of Singapore's National Dance Company, where she learned the varied dance forms from different cultures. This multicultural exposure and professional training were to become a turning point for her, as her training up to that moment had been focused on Malay dance traditions and preserving the Malay cultural identity within the larger nation-building context of Singapore. Mdm Som started her interest in Malay dance in school. It was her friend Sri Rahayu who introduced her to the cultural group Sriwana, from which she gained a deeper understanding of the fundamentals of Malay dance. The style that she learnt and that is most commonly practised in Singapore originated from Medan in Indonesia and was taught in Singapore by teachers like Mdm Liu Ah Chun and Tengku Rohanji Rosni. As the dance fundamentals of Malay dance came from Indonesia, she was challenged to make the dance more 'Singaporean'. Finding inspiration from Malay weddings she choreographed her first dance *Sekapur Sireh* (*Betel Nut*) in 1968.

Although her practice was mainly in traditional dance forms, she studied in 1983 in a dance creativity course under choreographer Bagong Kussudiardja based on the modern dancer Martha Graham's technique when she received a scholarship to study Indonesian arts in Padepokan Seni Bagong Kussudiardja (Arts Education Branch, Ministry of Education, n.d., Som Said PBM,[1] founder director of Sri Warisan Som Said Performing Arts Ltd.). When she returned to Singapore, she started choreographing traditional works with a more contemporary approach. In 1985, she choreographed *Hidup*, which means life, for the Singapore Arts Festival Malay Dance Night. This dance depicted a fragment of life experienced by an ordinary family and departed from the more traditional Malay dance choreography as it made use of different levels including the floor level, facial expressions and also included dialogue, which did not occur in traditional Malay dance (Jamari & Sirah, 1985, p. 3). In 1997, she started her own dance company, Sri Warisan, which aimed to have professional dancers and standardisation of Malay dance fundamentals. She acknowledges that it is difficult to have an exact definition of what makes a dance a Malay dance, as the younger generation of dancers are exposed to different forms of dance and create new mixed forms of choreography, but for *Hidup*, the work still followed the guidelines of the Five Pillars of Islam and so, for example, hugging and carrying between dancers of opposite genders was not allowed (S. Said, personal interview).

Sri Warisan consists mainly of dancers of Malay heritage who are trained in Malay dance forms, but the multicultural experiences from Mdm Som Said's earlier years as a dancer are demonstrated in the repertoire of her company's Arts Education Programme (AEP) performances for primary and secondary school students. "Unity in Diversity" (reminiscent of Singapore's nationalistic and multicultural slogan of the 1970s) is described as bringing together movements from Chinese, Indian and Malay dances to present a dance called *Dance Harmony* (Sri Warisan Arts Education Programme brochure, n.d.). They include works by Mdm Neila Sathyalingam, Mdm Yan Choong Lian (both integral members of the National Dance Company) and Mdm Som Said that depict a story of respect and care for the cultural and aesthetic values of these choreographers.

FIGURE 2.3A *Unity in Diversity*: The photo in the catalogue shows dancers, possibly from these other backgrounds in corresponding costumes

Source: Sri Warisan Arts Education Programme brochure

Works such as these allow interactions among dancers from different cultural backgrounds in rehearsal and performance contexts, but mostly occur based on demand. These performances are particularly popular on the government-created Racial Harmony Day[2] and successfully present the various performance styles side by side, but they are limited in their ability to demonstrate the daily interweaving of cultures. This adds to the complexity of maintaining an intercultural practice and the need for it to be dynamic and relational. If these dances and the 'composite dances' of the National Dance Company are witnessed in isolation, then the very choreography meant to capture the interweaving of cultures runs the risk of being perceived as reducing the processual nature of culture to a fixed format, making an audience misunderstand the dynamic weaving of cultures as circumscribed and as opposing the nature of the "inter". Indian theatre director and cultural theorist Rustom Barucha's insight that governments may have the ability to formulate multicultural policies, but they do not have the ability to develop an intercultural policy because the "inter" cannot be regulated (Barucha, 2000, p. 33), points to the fluidity and dynamic nature of performance of which we speak. Such intercultural performances require an understanding of the lived culture, so the AEP programmes are curated to include information on the historical background of the dances, an explanation of the movements and props. Performances are still limited in what they can share about an intercultural practice, as practice cannot only be shared as repertoire alone but requires a more holistic experience grounded in relationships and daily practices.

Intercultural friendship in Goh Lay Kuan's *Returning*

Even before the formation of the National Dance Company (Mdm Som was a key figure within the company but Mdm Goh and Mrs Bhaskar were not members), the need to forge their own paths also allowed the dance-makers freedom to follow their appetite to learn about their dance compatriots from different cultural groups, even as they tried to be proponents of their individual dance forms. So, while the performances in the early years of Singapore's independence laid a multicultural structure for the dance artists, it was their choice to actively engage their friendships through informal dinners, collaborations in future works and a desire to incorporate what they learnt from these interactions into their teaching and choreography that would make it an intercultural practice.

The dance pioneers sought and found the 'inter' in the relationships – whether friendships or artistic partnerships that they developed between themselves – and believed it necessary to develop among the field and community at large. Mdm Goh was of the view that making friends with people of all ages and backgrounds not only enriched her personal life but was also a professional responsibility because "when you start to create you will know their lives from the root and not just the surface" (Walker, 1982, p. 3). As she adopted this philosophy within her creative practice, she exemplified an ability to acknowledge what is "currently ours, within us and around us" (Kuo, 2005, p. 253). The practice of which Mdm Goh is a proponent does not subscribe to the shared universality that Barucha wrote of in 2000, first because she does not presuppose an "empty space" as the intercultural meeting ground (Barucha, 2000, p. 35). Quoted in a *The Straits Times* newspaper article on 13 June 1982, Mdm Goh said that "you have to find yourself in your culture" to achieve a distinctive expression and that "we must meet all sorts of people. You have to know what's going on around you, how people live" (Walker, 1982, p. 3). She does not see intercultural contact as being a contact which is without ethnicity. It is not a "first contact" between "essential human beings" that presupposes a universality that erases cultural roots (Barucha, 2000, p. 35). Mdm Goh's practice is more in keeping with husband and playwright Kuo Pao Kun's (1939–2002) notion of Open Culture that advocates keeping one's own culture and "freely adopting other cultures" (Kuo, 2005, p. 252).

Cultural intersections and mixing has been the norm of daily life in Singapore since the 1970s and 1980s, but the performance of culture still often presents it as self-contained or monadic, with separate arts festivals devoted to specific cultural groups, or even when dances of different ethnic origins are brought together, they are presented as different but existing harmoniously. In 2015, Mdm Goh proposed *Gui* – or known by its English title *Returning* – for that year's Singapore International Festival of the Arts (SIFA). The artistic vision for this work can be considered as an attempt to, as Rajendran describes Open Culture, "rekindle a primary impulse in cultural belonging and ownership through cultural reconnection, reclaiming and adoption" (Rajendran, 2016, pp. 447–448). This work was meant to recapture the exchange of dance forms and foster the open exchange that Mdm Goh believed was the foundation of dance in Singapore and something that had been missing in recent years. When discussing the impact of *Returning*, dancer Clarissa Poh says the work is evidence of how siloed many dance students have been in their learning of dance forms in Singapore when she states that she "gained a much deeper appreciation for the different cultural dance forms. Prior to this project, I hadn't really paid much attention to them" (C. Poh, personal interview, 18 June 2022). If successful, *Returning* would be the kind of "collaborative and process-oriented theatre" that Rajendran writes about which within the creative process seeks and engages with multiple views on culture and is able to "contribute to an understanding of difference as productive in the development of cohesive society" (Rajendran, 2016, p. 446).

Goh Lay Kuan's dance background was itself a mix of cultures. She learnt some Chinese dance in primary school but was formally introduced to ballet by Goh Soo Nee when she was 17. She furthered her ballet training in Melbourne's Victoria Ballet Guild and returned to Singapore after a brief career in Australia, including being the principal dancer of Ballet Victoria. In 1964, she married playwright Kuo Pao Kun and they started the Singapore Performing Arts School. Goh wanted to be a dancer and choreographer, but she found limited opportunities while having to train her own dancers. Later, she learnt Indian dance from her friends the Bhaskars and it was commented in a newspaper review of a dance show from her school that the Indian dance piece was the best item because Goh danced in it (Oon, 1972, p. 3). She also learnt Indonesian dances from Mdm Liu Ah Chun, traditional Chinese dance from Lee Shu Fen and modern dance at the Martha Graham School in 1983 and 1985. She created Singapore's first full-length modern dance piece, *Nu Wa (Mender of the Heavens)*, with more than 50 dancers picked from eight dance groups in Singapore, with more singers and musicians for the Arts Fest (1988). Nu Wa was described as evoking a cosmic atmosphere and coherently telling the story of a fecund creator using instruments in a manner that was reminiscent of American contemporary dance choreographer Alwin Nikolai. With the large cast of dancers, many of whom were amateurs, *Nu Wa* was not memorable for the dance technique of the performers. Malaysian playwright, director and critic Krishen Jit's guest review noted the poor technical abilities of the dancers in the mass dancing portions (Jit, 1988, p. 2). Its strength was in creating a platform for strong relationships to be formed. Christine Khor's overview of the dance performances in the Singapore Festival of the Arts that year emphasised the fact that the bond developed between the performers was reportedly enough to make them cry after each performance of *Nu Wa* (Khor, 1988, p. 5).

This same idea of developing relationships underpinned the design of *Returning*. With *Returning*, Mdm Goh made transparent the interweaving of the various cultures through the rehearsal and choreographic processes. The dance showed the various stages of the salmon as they grow from egg to adulthood. Similarly, the roles within the project reflected the career trajectories of the pioneers and demonstrates how Mdm Goh views the evolution of a choreographer's practice. She created a multi-generational design that brought together dancers at different stages of their careers and working in different dance traditions that represented the main ethnic groups of a multicultural Singapore. The dance reflected that working across cultures is not necessarily a smooth and organic process. *Returning* was originally to be called *Homecoming*, but Mdm Goh and the other advisors believed that this signified something too comfortable and safe. The story of the salmon is that it returns to certain death. In their research, the dancers saw the fish jumping and smashing their bodies against the rocks until they were torn and bloody. Those that survived only lived long enough to spawn. Would *Returning* be able to spawn a new generation of dancers who desired to embrace Open Culture in their artistic practices?

In the multi-generational design of *Returning*, the most senior tier consisted of Mdm Goh as the artistic director, and with her were her peers Mrs Bhaskar and Mdm Som Said as the advisors. As Mdm Goh acknowledged a desire to first be rooted in the more constitutive cultures of the Chinese, Indian and Malay cultures, Mrs Bhaskar and Mdm Som, along with Mdm Lim Moi Kim, were the mentors for the choreographers of the Indian, Malay and Chinese dance strands, respectively.

In the middle tier were the five choreographers from different cultural and dance disciplines, one for each segment: 'Eggs-Alevin-Fry' by Bharatha Natyam choreographer and Mrs Santha Bhaskar's daughter Meenakshy Bhaskar, 'Fry-Fingerlings' by current Singapore Chinese Dance Theatre (SCDT) artistic director Jenny Neo, 'Fingerlings-Smolt' (Freshwater) and 'Smolt' (Ocean) – 'Adult' by Era Dance Theatre's artistic director Osman Abdul Hamid, and 'Adult-Spawning-Start of New Cycle' by Chinese martial arts–based choreographer Low Ee Chiang.

Mdm Goh did not want the choreographers to stay within their own traditional forms alone. She wanted them to be rooted in their traditions but to develop a movement language, vocabulary and dance that would align with the story. The piece's dramaturgy had the choreographers and dancers of each segment working together to transition between the dance forms of one segment into another such that in the transitions, something new could be formed. As Open Culture does not link language (we extend it to movement language) with race, making it possible for individuals to identify with and be rooted in any culture (Kuo, 2005, p. 253), the choreographers were expected to have an understanding of their forms and to be able to transition out of it without losing the roots of the form. This new vocabulary brought about by the interweaving of cultures would not belong to either of the dance traditions, nor would it erase them but could be both at the same time.

FIGURE 2.3B *Returning* – 'Smolt (Ocean)' segment (2015); Chinese and contemporary dance–trained Li Ruimin and street dance, Bharatha Natyam and contemporary dance–trained Sufri Juwahir

Source: Photograph by Ng Yuan Jie

Significantly, the longest amount of time in the creative process of this project was devoted to training the dancers. The 22 dancers were first trained in the different genres by the choreographers, auditioned for the various scenes, then had further training in the dance forms they were selected to perform – and only then did rehearsals begin. The focus of this project was to give the young dancers a taste of what the early years of dance development had been like for Mdm Goh, Mrs Bhaskar and Mdm Som Said by putting them in a similar environment.

Through *Returning*, Mdm Goh demonstrates that the practice of Open Culture in dance cannot be taught as specific content but can be encouraged and proliferated by providing a conducive environment in which to witness or experience it. After the process, choreographers Meenakshy Bhaskar and Jenny Neo both spoke about how they looked forward to working with the other choreographers again and that working together was the highlight of the project. Dancer Clarissa Poh's response shows how *Returning* gave her the opportunity to develop close friendships with dancers from different cultural and dance backgrounds, subsequently altering the way she thought of dance. Her use of the word "spiritually" further points to the intangible aspects of Open Culture in practice.

> I think each of us gained something through learning from each others' movements, both physically as well as spiritually. It's like we were welcomed into sacred spaces and across boundaries that we were aware of but weren't allowed to speak about. We grew much closer.
>
> *(C. Poh, personal interview, 18 June 2022)*

If the practice of Open Culture is characterised by "an earnest desire to enter into other cultures and take them as part of one's own as well or extending oneself beyond one's own culture to evolve a larger, diverse one" (Kuo, 2005, p. 252), then *Returning* was designed to give a new generation of dancers the opportunity to make that choice for themselves, not only in their daily lives but also in their dance practice. Sufri Juwahir chose to build on his experiences in *Returning* and credits it as the start of finding his own way of deconstructing and exploring possibilities of Bharatha Natyam movements. This approach to choreographing led to the creation of his award-winning duet *Decipher*, which draws on his street dance and contemporary dance influences.

Open culture and intergenerational transfers

The final advisor for *Returning* was Santha Bhaskar, whose intercultural work started early in her career in Singapore. Her husband had taken her to watch a Chinese movie, *The Butterfly Lovers, Liang Shang Buo, Zhu Yingtai*, in 1958. This movie was very popular in Singapore and interested Mrs Bhaskar so much that the same year, they decided to stage an Indian dance version of *The Butterfly Lovers*. This was Mrs Bhaskar's first time choreographing a dance piece, and in a 2019 interview with the authors, Mrs Bhaskar acknowledged that she was young when she did the choreography and was not exposed to many things.

Yet, this work was innovative for its time. The piece was based in Bharata Natyam but since classical Bharata Natyam is presented as a solo dance, this production broke new ground by staging it as a full-length dance drama with an all-female cast taking on the various roles. It was also an innovation to present a Chinese tale, using Indian dance with the dancers dressed in costumes inspired by Chinese history. Years later, restaging this work would be a vehicle for Mrs Bhaskar to create a situation in which she could pass on her practice by designing a similar intercultural experience of interweaving performance cultures for her daughter and granddaughter.

Santha Bhaskar and her husband K.P. Bhaskar were both from Kerala and the dance forms she was originally trained in were Mohiniyattam and Kathakali. In an interview, she explained that when she first came to Singapore, Bharata Natyam was the most popular classical Indian dance as the Indian community mainly came from Southern India, so she would be expected to teach this form. For Santha Bhaskar to be able to teach Bharata Natyam, she had to undergo intensive training during a three-month crash course in India. To understand her teacher, she also had to quickly pick up the Tamil language, as her mother tongue was Malayalam. In Singapore, she found that her husband was friends with dance practitioners from different cultures and she learnt Malay dances, Chinese dances and ballet. This exposure to different dance forms added to her unconventional approach to choreography. As a result, instead of presenting the Bharatha Natyam dances as solo works, the Bhaskars were presenting their dances as group works that made use of formations and paid attention to the dynamics and shaping of the bodies. Mrs Bhaskar continued with her interest in dance forms from other cultures, and in 1995, she studied Thai dance and music at Chulalongkorn University in Bangkok on an ASEAN (Association of Southeast Asian Nations) exchange programme. Subsequently, in 1996, she adapted a Thai mythological story, 'Manohra', into a dance drama for Indian and Thai dance styles with Thai music.

In 2022, more than 60 years after the original production, Mrs Bhaskar proposed a new production of *Butterfly Lovers* by Bhaskar Arts Academy to be presented by the Singapore Chinese Cultural Centre. She was the artistic director, but rather than a faithful restaging of the original, the new production would be created by a younger generation of artists within the same framework. The production engaged Mdm Lim Moi Kim, founding artistic director of Singapore Hokkien Huay Kuan Dance Troupe (now SCDT), to teach the company the basics and grace of Chinese dance movements over six weeks. The programme book explained that both the original and 2022 versions followed the Yue Opera tradition of using an all-female cast, and that the new production was choreographed by Mrs Bhaskar's daughter Meenakshy Bhaskar and the title role of Liang Shang Buo was played by Malini Bhaskar, Mrs Bhaskar's granddaughter, who had also participated as one of the dancers in *Returning*. Mrs Bhaskar, unfortunately, passed away in February of this same year and did not see the production.

FIGURES 2.3C–D *Butterfly Lovers*: the initial production of *Butterfly Lovers* (left) and new 2022 production of *Butterfly Lovers* (right)

Source: Photograph by Bhaskar's Arts Academy

The new production still featured Bharata Natyam dance with new Chinese dance-inspired costumes. According to SCDT artistic director Jenny Neo (who was a choreographer for *Returning*), she had given some costuming ideas to the creators of *Butterfly Lovers*, who initially wanted a full Chinese costume. She cautioned that some Chinese dance costumes hide the feet and that would obscure much of the beauty of Bharatha Natyam, which to her lies in the footwork (J. Neo, personal interview, 1 July 2022). The music by Rajkumar Bharati was newly commissioned and featured a blend of Indian Carnatic music with the Chinese Ruan played by Neil Chua. Multimedia, which was not available in 1958, was also used in creating the stage. Mdm Goh Lay Kuan was invited to be an advisor together with Chua Soo Pong, who had witnessed the original. Compared to the original, this new production – which employs the instruments that are associated with the different cultures – further blurs the distinctions between the fixed cultural identities and rejects a concept of the intercultural that presupposes that the cultural origins of each element can be distinguished between "what is 'ours' and what is 'theirs'" (Fischer-Lichte, 2010, p. 14).

In this way, the remake of *Butterfly Lovers* was also a re-imagining and development of Mrs Bhaskar's approach to an intercultural practice – this time by a new generation of Singaporean artists within a context that has begun to acknowledge the fluid nature of cultures.

Conclusion

The practice of Open Culture hinges on the idea of extending itself. Although Mrs Bhaskar has departed, her legacy lives on through her daughter and those she has taught. The very porosity of the artistic practice of the three pioneers is what makes it transformative. Meenakshy Bhaskar noted that she imbibed Mrs Santha Bhaskar's philosophy towards dance and life through 'osmosis'. By watching her mother interact with others and by being brought up in a cross-cultural environment, she learnt to be open to all cultural concepts and ideas in her own artistic practice. This continues into the approach that the Bhaskar's Arts Academy dancers take. She has noticed that the dancers who were in cross-cultural works such as *Butterfly Lovers* are more receptive to learning other styles of dance and are also now exploring other artistic mediums. They now pick up on nuances in other styles very quickly and have learnt to identify the intrinsic differences in the styles.

These three dance pioneers allowed the mix of their lived cultures to influence their artistic output and their practices live on through the sharing of the approaches and not just the forms. Through Sri Warisan, Mdm Som Said continues to actively apply the beliefs that she values in her teaching and choreography. As an artistic advisor to the theatre company and performing arts space the Theatre Practice, Mdm Goh's ideas and philosophy continue to influence generations of learners.

Note

1 PBM stands for Pingat Bakti Masyarakat – it is a Singaporean national honour.
2 Racial Harmony Day was launched in 1997 as part of Ministry of Education's National Education programme. It is held annually on 21 July to commemorate the communal riots of 1964.

References

Arts Education Branch MOE. (n.d.). *Som Said PBM, S SN, Founder Director of Sri Warisan Som Said Performing Arts Ltd*. My Skills Future. Retrieved from www.myskillsfuture. gov.sg/content/student/en/preu/world-of-work/industry-landscape/industry-articles/ SOM-SAID-SRI-WARISAN-SOM-SAID-PERFORMING-ARTS-LTD.html

Barucha, R. (2000). *Thinking through theatre in an age of globalisation*. Middletown, CN: Wesleyan University Press.

Chan, S. K. (2013). Multiculturalism in Singapore: The way to a Harmonious Society. *Singapore Academy of Law Journal*, 25, 84.

Fischer-Lichte, E. (2010, August 11). Interweaving cultures in performance: Different states of being in-between. *Textures*. Retrieved from www.textures-archiv.geisteswissenschaften. fu-berlin.de/index.html%3Fp=961.html

Jamari, O. Z., & Sirah, M. K. (1985, December 3). Som Said buat eksperimen dalam *Hidup*. *Berita Harian*. p. 3. Retrieved from https://eresources.nlb.gov.sg/newspapers/Digitised/ Article/beritaharian19851203-1.2.24.2?ST=1&AT=search&k=hidup%20som%20said& QT=hidup,som,said&oref=article

Jit, K. (1988, July 1). Big endeavour, beautiful beginnings. *The Straits Times*, p. 2. Retrieved from https://eresources.nlb.gov.sg/newspapers/Digitised/Article/straitstimes19880701-1.2.77.4.3?ST=1&AT=search&k=Nu%20Wa%201988&QT=nu,wa,1988&oref=article

Khor, C. (1988, July 1). The last word: The straits times' team of critics sums up the fest "dance". *The Straits Times*, p. 5. Retrieved from https://eresources.nlb.gov.sg/newspapers/Digitised/Article/straitstimes19880701-1.2.77.4.6.2?ST=1&AT=search&k=Nu%20Wa%201988&QT=nu,wa,1988&oref=article

Kuo, P. K. (2005). Contemplating an open culture: Transcending multiracialism. In B. L. Tan (Ed.), *The complete works of Kuo Pao Kun: Volume seven – papers and speeches* (pp. 248–257). Singapore: World Scientific.

Ministry of Community Development. (1985). *Press release: Public performances of the National Dance Company*. National Archives of Singapore.

Oon, V. (1972, January 12). Enthusiastic show. *New Nation*, p. 3.

Rajendran, C. (2016). Multicultural play as 'open culture' in 'safe precincts': Making space for difference in youth theatre. *The Journal of Applied Theatre and Performance*, *21*, 443–458.

Sri Warisan Arts Education Programmes Brochure 2021. (n.d.). Retrieved from www.sriwarisan.com/arts-education/arts-education-programmes-brochure-2021/

Walker, P. (1982, June 13). Creativity comes with wider social contact. *The Straits Times*, p. 3.

Yeoh, F. (2019). The Singapore national dance company: Reminiscences of an artistic director. *SPAFA Journal*, *3*. doi:10.26721/spafajournal.v3i0.610

Žižek, S. (1997). Multiculturalism or the cultural logic of multinational capitalism. *New Left Review*, *225*, pp. 28–51.

2.4

(K)NOT IN DANCE

Bodies and dancing as states of becoming

Gerard M. Samuel

Introduction

I have a knot in my stomach. I am not even on stage, as one of the performers in *Knot* choreographed by Cape Town–based artist Grant Van Ster. My dual roles in this moment are: agile guide (I am, after all, his supervisor), and experienced and receptive audience member (I am 50-plus years old, and a regular attendee at public dance and arts events in Cape Town). But what am I anxious about in this sickening moment before a curtain up? Is the inclusion in this performance of dancers who are older than 35 years going to stir the conservatives in the house? What are the stereotypes and assumptions that these audiences hold, and where does their under-standing find its roots? How has the hegemonic discourses in dance such as the ideal dancing body and hierarchies of elite arts vis-à-vis cultural practices drown out the voices of some? How can dance by the excluded dance artists be read as a kind of social activism? How can I, as an author and witnessing audience member, remain neutral in my role as academic/senior dance researcher when I share a keen interest in the ontologies of contemporary dance in South Africa and its intersections with notions of hope or states of becoming? How should *Knot* and performances of this new category of contemporary dance performances by older artists be viewed as it seeks to question tropes of indestructible youth/age defiance? In this chapter, I lean into the narrative frames of Bagele Chilisa (2020) and Rachelle Chadwick (2017) as a way of offering multiple and intersectional accounts from both mature performers and myself who can be situated in 'older dancing' (a term to which I will return). I offer a brief testimony of how such performances over the past decade; i.e., since the 2010s) are gradually also beginning to emerge in Cape Town. This rich per-spective is provided through a dialogue with a choreographer and one of the artists in the work *Knot* that was first performed at the University of Cape Town's Centre for Dance, Theatre and Performance Studies department[1] under the direction of Grant Van Ster and his team. I contend that *Knot* can facilitate a key discussion of

DOI: 10.4324/9781003307624-15

ageism and its intersection with dance through its critique of the chasm, absence and the deathly silence surrounding the presence of dance performances by, with and for older dancers in South Africa. I also embrace the use of the term 'mature dancer' as a nod to the self-marked category that is taking place in the local industry. I have explored the potentialities that 'older dancing' offers, and the erasure of toxic hegemonies found in dance in South Africa which often relegate the older dancer to the margins (Samuel, 2016). What are those possibilities that older dancing opens that warrant our further attention? How can these forgotten artists be supported in financial terms, and with infrastructural resources and psycho-social care so needed in a highly flammable career? What needs to be made available to these artists so that all their dance at various stages of life can be seen and understood?

Rethinking patterns for mature dancers

Duke University's Dr Erdman Palmore invites a rethinking and moratorium for terms such as old and ageing, and their common association with deterioration, fragility, senility (and I add) collapse (Palmore, 2000). In the context of this research, the term 'older dancing' will be set aside for performances by former professional dancers – many of whom have left the world of the stage by the age of 35 and some of whom have remained in new roles as dance teachers, choreographers, and directors but who are still wanting to perform. These dancers are also referred to by Van Ster as 'matured dancers' who I argue seem to be ripe or full in terms of their performance experience and wisdom and also continuously evolving.

FIGURE 2.4 An intersectional reading of *Knot* reveals ageism, gender and race as well as notions of privilege and access

Source: Photograph by Lindsey Appollis, October 2021

Revisiting the work *Knot* which Van Ster had first created amid the COVID-19 year of 2021 as part of his postgraduate study in dance at the University of Cape Town, I asked why he wanted to include older dancers into his work. His replies explained the context of an ongoing research project into dance as performance studies in which a deepening research of the 'body as archive' and what remains (Schneider, 2001) was being investigated to suggest a value of the older dancer. For Van Ster, "It was research into the value of their body . . . for the body to be heard in that [performance] space" (Van Ster, interview, 2022). This early remark that was followed by "refreshing . . . the work acts as . . . [and] addressed the need and want of the dancers to come up to the surface for air" suggested to me a strong suppression of voices and concerns of older dancers. He argued for its importance and exposure of superficial understanding of who these dancers might be. Or as the oldest dancer in his cast, Adele Blank quipped not to be seen as the 'golden oldies'. Adele was very frank about this re-entry to the stage, given her long and fruitful career in dance. As a proud octogenarian, she has been dancer, choreographer, dance judge, director of the acclaimed Free Flight Dance Company[2] for more than 30 years and a beloved mentor to many. Fresh from her work with Zip Zap Circus, she laughed in an interview (Blank, interview, 2022) at how she was initially "petrified, and then thought 'What the hell? Let's do it!'" when approached by Van Ster, for whom she has much admiration.

I was curious as to how this choreographic process may have been different, so I asked Van Ster about this important creative moment. In his answer, I found expressions of an intimacy or as he described it as new "expressions of care". He said, "I began with one-on-one sessions in which I could go deeply into who each dancer was and what urge was driving them to be on stage [now]" (Van Ster, interview, 2022). He noticed how the dancers seemed to relish that they were not alone in their anxieties and isolation and reassured them – "this is a safe space to land". First, a recognition of their self-worth and previous 'high-flying' careers seemed to have opened a floodgate and tabernacle of memory. How was he going to relay these loose and forgotten threads that stemmed from Adele, who again took out her ubiquitous crochet needle during our interview? I began to appreciate where the impulse for oversize balls of yarn that were strewn across the *Knot* stage stemmed from, and which were linked and decoupled by subtle interweaving vignettes in the work. The dancers in *Knot* comprised Adele, in her late 70s; two female dancers, Louise and Lee, in their 30s and 40s; two male dancers, Shaun Oelf and Grant Van Ster, in their 30s and 40s; and two much younger dancers in their 20s, one female dancer and one male dancer. The young dancers were both trainees with the Jazzart Dance Theatre company, where both Oelf and Van Ster had begun their own dance careers prior to their more recent formation of Figure of Eight (F08), their independent, contemporary dance company. The ensemble spans the age ranges from 23–80 years, and from a cultural demography perspective comprised both white and coloured dancers. This latter categorisation, multi-/inter-racialism, becomes significant as we begin to unpack the tapestry that is the South African contemporary dance milieu and its histories and performance genealogies (Samuel, 2015).

A respectful relationship with one's elders lies at the heart of Van Ster's approach and therefore we can notice his nod to Blank, who also provided an eagle/outsider's eye in the development of *Knot*. Similarly, he layered his latest experiment *Embody You* (2022) with input and critical feedback from choreographer and former Jazzart teacher Ina Wichterich. Both artist-teachers Van Ster acknowledges with a deep respect that we can argue is beyond his cultural habit towards the aged. Many cultures revere the older members in the group, and numerous ethnographic entries can attest to this (Jolliffe & Worland, 2018). We can observe how Van Ster valued feedback from certain members in his audience such as Averil Barry-Hughes, a senior member of the management team at Jazzart. The wisdom and experience of the older dancer was mentioned by both interviewees, as was a disdain for older dancers and their apparent uselessness. Van Ster was thus noticeably excited that for especially the two younger/trainee dancers during *Knot*'s choreographic process that they had begun to unpack their own inevitable mortality, realising "this could [also] happen to them". Here he observed that a new perspective of the ageing processes became possible as the trainees could witness at close range Blank's negotiation with physically demanding movements and how she could access a range of fine gestural language to suggest a movement thrust or energetic impulse that was similar to their athletic and swift movements. A decline in movement ability was replaced by a new fascination with the possibilities which a mature/older dancer could expose. Blanks' opening salvo "I did move, I did do . . . what I could do . . . I can move in my own way" is telling for me, as I interpreted this statement as an assertion of her continued dancing ability and a refusal of imposition of ineptitude or incapacity by persons who are older in an ensemble.

This need to create a deepening awareness of older dancers was shared by founder of the Nederlands Dance Theatre 3/NDT3, Jiri Kylián, in 2000. Whilst that company, an ensemble of three professional dancers including Sabine Kupferberg, Gerard le Maître and South Africa–born David Krugel had many major successes within and outside of Europe. Sadly, they have closed their doors as new goals became of greater import to decision-makers and as resources shrivelled. This prompted Blank's counter-question "Where is the place for them?". When I had enquired "Why do you think so many dancers stop performing at around age 35?", I wanted to know more about the perennial questions of dancers and retirement which in a South African context begins in their early 30s. For Blank, dance companies would need to be set up and comprised of dancers who are "confident in who you are . . . . They are ready in their lives, artform and in their skills". She felt very strongly that "They are ready to give and come with a different maturity". I dug a little deeper wanting to know what content these companies could produce and explore briefly recounting the often tongue-in-cheek work of Artistic Director Ann Dickie, and her UK-based company, From Here to Maturity. Blank's reply intrigued me when she said, "Yes, to use the light and the frivolous. Frivolous is relevant, too. It can be simple and entertaining, too" suggesting that some of the issue may lie in the nature and content of older dancing performances.

Neither of the interviewees spoke at length or directly to issues of gender, though Van Ster commented that for the older dancer who is female, he sensed the whole question of ageism presented a "more prominent battle". This echoed Richards et al.'s (2012) study of photographic alternative images of older women which revealed Laura Pannack and Monica Fernandez's defiance of "the old [who] are reduced [to their] observable physical features or their attire" (Richards et al., 2012, p. 76). Furthermore, they argue how both these photographers "resist locating women as mothers, grandmothers or aunts, [as] a conventional representational trope" (Richards et al., 2012). Richards and colleagues point out the rupture between images of old persons as dependent and in decline, versus celebrated and with an ability to laugh at themselves, which for some may be atypical. Through their analysis of the photographic projects, we can learn how tropes for older persons are maintained. Van Ster suggested that the typical relationship between older male dancers and their younger counterparts was easier for him to understand as a kind of intergenerational space. In his understanding, seniors passed on the baton to junior dancers – and this was expected. Interestingly, he also hinted at a sexual frisson between the two males that was present. More research and investigation would need to be unpacked of the roles between master and apprentice and for both females and males. For me, an entrenched intergenerational exchange seems to be a central feature in dance worlds as characters/roles are often passed down to so-called newbies and via oral tradition. This bequest or inheritance is highly valued and so it was that to be coached by on older dancer, someone who had excelled in a particular role, was a prized moment for many younger dancers. Such parent–child, custodial relationships can be found in many rehearsal studios and shared between both male and female directors and their dancers – and, I would argue, exist for both gay and straight dancers. Our discussion of pathways and transfer of knowledge quickly led to notions of the high speed/traffic and volume of (dance) information that is available to audiences today and the role that social media currently plays in terms of promoting a culture of aspiration and consumerism. For Van Ster, social media "is always in the future tense" and less about "what wealth comes from behind you". I took from his tone and criticism that in his observations and experience of social media platforms such as Facebook, Instagram, and Twitter fictional selves and lives seem to mushroom and can become globally viral within hours. This quest to be the most affluent and most popular both in the present and future tense has been widely critiqued, with further research needed to determine the pitfalls and or progress that social media generates (Kross et al., 2021). The issue of a battle weariness and consequently his inference of scars recurred frequently in Van Ster's retelling of his creative process. This seems to support a widespread condition for older persons (and dancers) who fight against systemic, ableist norms and an accompanying stereotype of a frailty and dependency which I, too, have critiqued elsewhere (Samuel, 2016). Such hegemonies for older dancers in South Africa was also found around the globe. Concomitant with the anti-ageism war is the hedonist promotion of youth culture (Samuel, 2011) and an ever-advancing posthuman world, that of robotics and artificially intelligent beings as if rising from a primordial swamp of the 20th century. Blank seemed to revel in what she described as "the inexperience experience of the kids", reflecting on the dialogic nature of her exchange with both Van Ster and the rest of the ensemble. In her view, such openness and collaboration would stand Van Ster in good stead as she framed it to be able to "shoot for the stars". But, accelerated technological advancements which have launched us into new spaces – including an international space station – can also easily obscure the wisdom that can be found in older performers and when located in dance, negate the value of embodied knowledge and "body as archive" (Parker, 2020). I have written before about the cliché that with age comes a certain wisdom and I return to that statement briefly in this context, as I notice Blank's "ripe and ready" remark for the older dancer whose potentiality she implies. This is not to suggest that all younger dancers are somehow inherently vacuous and rely on their spirited athleticism and virtuosity, but rather to demand a recognition of knowledge from and *in* the body. Maree had reminded me of our witness of an AmaPondo music and dance group in Durban and of a notion of longevity in the arts that was commonplace for these artists (Samuel, 2016). She also pointed out that in many other cultures such as in Indian dance "Pratab and Priyah [Pawar] who danced well into their 50s" (Maree, cited in Samuel, 2016) a premise of which was also based on the one's state of fitness and overall health and not a marker/cut-off age limit for the enrolment of dancers. I concurred with Lynn Maree[3] and later David Krugel[4] of the guru status and reverence for older dancers in Butoh, a contemporary Japanese art expression. Older dancers in all these spaces are regarded as custodians of culture and viewed as wise sages with access to vaulted choreographies and repertoire in their so-called frail bodies. Mamela Nyamza,[5] who had also generously shared with me her experience of working with older persons noted, "What I liked about an older person . . . they're open, they're not shy. I feel like there's something about actually people appreciating their selves later on in life. They are not afraid of anything" (Samuel, 2016, p. 144). This reminded me of the role of the fragile ego which the artist (young and old) must navigate.

Reflecting on her own choreographic process, Blank explained how an earlier Enrico Cecchetti, Graham and Horton–based dance training[6] are all interwoven into her creative and artistic approaches to dancing making today, and that she acknowledges that lack of support for the arts worldwide. In re-imagining a future, she envisaged a "senior dance company", one that included dancers who were "ripe and ready". I was intrigued and wondered what works such a grouping initiate, and what type of dancers would comprise this company. For her, they would have to be mature individuals who had "synergy with their fellow dancers, synergy with their age . . ., and synergy with their dance", as the common goal would be about making art. She echoed my much earlier interview in London in 2013, with Dickie and Pasch[7] and a reference to "who wants to see the golden oldies". (Samuel, 2016). This self-deprecation indicated to me once again how much of the stigma of old age and its intersection with dance remains a knot in my stomach even now.

Notes

1   The study of Dance at the University of Cape Town (UCT) can be traced to 1934 and its beginning as a conservatoire for ballet with white students only. The UCT Ballet School evolved to UCT School of Dance in 1998 where other forms (such as African dance and modern dance) and approaches to a study of dance were introduced and celebrated. This period also saw the first Black students access dance training at tertiary institutions By 2008, postgraduate dance programmes were beginning to explore whole new areas and intersections of dance. Topics including dance notation, dance pedagogy, dance and the archive, community dance, ballet in transition, Butoh and Bharathanatyam. A period from 2015 saw a further and deepening enquiry into performance studies. This has also led to the new department and a latest iteration: in 2018, the School of Dance merged with the Drama Department to form the Centre for Theatre, Dance and Performance Studies (CTDPS).

2   Free Flight Dance Company was part of many smaller multi-racial, modern dance companies that emerged in South Africa in the waning years of apartheid (late 1980s). Other significant dance companies of similar ilk include Jazzart Dance Theatre company formed in Cape Town in 1974, and the Moving Into Dance company based in Johannesburg, and formed in 1978. The ethos of most of these companies was built around principles of collaboration across racial, ethnic and cultural divides. The term 'Afro fusion' was widely used by its pioneers that includes Sylvia Glasser (of MID), Alfred Hinkel (of Jazzart), Sharon Friedman (at UCT, Jazzart and Silverleaf Youth Dance Co.).

3   Lynn Maree was former director of The Playhouse Dance Company in the 1990s and a key figure in the interviews for my PhD study. She had self-exiled in England during the height of apartheid and returned to South Africa, bringing with her with a wealth of experience in community dance and Asian dance.

4   David Krugel is a South Africa–born dancer with an illustrious career as dancer, choreographer, and artistic director especially in the Netherlands and South Africa. He was a founder member of the renown NDT3 company under Jiři Kylián's leadership in the 1990s. Krugel and I danced together at NAPAC Ballet in Durban in the late 1980s.

5   Mamela Nyamza is widely considered to be one of the first Black women studying ballet to have joined the professional dance companies in the Performing Arts Councils of South Africa in the 1990s before the collapse of apartheid in 1994. She is an award-winning choreographer based in Cape Town and producing highly controversial, contemporary dance and live performance artwork today.

6   What may belie the "multiple dance training styles" comment in the South African context reveals that to train in multiple dance styles was not an option for many black dancers who had little access to e.g., ballet. This was part of the segregationist practices which denied access to dance spaces such as the University of Cape Town School of Dance and the rich resources therein based on race. Only privileged white dancers could freely attend. As white, Jewish women, the roles and contributions of Blank, Mayo, Glasser and Friedman to contemporary dance (read modern dance) in South Africa have yet to be fully interrogated.

7   Ann Dickie is director of the From Here to Maturity dance company based in London. Jasmine Pasch is movement and play practitioner, and published author with her own company, London-based Phew Arts. Her work in early education and child development and movement and dance remains groundbreaking. Pasch is known to me for more than 20 years, and she pioneered the journeys into disability arts in Durban, South Africa in the late 1990s. She remains and inspiration into my foray into dance and ageism.

References

Blank, Adele. (2022). *Open interview*. Baxter Theatre Restaurant. Thursday 4 August.

Chadwick, R. (2017). Thinking intersectionally with/through narrative methodologies. *Agenda*, *31*(1), 5–16.

Chilisa, B. (2020). *Indigenous research methodologies* (2nd ed.). Thousand Oaks, CA: SAGE.

Jolliffe, P., & Worland, S. (2018). Honouring the elders: The common good among Karen communities – a multi-sited ethnography. *The Australian Journal of Anthropology, 29*(2), 158–170.

Kross, E., Verduyn, P., Sheppes, G., Costello, C. K., Jonides, J., & Ybarra, O. (2021). Social media and well-being: Pitfalls, progress, and next steps. *Trends in Cognitive Sciences, 25*(1), 55–66.

Palmore, E. (2000). Guest editorial: Ageism in gerontological language. *The Gerontologist, 40*(6), 645.

Parker, A. (2020). *Anarchival dance: Choreographic archives and the disruption of knowledge* [PhD thesis]. University of Cape Town, Cape Town.

Richards, N., Warren, L., & Gott, M. (2012). The challenge of creating 'alternative' images of ageing: Lessons from a project with older women. *Journal of Ageing Studies, 26*, 65–78.

Samuel, G. M. (2011, Winter). Dance is for the youth-filled body. *South African Dance Journal, 1*(1), 56–65.

Samuel, G. M. (2015). (Dis)graceful dancing bodies in South Africa. *Choreographic Practices, 6*(1), 107–124.

Samuel, G. M. (2016). *Dancing the other in South Africa* [PhD thesis]. The University of Cape Town, Cape Town.

Schneider, R. (2001). Performance remains. *Performance Research, 6*(2), 100–108.

2.5

DANCE IS "WHO YOU ARE; IT'S WHO YOU ARE KNOWN AS"

Amy Dean

Introduction

Within the context of Western classical ballet, this case narrative explores how 'dance' continues to play a role in the lives of four former South African professional ballet dancers. Through exploring their experiences of their career transition from a professional performing career to other careers or roles, I uncovered how dance had become an integral part of who they are and who they are known as.

I draw this from the interviews and analysis for my master's degree research study into the career transition experiences of four former South African professional ballet dancers transitioning from full-time professional performing careers to alternative careers or roles (Dean, 2022). Four themes had emerged from the data analysis of the four semi-structured in-depth interviews. One of these four themes – labelled 'loss, grief and coping processes' – discusses how dance played a role and continues to play a role in the identities and lives of the four former South African professional ballet dancers. The research study aimed to continue the growing international dialogues on dancers and career transitions from a South African perspective using a phenomenological case study research method.

This case narrative describes these experiences, suggesting that dance played a significant role in the lives of the dancers and did not disappear when they left their professional dance careers, but that their *assumptive worlds*[1] needed to adapt to this loss of dance.

The research study method and analysis

The key question for the research study was: "What is the experience of South African classical ballet dancers transitioning from a full-time professional stage performing career to alternative careers or roles?". The research study aimed to observe the lived experiences of the former ballet dancers during their career transition event

DOI: 10.4324/9781003307624-16

and therefore applied a phenomenological lens. A case study research method was applied to narrow the research study. I determined that qualitative data collected through semi-structured in-depth interviews with four former ballet dancers who are over the age of 18 years, had been full-time employed by Cape Town City Ballet (Western Cape, South Africa) for at least one year and whose career transition took place between December 2015 and December 2020 best suited the research design. The interviewees are referred to using the following pseudonyms Emma, Chad, Leigh and Sophie. Thematic data analysis (Braun & Clarke, 2012) was used to analyse the data and four themes emerged:

1   Loss, grief and coping processes
2   Preparation for an exit
3   Support systems
4   South African experience versus experience outside South Africa

The experiences of what dance meant and the role it has played and continues to play in their lives stems from the analysis of theme one: loss, grief and coping processes. The overall observation of this theme describes how dance was the primary loss for the former dancers and this created multiple secondary losses. These secondary losses suggest what dance meant to each dancer, and it was these secondary losses with which the former dancers needed to cope through grief and restoration (Dean, 2022).

I also reviewed current American, European and Australian scholarly and popular literature and, through this review, I designed the research study. Joan Jeffri (2005) writes that when researching the experiences of dancers' career transitions, there is a link between the themes observed. However, these themes are identified in differing order of priority between different countries. This shows the individuality of the experience based on the circumstances of dancers (Jeffri, 2005) which is echoed by Irina Roncaglia (2008), and this is the gap the research study took advantage of.

Dance is who you are

All four former dancers at some point in their professional performing careers had a strong association with their dancer identity. This identity stems from Britton Brewer, Judy Van Raalte and Darwyn Linder's idea of athletic identity, which is defined as "the degree to which an individual identifies with the athletic role" (Brewer et al., 1993, p. 237). Although the research study did not use the Athletic Identity Measurement Scale (AIMS), their answers to the various questions showed that there was a significant association during their careers with their role as a dancer. The interviewees had the following to say about dance and their identity.

> I think it's all encompassing, it becomes your life, it becomes who you are; it's who you are known as.
>
> *Emma (personal interview, July 22, 2021)*

Alright . . . it was really very difficult because you do associate yourself as the dancer, you are the dancer in the family and now you are not dancing, o but then what are you?

Leigh (personal interview, July 11, 2021)

I would say there were phases where I strongly identified with it on all levels and then there were other times that I was like, no, this is just what I do.

Sophie (personal interview, June 30, 2021)

Collin Parkes's (1998) ideas on Psychosocial Transition Theory describe how a person's internal view of the world needs to adapt when faced with an external change. These former dancers' dancer identities formed part of their assumptive (internal) worlds.

Some of the former dancers personified their primary loss of dance as a relationship loss (a break-up, a death or being heartbroken). This shows the extent that dance played in the assumptive world of these former dancers and "[e]xplaining their experiences in such a way helped them understand and articulate their feelings of grief and deep sadness" (Dean, 2022, p. 108). This primary loss resulted in secondary losses, which are identified as a loss of identity, social network, place and belonging, structure (comfort and familiarity), greatness and significance, expressive outlet and physicality. The interviewees shared some of these experiences, while some were unique. These secondary losses suggest the role dance played in the lives of the former dancers and formed a significant part of the dancer's assumptive world.

Dance is who you are known as

Brewer and colleagues explain the social aspect of athletic identity by stating "that the extent to which one labels oneself as an athlete may be strongly influenced by family members, friends, coaches, teachers and the media" (Brewer et al., 1993, p. 238). It was made clear by the interviewees that others – being their social networks, friends and families – saw them as dancers. Dance had become who they were known as. Sophie (personal interview, July 11, 2021): "I think it was very clear from other people's perceptions that that's the little box that they had put you in and you would then be their stereotype of what a dancer was".

After dance, who are you and who are you known as?

After the dancers transitioned from their full-time professional performing careers, their assumptive worlds needed to adapt and shift. As Parkes (1998) describes, adapting to an external change – whether a positive or negative change – can cause grief. Each former dancer describes experiencing grief at different points in their career transition some months before the actual transition took place and others after the transition. To cope with this grief, the dancers explained a process in which they reinvented, restored or added to themselves as they adapted to the primary loss of dance and the secondary losses. When asked if they still considered themselves dancers, they responded:

> I am still in the deepest, deepest, deepest of hope in my heart, I am still a dancer – but in reality, [slower] I am not.
>
> *Chad (personal interview, July 22, 2021)*

> Yes, it's made me who I am today. All that discipline, time management, [being] goal-driven, discipline, discipline, discipline has carried through and it's definitely shown in the workplace now.
>
> *Leigh (personal interview, July 11, 2021)*

> I remember it's the people that I met and the friendships that I made that are a lot more important to me . . . the life lessons that I gained, the character traits that it built.
>
> *Sophie (personal interview, June 30, 2021)*

> I think it, it carries on with you even though you don't dance.
>
> *Emma (personal interview, July 22, 2021)*

A part of dance remains in the assumptive worlds of these four former dancers, regardless of their current connection and physical interactions with dance. For some of these dancers, what remains is the life lessons and character traits, the love and passion, the social networks and friendships, the feeling of fulfilment because they had achieved something great, the random movement outbursts or – for Chad – a complete return to the professional dancing stage.

Conclusion

What the four former ballet dancers experienced was that dance did not only mean the physical act of dancing, but it filtered into varying aspects of their lives and formed a large part of their assumptive worlds. Dance informed their identities, their social networks, their behaviours, their priorities and their self-worth. Once these dancers lost this primary loss and the accompanying secondary losses, they had to renegotiate and restore their assumptive worlds. Although the former dancers continue to maintain various connections and physical interactions with dance, dance has continued to inform aspects of their new assumptive worlds.

Note

1 A term coined by British psychiatrist Collin Murray Parkes which describes a person's internal view of the world and is defined as "everything that we assume to be true on the basis of our experiences" (1998, p. 56).

References

Braun, V., & Clarke, V. (2012). Thematic analysis. In H. Cooper, P. M. Camic, D. L. Long, A. T. Panter, D. Rindskopf, & K. J. Sher (Eds.), *APA handbook of research methods in psychology, Vol 2: Research designs: Qualitative, neuropsychological, and biological* (pp. 57–71). Washington, DC: American Psychological Association.

Brewer, W., Van Raalte, J., & Linder, D. (1993). Athletic identity: Hercules' muscles or achilles' heel? *International Journal Sport Psychology*, *24*(4), 237–254.

Dean, A. D. (2022). *A South African perspective on professional ballet dancer's career transitions (2018–2021)* [Unpublished MA in dance dissertation]. University of Cape Town, Cape Town.

Jeffri, J. (2005). After the ball is over career transition for dancers around the world. *International Journal of Cultural Policy*, *11*(3), 341–355. doi:10.1080/10286630500411499

Parkes, C. M. (1998). Bereavement as a psychosocial transition: Processes of adaptation to change. *Journal of Social Issues*, *44*(3), 53–65.

Roncaglia, I. (2008). The ballet dancing profession: A career transition model. *Australian Journal of Career Development*, *17*(1), 50–59.

2.6

A FULL AND CREATIVE LIFE

Mary Davies

A pivotal moment for me in my creative practice was provoked by an accident in childhood when a bad break resulted in an inability to straighten my right arm. This permanent misalignment dogged my early dance career until choreographer Lea Anderson reshaped *Flesh and Blood* (1989) around my difference, creating a piece in which all the dancers' arms aligned to mine and had a curve. Embracing difference and using it to inform a creative response led to a career of integration and inclusive practice with a focus on movement for older people.

Community groups flux over time and are unique by nature – and groups of older people are no exception. They are a group of individuals bound by a common desire to take part, motivated by a myriad of different reasons. Not held or shaped by a common thread of training, without a common language of movement, any creative practice must embrace the specific differences and strengths of the population within the group for it to thrive. Sian Williams observed as a movement director we "inspire and encourage actors in their particular way of moving" (Tashkiran, 2020, p. 94). This principle is the foundation for work in the community setting; as the group itself is organic in nature, this process is both collaborative and exploratory. Individuals are inspired and encouraged within themselves and by one another. As a movement director and choreographer, I am inspired by the creative process of seeking out opportunities to extend and explore innovative ways to create movement within that context.

One can speak about movement as a language of communication. The body has its own way of speaking with the five senses telling and interpreting a story. There may be any number of communication barriers, but we can listen and be listened to through the body. As a movement practitioner, my focus is to navigate, flex and inform through movement. Primarily, this is learning through observation to facilitate ideas and impressions on the group's movement as an intuitive process within a community setting. I use trust and creativity to 'facilitate' a space for the group

DOI: 10.4324/9781003307624-17

to discover movement and qualities *within* themselves, seeking ways to encourage them to extend their individual movement vocabulary.

I acknowledge that careful use of language can inform and extend that exploratory process. Labels such as 'older people' or 'older adults' often used for this demographic can be subtly limiting by perception and association. The renowned Company of Elders leaves this entirely out of their company description whilst simultaneously using the word 'elders' in their name with its implicit associations of wisdom, experience and knowledge.

The relevant information they choose is 'non-professional'. Only when describing their diversity policy does 60-plus reveal their age. Limited expectations and the gentle use of language concerning movement and the older dancer denies the participant aspects of their resilient and intelligent selves. Quite often, the only aspect that differs from their younger selves is their physical range. Labelling is "contingent, imprecise and can infer allegiance with an objectification of a group of people" (Whatley & Marsh, 2017, p. 6). Imposing views based on preconceptions is problematic and disabling in effect. My work is a process of practice research through observation and participation.

Working extensively with the community performance group EncoreEast for more than ten years, we explored methods to encourage creativity and develop performance skills, alongside delivering creative and choreographic workshops at DanceEast's *Host* sharing ideas and problem solving. Recently invited back as a mentor, I witnessed some wonderful choreographic work by and for EncoreEast members. The process I adopted saw five company members step forward to take a choreographic lead, while the remaining participants volunteered as dancers. Delivered on Zoom over six months, this culminated in a sharing of four choreographed works. For some participants, changing their focus from dancer to choreographer was challenging but rewarding, and individuals discovered a broader set of creative possibilities to pursue. It is widely understood that encouraging expression through creativity aids self-belief and wellbeing, and feedback from the process revealed unique and surprising developments. It proved to be a hugely positive experience as members expressed feelings of joy, admiration and support for the work and for each other and much of this work now sits within their repertoire.

> Many movement directors acknowledge that working habitually with actors of various ages, physical capacities and body types develops multimodal, inclusive movement practice that can be redeployed to create work with non-professional performers.
>
> *(Tashkiran, 2020, p. 189).*

When working with EncoreEast, I committed to facilitating a creative environment for the company members to surpass themselves; with careful listening and appropriate responses, I nudged participants along the road of discovery to embrace opportunities and have agency over their work. In their profile, the Company of Elders choice of words draws attention to a large group of non-trained dancers

FIGURE 2.6   *Night Alarm* (2014), EncoreEast Dance Company (formally The Elderberries)

Source: Photograph by Anthony Cullen

celebrating community dance and quality of work. This considered and subtle choice of language implies progress.

My own work with EncoreEast and older dancers demonstrates that given the appropriate facilitation and creative ways to explore a 'language of movement', the process is in itself inclusive. I am an advocate of inclusive practice within a movement space that is enlightening and educational, and a rich source of inspiration with enhanced benefits to health. This in itself opens up access to groups and individuals who might otherwise struggle to reach their full potential, unable to express their identities and continually damaged by the challenges of accessing spaces and taking part – all barriers that lead to severe isolation and represent marginalisation. As a movement director, inclusive practice offers significant shared educational benefits for participants, for the movement director/facilitator and for the audience. Movement direction allows me to read and respond to the pace of the engagement and offer variations within the room. This delivery and engagement process becomes organic, framed by suggestions and malleable to providing a variable temporality enabling a deep exploration and expression, a necessarily considered approach and one that relies on acute observation and quick thinking. By facing challenges and problem solving together, the group and individual participants can learn and grow, building the confidence and resilience over time to extend their own and the group's movement boundaries – I argue that this context creates a forgiving landscape of trust whereby learning and progress can be made. Through navigating mistakes and questions, progression takes place, with the movement director's skills in suggestion and observation identifying the route to eke out the discoveries. Through my practice, I am committed to creating spaces for appreciating and respecting individual abilities, listening to the identities of those in the room and suspending all preconceptions to create the environment for mutual and professional growth. Accepting oneself and those around yourself breaks down barriers, affords access and leads to greatly enriched experiences within communities.

References

Tashkiran, A. (2020). *Movement directors in contemporary theatre conversations on craft*. London: METHUEN DRAMA Bloomsbury Publishing Plc.

Whatley, S., & Marsh, K. (2017). Making no difference: Inclusive dance pedagogy. In S. Burridge & C. Svendler Nielsen (Eds.), *Dance, access and inclusion: Perspectives on dance, young people and change*. London: Routledge.

SECTION 3

Community dance practice and performance

FIGURE 3.0   Dancer: Katrina Rank, choreographer for Fine Lines

Source: Artist's personal collection

DOI: 10.4324/9781003307624-18

3.1

AN IDEA, A PASSION, A SHOT OF TEQUILA AND A WHOLE LOT OF LOVE

Liz Lea

This is how the dance festival BOLD came about

Canberra's only professional dance festival, BOLD, is an international presentation of intercultural, inclusive and intergenerational dance programming. BOLD draws on the legacies of our cultural elders, celebrating the empowerment of ageing.

Established in 2017 as a platform for dance elders, BOLD is an ever-evolving platform, directly responding to the changing needs and sector diversity of practice with an intergenerational, intercultural and inter-ability vision. It provides a platform for older artists to celebrate their longevity and nurtures intergenerational exchange, seeding new works from emerging artists and their cultural legacies.

BOLD is unique in Australia, providing an invaluable dance hub embodying a solid reputation over its five-year lifespan. Interdisciplinarity is explored through connections between movement, science, multiculturalism and art, with an emphasis on First Nations heritage. BOLD's key objectives are providing development, performance and profile opportunities for professional and community dance artists in the Australian Capital Territory (ACT) and beyond. The powerhouse of artistic excellence presenting and attending the festival builds our audiences of dancers, artists, critics and health professionals, seeding future collaborations locally, nationally and internationally. BOLD's programming strength is built around innovation, community benefit and economic potential, enabling artists to connect and showcase their work nationally and internationally.

I conceived the event in 2014 when I first read about the Elixir Festival presented at and by Sadlers Wells in London. The rockstars of dance were taking to the stage, the crowds were going wild and this was creating space and support for elder community dance companies. I was deeply inspired and motivated. The rockstars are people like Kenneth Olumuyiwa Tharp, Mats Ek, Ana Laguna, Geraldine Morris, Linda Gibbs, Brian Bertscher, Anne Donnelly, Christopher Bannerman,

DOI: 10.4324/9781003307624-19

Lizie Saunderson, Betsy Gregory and Namron. These are the dancers I had looked up to when I began training at London Contemporary Dance School, and 25 years after graduating, I still find inspiration in how they move, inform us and inform the sector with their wisdom. Their experience and power onstage is just as real offstage as they take their experience backstage, producing, teaching and in the boardroom.

The name BOLD came from an in-person visit to Sadlers Wells. I was there on tour with Canberra Dance Theatre's GOLD Company. I was the artistic director of Canberra Dance Theatre from 2010–2016. My first task was to submit an application to the ACT government under the ACT Health Promotion Grants Program. I had just seen my colleague Chris Tudor working with Company of Elders dance company based at Sadlers Wells. Chris is another of my rockstars, and he and I danced together with English Bach Festival through Sarah Cremer and Stephen Preston. He had created a Baroque-inspired work on the Elders, and I was transfixed. My colleagues and I submitted an application for a ten-week performance project for over 55s in early 2011, designed for six people to learn a Baroque dance. In the event, we had 32 people register and partnered with the National Library of Australia and Belconnen Arts Centre. We kept the classes going, and for five years, I co-directed the company with Philip Piggin and Jane Ingall. GOLD recently celebrated its tenth anniversary.

Back to London

I produced a European tour for the GOLDs in 2015, connecting with older community elders' companies. A visit to Sadlers Wells and meeting the Company of Elders was a must. There, I met with a director to talk about the possibility of partnering with the Sadlers Wells team to run Elixir II in Australia. I was gently informed that the Wells are such a big organisation that this kind of partnership would not be possible, but I was asked if I would like a ticket to see Caroline Bowditch's *Falling in love with Frida*? "Yes I would", I said, and I was shown to a seat on the stage and given a shot of tequila. I knocked it back and the word 'BOLD' flashed into my mind. That's the name of this festival. And so it came to be.

This happened on the same stage that I had given my London premier of my solo *Inland*. The creation of that solo took place in the QL2 Theatre, Canberra. And so we come full circle as this is the venue in which we run our BOLD workshops and also present at least one show per festival. As the seeds of the festival began to grow, I began to expand my thinking. I moved away from a festival that focused on community dance only. I was on holiday and swimming laps and – in all honesty – disillusioned with the community dance sector. If I was going to build something big, then more of my passions needed to be involved, and I shifted the focus to professional dance practice also.

I turned to the grand dame of dance in Australia – Dr Elizabeth Cameron Dalman (see the Conversations section 1.3, page 18). Elizabeth is an Australian choreographer, teacher and performer. She founded Australian Dance Theatre and was its artistic director from 1965–1975. She is also the founding director of Mirramu Dance Company. She still performs, teaches, tours and choreographs. She is a legend, and she lives on the shores of Lake George in New South Wales, just on the border of the Australian Capital Territory. She agreed to become our Patron:

> The BOLD festivals not only celebrate dance in all its many forms, but they also acknowledge and pay respect to our dance elders, teachers and mentors. Making a career in the arts, particularly in dance, is not an easy pathway. It requires a flexible body and a flexible mind. It also calls for skill, determination, discipline, and a great deal of audacity. One needs to be 'BOLD'.

Elizabeth's words speak to our ethos of being BOLD, *not* Being OLD. It never occurred to me that this might be the thinking behind the name. One very well respected Australian choreographer was mortified and offended when I asked them if they would like to be involved, as they assumed the name was just that, a play on Being OLD. Heck, no. We are thinking BOLD, Bossy, Ballsy, Boisterous and Bloody minded. With this mindset, I went about connecting with the many national institutions here in Canberra. We now partner with the National Film and Sound Archive, National Library of Australia, National Portrait Gallery, National Gallery of Australia, Gorman House, QL2 Dance and Canberra Theatre Centre. We have also presented at Parliament House and worked with many businesses including wineries and Bloch.

The bedrock of BOLD is our artists. We have been able to connect with more rockstars – Anca Frankenhauser and Patrick Harding-Irmer have performed every year since we launched. Eileen Kramer performed in 2014 at Parliament House when she was 104, and she left people breathless. She also had a book launch that year at the National Library of Australia. For BOLD22, she presented one of our keynote talks assisted by the brilliant Sue Healey, whose work has also been presented each year. We have been privileged to present the work of Dr Stephanie Burridge, Rakini Devi, Ripe Dance, Somebodies Aunt, Australian Dance Party, Dance Makers Collective, Katrina Rank and many more. International performers have included Dancecology (Taiwan), Diverse Abilities Dance Collective (Singapore), Didik Hadiprayitno (Indonesia), Professors Eileen Standly and Mary Fitzgerald (US), Dr Dimple Kaur (India), Ryuichi Fujimura (Japan/Australia) and Lucky Lartey (Ghana/Australia) and Apsaras Arts (India/Australia).

The GOLDs are also a core part of our program; for example, every year, the brilliant Zest dancers who live with Parkinson's, run by my colleagues and dear friends Jane Ingall and Philip Piggin. The programming is deliberately eclectic – we look at the energy and mood of each work and also programming elders alongside emerging artists. The full gamut of dance is shared on our many stages, and this brings a sense of joy for audiences and performers alike. What has been a delightful surprise is that people older than 50 are seeking places and spaces to create and perform in – and there are not many of those. BOLD can provide this wherever possible. We have fabulous partners and a beautiful city that is easy to move around.

One of the most valuable and exciting aspects of BOLD from my perspective is that we work with and engender support for younger artists who are creating work inspired by their heritage or research into historical events and places. Tammi

FIGURE 3.1 GOLD Men, choreographer Liz Lea, BOLD Festival 2022

Source: Photograph by Lorna Sim

Gissell, Dance Makers Collective, Alison Plevey, Jolanda Lowatta, Hilal Dance Australia, Rainbow, Project Dust, Agal Dance, Danny Riley and Chris Wade have all presented performances and talks which speak to a respect for legacy.

I was also motivated by my own advancing years. I felt a shift in my body and psyche – I no longer ached to be in the studio or on stage all the time, and I needed to address the changes that come with that shift, so I, too, have an event I can present my work, try new ideas and continue to explore and expand my practice.

At the heart of BOLD though is our conference presented at the National Library of Australia. Our speakers hail from across the world – Dr Michelle Potter, Karen Gallagher, Dr Padma Menon, Eileen Kramer, Dr Stephanie Burridge and First Nations leaders Gary Lang, Marilyn Miller and Tammi Gissell. We also introduced the BOLD lecture given in the name of the brilliant UK-based Australian choreographer Janis Claxton. Our first BOLD lecture was given by Claire Hicks and the second by Marc Brew.

I am delighted with how we are evolving: BOLD22 presented ten world premieres, eight national premieres and three established works alongside 40 talks, 12 workshops and 25 films across five days. We align with the Enlighten Festival and Seniors Week. Past presentations (2017 and 2019) each had over 140 participants, 90 delegates, 55 talks, ten workshops, 7–20 films and five performances in five venues with 1500+ audience members.

BOLD22 was also a hybrid event, running both in person and partially online, with BOLD ON DEMAND running after the festival, granting access for 22 days after the live event, allowing national and international access and participation. This initially arose because of the ongoing impacts of COVID-19. We postponed the event three times until the team finally decided we needed to go ahead – and by going online, we really opened up our audience network while also supporting greater accessibility. Artists who live interstate, regionally and internationally were able to participate, engage and connect over a sustained period of time. It also enabled artists who live with disability to have ease of access to the event over a sustained period for the first time. We transcend barriers such as isolation/distance/lockdown and build sustainability at the core of the event as a sustainable art offering.

From a programming perspective, it opened up new worlds – we had speakers from Ireland, the UK, Egypt, Kuwait, Scotland, Canada and across Australia. Likewise, we were able to open our programming for workshops, and this, too, meant teachers from around the world were able to connect with new participants. We also had our performance at the National Portrait Gallery livestreamed and filmed. BOLD came into people's homes, and this is something we are really proud of. We climbed the steep learning curve and are thrilled with the result. This is particularly because we offered captioning and live/filmed Auslan (Australian signing for the hearing impaired) to the talks. We offered audio description for ten of the films and adding these elements to an online on demand program. By offering an event with this level of inclusivity in an online format, enabling accessible content, we put BOLD and the ACT at the forefront of innovative and proactive arts presentation in an international context.

New events arising from BOLD

Another BOLD legacy is I Dance. I Dance Festival is a mini film festival of dance films, showcasing excellence in dance films curated and created by artists with disabilities across the ACT, Australia, and the world. The event is curated by artists with disabilities with a national focus that has international implications for the disability dance community. Hosted by Hanna Cormick, Matt Shilcock and myself, we launched on 3 December 2020, the International Day of People with Disability. The festival is fully accessible with Auslan, captioning and audio description. Creators were drawn from leading Australian companies such as Restless Dance Theatre, Marc Brew, Joshua Campton, Sue Jo Wright, Fayen D'Evie and Riana Head-Toussaint, along with Matt and Hanna themselves. I Dance II is scheduled to take place at the National Film and Sound Archive in April 2023.

BOLD also has its own commission, 'The Annie'. One of our earliest supporters is Annie Greig who, along with her partner Jen Brown, attended the first event in 2017. Annie and Jen became synonymous with our ethos of quality dance performances and presentations, raging sense of humour and quirky style. When I heard Annie's health was failing, I approached them with the idea of 'The Annie', a choreographic dance film commission in Annie's spirit supported by donations given to continue Annie's legacy. Annie Greig was a brilliant communicator, connector and supporter of artists. 'The Annie' continues her ethos of providing opportunities for newly developing choreographers. It was her wish to establish a choreographic commission for a short 5–7-minute dance film for a choreographer to work with dancers aged older than 50. This commemorates the MA in Dance video which Annie undertook in New York. The Inaugural 'Annie' choreographer was announced at the National Film and Sound Archive on 2 March at the launch of BOLD22. Daryl Brandwood will create a film with Perth's Momentum Dance:

> The land we live on, the cycle of life and the power of natural beauty are themes we will be exploring in this proposal for a 6-minute work. I will be choreographing on 15–20 mature-dancers all over the age of fifty, who will also actively contribute to the choreography. We will film at one of Perth's most famous beaches at sunrise, when the light is at its most brilliant.
>
> *(Daryl Brandwood, Perth, Western Australia, March 2022)*

BOLD has also had two children

I have been searching for a mascot for years and the brilliant Dr Katrina Rank has performed and taught at BOLD each year. This year she shared creature with us. Creature is a charmingly ridiculous exploration of a metamorphosis from Mary Quant fashionista into a full-scale human accessory. The creature's transformation is animated by an extraordinary performer and choreographer, a self-confessed obsessive and the creator of the ridiculously decadent plush material that turns into creature. Creature itself is utterly relatable. The elements humanise rather than dehumanise the character and make the message – do not waste, but also beware hoarding – palatable. Creature is proudly supported by FUSE, Darebin's multi-arts festival, and BOLD is a proud parent.

BOLD's other (love) child is the Chameleon Collective, Canberra's first inclusive dance company. The Chameleon Collective is a boutique offering of artistic excellence in the inclusive and accessible arts field. The collective epitomises the vision of a forward-looking Canberra and the next generation of artists being invested in by the current generation of artists living with and without disability. The Chameleon Collective was founded in 2020, named after the constellation and reptile, both constant and adaptable. The first of its kind in the ACT, Chameleon became the link between community/youth dance and professional practice. We commission internationally recognised artists of all abilities, sharing the work on stage, screen and online to develop awareness and networks with a view to employment, further engagement and networking opportunities. Chameleon commits to 70% of our commissioned and collective artists living with disability, chronic illness and/or PTSD. Chameleon arises from the need for community dancers living with disability to channel their energies and talents into a professional parts development program that is supportive, accessible and at the leading edge of contemporary performance.

BOLD arose from connections across the globe and my being inspired by the extraordinary dancers who make up our dance world, dancers of all ages, backgrounds and abilities. Caroline Bowditch fell in love with Frida Kahlo, I fell in love with her show, BOLD was born and now BOLD has babies. It is really, simply, a love letter to Canberra and a lovefest for dancers.

3.2

STILL RIPENING

Evolving a dance practice through reflection

Gail Hewton

Introduction

I had never envisaged having an encore career in dance teaching and dance education, but my own need to find dance suitable for my ageing body has taken me on a journey of joy, fulfilment and reward. This ten-year journey immersed in dance for older people with a strong health and wellbeing focus has generated a new practice. The development of this practice has been supported by ongoing reflection.

My entire career has been spent in the arts, mainly in dance as a performer, teacher/educator, choreographer and producer. From 1978–2002, I taught in high schools, tertiary institutions, professional companies and communities. When I stopped teaching in 2002, it was not long before I missed dancing and over the next ten years, I found it difficult to find a dance class to suit my age and physical needs. Then in 2012, I had an "aha!" moment in an aerobics class I was attending where people older than me (I was 54 at the time) were moving very well and I thought perhaps they might like to do a dance class that suited their bodies and mine. I was working in a four-days-a-week administrative role so was able to start a class on my day off based in jazz/contemporary technique, modifying the dance material to suit older bodies. And so, on 6 July 2012, RIPE Dance[1] was born – RIPE because as older people we are at our peak, and it is an acronym for 'Really Is Possible for Everyone'. I was aware of the benefits dance brought me and I wanted others to benefit too, but I had had a ten-year teaching hiatus and had lost confidence. What helped and guided me to initially rebuild confidence and to continually evolve this new practice was reflection. Just as my career has evolved, so, too, has my reflective practice – the two working in tandem, each responding to and influencing the other so that I am now using it more effectively.

DOI: 10.4324/9781003307624-20

FIGURE 3.2A   *Yes We Can Can!* public performance for Seniors Week 2017, RIPE Dance active and agile seniors; venue: The J (Noosa Heads)

Source: Photograph by Barry Alsop, Eyes Wide Open Images

From reflection to critical and forensic reflective practice

Reflection has always been integral to my work ethos since my high school teacher training in the late 1970s. Initially, my reflective practice was intuitive rather than guided by any specific academic theories. It was not until 2015 when I enrolled in a doctoral degree programme that included study of reflective practice that I was able to name, analyse and unpack my past reflective practices. More importantly, I became aware of many different theoretical views and frameworks, such as those of Stephen Brookfield (1995), Arthur Costa and Bena Kallick (1993), Christopher Johns (2010), Jan Pascal and Neil Thompson (2012) and Donald Schön (1987), which took me into the world of what lecturer Brad Haseman (2015) referred to as forensic reflective practice, a much deeper and broader examination of our practices through reflection and reflexive thinking.

The theoretical framework for reflective practice that resonated with me most was that of adult education scholar Stephen Brookfield (1995) who proposes the use of four different lenses: the autobiographical; the students' eyes; colleagues' experiences, views and perceptions; and theoretical and research literature to examine and develop teaching practice. As I was working with older adults and in the early years of this new community dance practice, I realised that I needed to critically examine my knowledge and assumptions regarding older adults, in particular the needs of those older than me; an understanding about the ageing process; how older adults learn and/or engage; differences when catering for lifelong and novice dancers; and myself as an older teacher, artist and community practitioner. Brookfield's framework provided me with a foundation to examine, re-examine, develop and expand my practice.

Walking reflection – an effective personal tool

Incorporating Brookfield's four lenses as tools in reflection provides me with new knowledge and insights, and a range of perspectives, observations and experiences. Each lens is of equal value and importance in my practice develop-ment. Many theorists and authors on the subject of reflection, such as David Boud (2001) and Jennifer Moon (1999), suggest journaling as a tool to assist reflection. As a dance practitioner, what works for me is reflection while walking alone in nature. Fortunately, I live in a coastal area that enables me to regularly walk on or alongside beaches, on river paths and in varied sections of a forested national park. Movement and nature are the main mechanisms that positively affect my mental health and wellbeing. Their calming effect gives me thinking space to mull over, analyse, evaluate and synthesise learnings and insights pro-vided by the four lenses, enabling "aha!" moments and the generation of new ideas, strategies and solutions. My walking reflections have been and continue to be of paramount importance and instrumental in guiding and honing my journey of practice.

RIPE blossoms

RIPE Dance has flourished through these reflective practices over the past ten years, growing from one class per week to six classes with high participant reten-tion and adherence. I now have approximately 90 community dwelling participants aged 60–96 years attending my classes regularly, some still with me from the very first 2012 class. There have been numerous discoveries, breakthroughs, watershed moments and turning points throughout the development of RIPE Dance; hence, I have selected what I see as a few major milestones to discuss and how reflective practice influenced or led to them.

Birth of a new practice and its early development

RIPE Dance's beginnings were very much led by the autobiographical lens. I initi-ated a class to meet my need to dance. Early classes were for active and agile over 50s and were devised and delivered drawing on my experiences both as a teacher and student and as an ageing lifelong dancer. However, the diversity of participants and their different needs presented an immediate challenge. They were all older than me – being in their 60s, 70s and a some in their 80s – and most were novice dancers. My reflection centred around the question, "Is what and how I offered and delivered dance in the past for teenagers and young adults appropriate for older adults?". While I knew I needed to modify the movement I taught to cater for older adults, I contemplated how such a class with format and dance content based in contemporary and jazz dance techniques would be of interest and appropriate for this new cohort. I turned to the student lens. I relied on corporeal feedback through observation of participants in class as well as seeking their verbal feedback during and after classes. While they enjoyed the class structure, the dance style and content, and the music, I realised that in order to cater to participant needs safely and effectively, I needed to know more about older bodies, issues pertinent to older people and the implications of these for devising and delivering dance for older adults.

I employed the lens of literature and research for information about the ageing process and implications for dance for active and agile seniors, the specific cohort with which I was working. There was a wealth of information available regarding the ageing process but not the implications for dance. Liz Lerman (1984) provided some good foundational information; however, its use for me at that time was limited due to its narrow focus on modern dance and for less mobile seniors. Lerman did, however, trigger my interest in the holistic nature of dance's benefits for older people. "Dance magically combines exercise, self-expression, fun group activity, intellectual stimulation, and spiritual uplift" (Lerman, 1984, p. xiv).

I engaged in conversations with long-time dance colleague, Julie Chenery (who happens to be a few years older than I). Julie is a critical friend with whom I am able to have honest and confidential dialogue, which always helps me to clarify my thinking. Julie occasionally attended some classes, enabling her to provide valuable feedback to affirm my delivery, as well as offer suggestions or different viewpoints for me to consider. This helped to rebuild my confidence and challenge my thinking in developing my new practice. I also searched online for dance classes and programmes for older people to affirm my work and glean ideas – there was not a lot to be found at that stage.

Reflection assisted me to refine classes taking into consideration newfound knowledge about the ageing process, and about participant and collegial feedback. Those early classes were a cycle of trial, reflect and evaluate, reflect and refine.

FIGURE 3.2B   Weekly class, 2021, RIPE Dance, *Dance Capers for active and agile seniors*; venue: Noosa Leisure Centre, Noosaville

Source: Photograph by Barry Alsop, Eyes Wide Open Images

Expansion and contraction of the practice

During a short period of unemployment in 2010, I volunteered one afternoon each week in a local aged care residence where I was tasked with leading a group of low-care residents in playing cards and bingo. I thought these were uninspiring activities and wondered if a dance class might be more engaging and beneficial. My lack of experience and confidence in working with this cohort of older people stopped me venturing into this area of dance at that time. When I discovered Lerman's text – which provides numerous examples of seated and assisted standing dance – in 2013, the notion of a seated dance session for aged care began to formulate. In May of that year, I attended the inaugural Australian Introductory Training Workshop on Dance for PD® with long-time dance colleague, Sonja Peedo.[2] The workshop, facilitated by David Leventhal, affirmed the concept of seated dance and gave me confidence in my ability to translate a similar approach to the aged care context. I asked Sonja to join me to offer a dance programme for aged care. I approached a local aged care facility, which resulted in us co-devising and co-teaching a trial pro-gramme once a week for ten weeks. We delivered the trial for free, as it was a new concept for facility management, staff and residents, and it gave us the opportunity to try our ideas and build our confidence. There were 20–25 participants each week representing a diversity of backgrounds, personalities, abilities and engage-ment levels. Each week, we discovered more about individual participants, which provided stimulus for music selection and dance content. Sonja and I would debrief after each session to reflect on, evaluate and refine the content. It was a success leading to me being engaged (and paid) by the aged care organisation at the start of 2014 to deliver dance, which I did fortnightly for the next five years.

When the aged care facility opened the sessions to residents from the dementia unit, I realised a much less structured approach was required, as was the need to involve more care staff and volunteers to assist one-to-one those participants liv-ing with dementia. I learned that having sufficient numbers of people to assist can greatly affect the content and engagement of aged care participants and ultimately the success of sessions.

Several factors influenced a major decision to cease my work in aged care in 2018. Despite recognition by the allied health workers of its value, management only saw dance as entertainment. Participant numbers were becoming unmanageable – up to 40 residents at times and without enough staff to assist. These factors – in addition to learning that only 5.2% of Australians over 65 years live in aged care with the remain-ing 94.8% living in community (Australian Bureau of Statistics, 2016) – provoked some earnest and painstaking reflection. Whilst I loved working in aged care and supported and recognised the need for dance programmes there, I made the decision to concentrate my practice in the community. This is where I believed I could affect the lives of more older people to help them live well in their community.

The success of the initial aged care trial also gave me confidence to expand my offerings for community dwelling seniors with mobility challenges. After success-fully approaching a retirement village for use of their venue, I began a weekly class in March 2014 for village residents and those who lived externally.

FIGURE 3.2C   Class with options to cater for different mobility levels, 2021, RIPE Dance, *Yes, You Can Dance! for seniors with mobility issues*; venue: Laguna Retirement Village, Noosaville

Source: Photograph by Barry Alsop, Eyes Wide Open Images

Further along in my years practising, in response to high demand, I added more classes for active and agile seniors and people with mobility issues. Also, through reflection, I identified a gap in my practice provision. There appeared a need for a class to meet the needs of active, yet less agile seniors who could manage an all-standing session. When I received a request from a mobility class participant for a second class to add to her week and one that was more challenging, it confirmed my thinking to start a class. This has proved a good decision, as the class has been at full capacity since 2017.

FIGURE 3.2D   Socially connecting and enjoying dancing together in weekly class, 2021, RIPE Dance, *Dance Capers for active (less agile) seniors*; venue: Laguna Retirement Village, Noosaville

Source: Photograph by Barry Alsop, Eyes Wide Open Images

Focus on falls prevention

Working with people with mobility issues in aged care and the community, I became aware that falls are a major issue for older individuals, families and society. I was astounded when I read the statistics at the time in terms of deaths and hospitalisations of older people due to falls and the enormous cost to our health system, and current statistics continue to paint a grave picture (Australian and New Zealand Falls Prevention Society, n.d.).

Through research, I sought out evidence-based falls prevention exercise programmes and found that the exercises of the FaME (Skelton & Dinan, 1999) and Otago (Campbell & Robertson, 2003) programmes developed by physiotherapists are similar to (or contained within) many dance technique exercises in ballet, contemporary and jazz dance, genres I use in my classes.[3] Good posture, alignment and balance, muscular strength and flexibility, joint mobility, coordination, proprioception and gait are hallmarks of both falls prevention and dance. What I had been doing unintentionally for falls prevention, I could now do intentionally whilst ensuring the essence of the dance remains.

I also read a number of peer-reviewed articles that researched the efficacy of dance for falls prevention, such as those of Alpert et al. (2009), da Silva Borges et al. (2014), Fernández-Argüelles et al. (2015), Keogh et al. (2009), Sofianidis et al. (2009). Research findings demonstrated positive outcomes and the potential of dance as an intervention for falls prevention. Reflecting on all of this and seeing the marked physical improvements of my participants, together with participant

FIGURE 3.2E   Working on stepping it out to improve posture and gait for falls prevention, 2021, RIPE Dance, *Yes, You Can Dance! for seniors with mobility issues*; venue: Laguna Retirement Village, Noosaville

Source: Photograph by Barry Alsop, Eyes Wide Open Images

feedback of reduced falls or falls averted, I made the decision to continue intentionally designing dance content to incorporate a falls prevention focus. I then felt further supported in my approach when I learned of the UK's Dance to Health[4] falls prevention programme that was also incorporating the FaME and Otago programmes within dance and having positive outcomes (Sport Industry Research Centre, 2019).

Whilst I believe that dance of any genre may contribute to falls prevention at some level, it seems reasonable to infer that dance programmes tailored for falls prevention may offer more optimal impact and therefore warrant further research. My falls prevention focus continues to grow stronger, and seeking research evidence to support my methodology is something I am currently working toward. Conversations about this led to a strategic collaboration inviting dance-trained colleague Bronwyn Claassen, an experienced physiotherapist, and Karly Pollard, an exercise physiologist, to join Julie and me to conduct a preliminary analysis of one of my classes, in order to evaluate content in terms of falls prevention contributing factors. Our findings (Hewton et al., 2021) showed that in the dance class, there were many repetitions of dance moves together with other falls prevention aspects that are similar to the content of the FaME and Otago programmes.

I then presented the success of the RIPE Dance programme – including its high attendance and adherence rates, something providers of exercise programmes find problematic – and the findings of our preliminary analysis at the 2021 Australian and New Zealand Falls Prevention Society conference. This has resulted in researchers from University of Sydney Institute of Musculoskeletal Health expressing interest and successfully applying for a research grant to conduct an impact evaluation of the RIPE Dance programme.

FIGURE 3.2F   Weekly class incorporating falls prevention with a relational approach, 2021, RIPE Dance, *Dance Capers for active and agile seniors*; venue: Noosa Leisure Centre, Noosaville

Photographer: Barry Alsop, Eyes Wide Open Images

Identification of a relational approach as the underpinning of my practice

During my time as a high school teacher, I realised that connecting with students was key to engaging them. Finding out what interested them not only told them they mattered, but gave me subject matter to weave into lesson content to engage them. Reflecting on that early career experience led me to believe this also to be relevant to my new context. Ascertaining older participants' music preferences, interests, life stories, cultural backgrounds, etc., gives similar outcomes. Yet, this feature of my approach is broader than just person-centred. I endeavour to ethically engage participants connecting them with each other and to the wider world in a fun, safe, supportive and welcoming environment.

When I expressed the need to name this feature for my doctoral study, Julie suggested it was a relational approach and to read psychologist Kenneth Gergen's *Relational Being* (Gergen 2009). I did, and his view that our wellbeing – both local and global – depends on positioning relationship at the forefront of concern resonated with me in a profound way. Subsequent inquiry reveals research evidence (Cacioppo & Cacioppo, 2014; Holt-Lunstad et al., 2015) supporting the value and benefits of social connectedness and that it is an important factor for successful ageing.

My doctoral study helped me identify a relational approach as a key feature of my teaching and leading dance. Further reflection has led me to acknowledge that it underpins my practice. Ongoing reflection allows me to hone its use and explore new strategies to keep it fresh.

Greater focus on health and wellbeing

I endeavour to design my dance sessions to optimise the physical, cognitive, emotional and social benefits dance can effect. However, sessions must be first and foremost a dance session. It takes time to devise content that creatively incorporates these health and wellbeing aims whilst ensuring the essence of the dance remains. Reflection plays a significant role in crafting my sessions. I believe that I am on the right track. Medical and health professionals refer their patients and clients to my classes, which have been endorsed by occupational therapists and physiotherapists who have attended sessions. Receiving testimonials such as the following from occupational therapist Lacey Styles (email correspondence, 2017) attest to this:

> The benefits of dance and music therapy are well documented, and to see Gail put all of this into practice showed me firsthand that this should be the way of the future for any rehab and maintenance program. The participation, retention and health outcomes for clients, I believe, far outweigh many other conventional therapy approaches.

FIGURE 3.2G Weekly class including participants living with Parkinson's, post-polio, cancer, rheumatoid arthritis, polymyalgia and ageing challenges, 2021, RIPE Dance, *Yes, You Can Dance! for seniors with mobility issues*; venue: Masonic Hall, Tewantin

Source: Photograph by Barry Alsop, Eyes Wide Open Images

Need to benchmark my work, continue professional development and build a collegial network

Despite receiving affirming testimonials, I felt the need to benchmark my work against others who have had substantial experience working in the field, as well as open myself to new information and other ways of working. I have regularly travelled nationally since 2014 to present at or attend arts and health gatherings, particularly those with a dance for older people focus. I also initiate meetings with key colleagues working in the field to help build a strong collegial network. These collegial interactions range from meetings to discuss our respective work to attending classes and rehearsals to observe them in practice and at times in response to invitations, leading classes or workshops with their older participants. Reflection on these experiences often leads to incorporating new learnings in dance sessions or sharing new information and/or research findings with participants and others.

Of significant impact was a six-week UK study tour I undertook in 2018 to investigate dance for older people. I met with more than 20 dance colleagues from 13 key organisations; observed through participation more than 25 classes and sessions, and I attended various professional development workshops. The main outcomes, learnings and reflections for me included the following. I was able to:

- Compare my thinking and practice developments in dance for falls prevention with the Dance to Health programme. Whilst our respective programmes were similar, a major difference, from my perspective, was that the Dance to Health programme was driven and somewhat constrained by having to include specific exercises of the Otago and FaME falls prevention exercise programmes in every dance session – rather than letting dance drive the programme whilst incorporating principles of these falls prevention exercise programmes across time.

- Benchmark my work against the work of highly experienced practitioners working in the field.
- Identify a common issue in the UK to one I see in Australia, which is that practitioners need professional development in order to fully understand an older person's body, the ageing process and the implications of these and health issues for dance that is safe physically, cognitively and emotionally.
- Further develop my network establishing numerous new contacts and relationships with key organisations and practitioners not only for my own work but also to share with the dance community in Australia.

RIPE bears fruit – the establishment of Gold Moves Australia

Interest in and demand for dance for older people for health and wellbeing is growing. I constantly receive requests for more classes, there is more media coverage and research into its benefits is increasing. However, as stated in an Ausdance Victoria (2018) research report, there are not enough practitioners qualified in this field to meet demand. Reflecting on the success of RIPE Dance and my many learnings from it, I felt that given my previous experience as an educator and a teacher trainer, I was in a position to share my knowledge and learnings with others in order to ultimately benefit more older people, so I invited Julie to join me in a partnership venture and we established Gold Moves Australia[5] in 2018 to provide education and advocacy for dance for older people for health and wellbeing. This, too, is an evolving practice utilising reflection.

FIGURE 3.2H Practitioner professional development workshop – *Introduction to Leading Dance for Older People for Health and Wellbeing*, 2021, Gold Moves Australia workshop participants; venue: St Paul's Uniting Church Hall, Mackay

Source: Photograph by Julie Chenery

Conclusion

I have developed the RIPE Dance programme through practice-based exploration supported by rigorous reflection. Reflective practice has enhanced my professional performance and self-development, by illuminating issues and concepts, enabling insight and assisting learning for new understandings. It has involved drawing on my knowledge and experience and that of others, responding to feedback and the perspectives of my participants and colleagues, and learnings from literature and professional development. It has resulted in RIPE Dance becoming a well evolved community dance practice and the establishment of Gold Moves Australia, a burgeoning dance education and training practice.

Notes

1 https://ripedance.com.au/
2 Dance for PD® is a program founded in 2001 as a collaboration between the Mark Morris Dance Group and the Brooklyn Parkinson Group in New York to offer specialised classes for people with Parkinson's disease.
3 The Falls Management Exercise (FaME) program is a structured evidence-based exercise class that contains age appropriate exercises for older adults. Otago – named for a region of the South Island of New Zealand – is an evidence-based program of strength and balance exercises delivered in the home to reduce falls for frail older adults.
4 Dance to Health is a UK-based falls prevention dance programme for older people begun in 2015 and devised and managed by Aesop. https://dancetohealth.org/
5 https://goldmovesaustralia.com.au/

References

Alpert, P. T., Miller, S. K., Wallmann, H., Havey, R., Cross, C., Chevalia, T., & Kodandapari, K. (2009). The effect of modified jazz dance on balance, cognition, and mood in older adults. *Journal of the American Academy of Nurse Practitioners, 21*(2), 108–115.

Ausdance Victoria. (2018). *Leading and teaching dance to ageing populations.* Retrieved from https://ausdancevic.org.au/wp-content/uploads/2021/02/Ausdance_LeadingTeaching DancetoAgeingPopulations.pdf

Australian Bureau of Statistics. (2016, October 18). *Disability, ageing and carers, Australia: Summary of findings, 2015.* Retrieved from www.abs.gov.au/ausstats/abs@.nsf/Lookup/4430.0main+features302015

Australian and New Zealand Falls Prevention Society. (n.d.). *Why we need to pay more attention to falls.* Retrieved from www.anzfallsprevention.org/

Boud, D. (2001). Using journal writing to enhance reflective practice. In L. M. English & M. A. Gillen (Eds.), *Promoting journal writing in adult education. New directions in adult and continuing education No. 90* (pp. 9–18). San Francisco, CA: Jossey-Bass.

Brookfield, S. D. (1995). *Becoming a critically reflective teacher.* San Francisco, CA: Jossey-Bass.

Cacioppo, J. T., & Cacioppo, S. (2014). Social relationships and health: The toxic effects of perceived social isolation. *Social and Personality Psychology Compass, 8*(2), pp. 58–72.

Campbell, A. J., & Robertson, M. C. (2003). Otago exercise programme to prevent falls in older adults. *ACC Thinksafe.* Retrieved from www.livestronger.org.nz/assets/Uploads/acc1162-otago-exercise-manual.pdf

Costa, A. L., & Kallick, B. (1993). Through the lens of a critical friend. *Educational Leadership, 51*(2), 49–51.

da Silva Borges, E. G., de Souza Vale, R. G., Cader, S. A., Leal, S., Miguel, F., Pernambuco, C. S., & Dantas, E. H. M. (2014). Postural balance and falls in elderly nursing home residents enrolled in a ballroom dancing program. *Archives of Gerontology and Geriatrics, 59*(2), 312–316.

Fernández-Argüelles, E. L., Rodríguez-Mansilla, J., Antunez, L. E., Garrido-Ardila, E. M., & Muñoz, R. P. (2015). Effects of dancing on the risk of falling related factors of healthy older adults: A systematic review. *Archives of Gerontology and Geriatrics, 60*(1), 1.

Gergen, K. J. (2009). *Relational being: Beyond self and community*. New York: Oxford University Press.

Haseman, B. (2015, February 28). *Forensic reflective practice: Effecting personal and systemic change* [Lecture]. Doctorate of Creative Industries Semester 1, Module 1, Queensland University of Queensland, Kelvin Grove, Brisbane, Australia.

Hewton, G., Chenery, J., Claassen, B., & Pollard, K. (2021, December 2). *Falls prevention through dance: A community program case study* [Conference presentation]. 9th Biennial Australia and New Zealand Falls Prevention Conference. https://goldmovesaustralia.com.au/co/

Holt-Lunstad, J., Smith, T. B., Baker, M., Harris, T., & Stephenson, D. (2015). Loneliness and social isolation as risk factors for mortality: A meta-analytic review. *Perspectives on Psychological Science, 10*(2), 227–237.

Johns, C. (2010). *Guided reflection: A narrative approach to advancing professional practice*. Chichester: Wiley-Blackwell.

Keogh, J. W., Kilding, A., Pidgeon, P., Ashley, L., & Gillis, D. (2009). Physical benefits of dancing for healthy older adults: A review. *Journal of Aging Physical Activity, 17*(4), 479–500.

Lerman, L. (1984). *Teaching dance to senior adults*. Springfield, IL: Charles C Thomas.

Moon, J. A. (1999). *Learning journals: A handbook for reflective practice and professional development* (2nd ed.). London: Routledge.

Pascal, J., & Thompson, N. (2012). Developing critically reflective practice. *Reflective Practice: International and Multidisciplinary Perspectives, 13*(2), 311–325. doi:10.1080/1462394 3.2012.657795

Schön, D. A. (1987). *Educating the reflective practitioner*. San Francisco, CA: Jossey-Bass.

Skelton, D. A., & Dinan, S. M. (1999). Exercise for falls management: Rationale for an exercise programme aimed at reducing postural instability. *Physiotherapy Theory and Practice, 15*, 105–120.

Sofianidis, G., Hatzitaki, V., Douka, S., & Grouios, G. (2009). Effect of a 10-week traditional dance program on static and dynamic balance control in elderly adults. *Journal of Aging and Physical Activity, 17*, 167–180.

Sport Industry Research Centre, Sheffield Hallam University. (2019). *Dance to health 'phase 1 roll-out [test and learn]' evaluation: First report*. Dance to Health. https://ae-sop.org/wp-content/uploads/sites/63/2019/06/SHU-SIRC-1st-report-FINAL.pdf

Styles, L. (2017). *Testimonial for RIPE dance classes for older people with mobility issues*. Emailed correspondence.

3.3

FROM VIRAL HIT TO VITAL TROUPE

The "dancing grannies" of Angthong and their revival of Lakhon Chatri during a pandemic

Pornrat Damrhung

Introduction

Under the COVID-19 pandemic lockdown in the spring of 2020 in Thailand, a group of elderly women in the Angthong province, Central Thailand turned their old "Lakhon Chatri" Thai dance-drama knowledge into live streaming and viral hits that inspired them to move and also moved the country, winning the hearts of the homebound audiences looking to screens for signs of life and pleasure during the uncertainties of that time. These elderly dancers' interest in and the interest of others in their dance since late 2020 have come to settle into a regular set of dance activities in public settings as vaccines became more available and as COVID-19 has become less of a threat in 2022. Yet, the women are still looking for new opportunities to dance for others in a world less bothered by COVID-19. How did that evolution come about, and what does that say about the relations of dance and the elderly in Thailand in a post-pandemic world?

This chapter will first outline the evolving "Lakhon Chatri" performance tradition in Thailand. It will then examine how the place and time of COVID-19 affected this group of women as they emerged as a viral hit among Thais during the early pandemic, and finally assess how they solidified their place in their local area while strengthening their own bodies, minds, and collective cultural power by practising dance. To focus on the evolution of these "dancing grannies" from Angthong, I first observed their Lakhon Chatri dancing on their social media and mass media accounts from May 2020. I also saw them perform live and spoke with them in June 2020. In addition, I interviewed and discussed their activities with their adopted grandson, Mr Suatha Senamontri, who has been their coordinator and manager since late 2020. This was followed up by watching how the Thai mass media presented these women and their dance in 2020–2021. I also visited and interviewed them individually and collectively in 2022. This multifaceted approach

DOI: 10.4324/9781003307624-21

has allowed me to see how the dancing grannies first entered the public spotlight, how the media presented them and how they have evolved as an active and brave group of women dancers under COVID-19.

"Lakhon Chatri" performance culture in Central Thailand and in Angthong

The dance tradition embodied by the elderly dancing ladies at the focus of this chapter is "Lakhon Chatri" (meaning "Bold [or Courageous] Dance"), one of the oldest forms of dance in Thailand (Nicolas, 1924; Grow, 1992; Department of Cultural Promotion, 2009). It consists of dance drama and singing performances from a repertoire of folk legends, accompanied by traditional music ensemble, and it is framed by a ritual structure that pays homage to the tradition's founders and honours important spirits.

Since the late 19th century, women "Lakhon" court dancers from Bangkok spread their refined court dance forms through parts of Central Thailand, altering Lakhon Chatri and increasing its popularity in town and temple celebrations, weddings, and funerals, while keeping its function in paying homage to spirits and ancestors. It evolved into distinct local traditions with unique styles in provinces of Central Thailand, such as Phetburi, Angthong, Nakhon Pathom, Chachoengsao, and east in Chanthaburi and others, becoming a female performance art mostly performed for spirits and gods at temples and shrines. In recent times, dance drama as local entertainment has shifted to more lively and improvisational forms like Likay (Thai folk opera), which had both men and women performers. Women performers mainly performing Lakhon Chatri for gods and spirits often had the right skills and knowledge to let them perform in Likay troupes (Damrhung and Skar, Forthcoming).

For more than half a century, Lakhon Chatri has been performed by women who mostly perform in *Ram Kaebon* (thanksgiving dances) for gods and spirits at temples and shrines in various parts of Central Thailand.[1] Lakhon Chatri honours and entertains gods and spirits given as gifts by sponsors and patrons who wish to show their thanks to the spirits for receiving a wish or goal they had previously requested. Lakhon Chatri performances are mostly done in temples and shrines each day in cities and towns.[2]

The taste and preferences of sponsors and performers of Lakhon Chatri have evolved and typical performances have changed. Younger sponsors prefer younger dancers, so many older performers often retire in their 50s or 60s. They sometimes perform as part of entertainment families or because their main patrons were spirits who seemed to prefer old styles and forms, but some still had fans of their unique styles.

Short Lakhon Chatri dances are done to honour the spirits in places like Angthong, often by young people, but if a patron desires a more elaborate performance, more experienced performers stage more complex Lakhon Chatri performances. Elaborate Lakhon Chatri performances may even include elements from the Likay tradition (and may include popular Luk Thung "country" songs), which are often sung by young performers, both since young performers may not know much of the old dance drama, and because their patrons may consider the old form as slow-paced and filled with complex plots and unfamiliar characters. These changes have contributed to a demise of knowledge of old dances, stories, and singing, but these forms are kept by older members of Lakhon Chatri communities, such as in Angthong, located 115 kilometres northwest of Bangkok.

While agriculture is still common in and around Angthong, industrial estates and government agencies now employ most of the population there. Lakhon Chatri now often uses young performers who dance more simply, often include popular Luk Thung songs to express thoughts and sensibilities. Performances for gods and spirits are done to suit the taste and knowledge of the younger patrons and sponsors. The Thachang community in Wisethchaichan district of Angthong retains a distinctive older Lakhon Chatri dancers and traditions, with musicians able to play both old-style Lakhon Chatri and more popular modern Likay forms.

Although the old Lakhon Chatri has gradually changed with the times, it is still connected to community legends and beliefs, and rooted in "the blood and the bones" of the elderly performers who are masters of the tradition. Elderly women are connected by marriage, by training and by communal performance, but for most of their adult lives, they performed in different Lakhon Chatri troupes. After entering their 60s, most had given up performing. In the late 2010s, Lakhon Chatri seemed to be waning as its practitioners aged.

To the surprise of many, the COVID-19 pandemic helped to bring about a viral – but real and enduring – revival of Lakhon Chatri in Angthong by this group of retired elderly dancers.

The viral rise of Lakhon Chatri from the dancing grannies of Angthong province during the COVID-19 pandemic

Lakhon Chatri is practised by many families in Thachang village in Angthong, but since many of its practitioners are now elderly, they had given up performing. The COVID-19 pandemic changed this situation. When Thailand's first national lockdown for the pandemic began in March 2020, social distancing kept people at home and closed most workplaces and schools. With Thai universities closed, Mr Suatha Senamontri, a native of Angthong, returned from Bangkok. He had grown up in a network of interconnected Lakhon Chatri performers as an adopted grandson. Seeing no work in his area, he wondered what he could do to bridge the Lakhon Chatri community to their locked down audiences. Performers of other dance-theatre forms like Likay or Morlum had begun performing short dance pieces online via live streaming, posting them on YouTube channels, or using social media platforms to communicate with their audiences and to provide temporary work for performers. Fans of specific stars wanted to watch them live and contribute to them by online payments for virtual "tickets" and digital "garlands."

Mr Senamontri looked to do the same with Lakhon Chatri, even though its local performers had no popular local stars or fan base. He wondered if live-streamed performances of Lakhon Chatri would attract viewers or what kind of performance could they develop to show people and have them enjoy seeing it. He hoped the older artists could perform pieces live in their own unique Angthong style online, giving them a chance to dance in the style they used to do years ago before they stopped performing. This could help to show a unique but disappearing art form that was still alive in the elderly ladies, which had become a rare thing to watch.

He first discussed it with his aunts and grand-aunts who performed the dance, but the idea of performing live on a social media channel met with a resounding "No." They did not see themselves as beautiful, capable, or being of interest to others, and they believed that their dancing skills had waned and their bodies were weak. They did not believe that people would want to see old dancers on their screens, even if they danced rarely performed pieces. They did not want to publicly make fools of themselves. Their lack of confidence in their abilities and their knowledge made them hesitate.

These elderly women reconsidered their initial answer and changed their minds, deciding to take this risk and work on some scenes to perform. Why? Mr Senamontri told me that he wanted them to "share their knowledge of the past to help generate income and raise funds for their families who could not work; they were very skilled artists and could help support their families with their special knowledge." Dancing to support their families and community with their art was the argument that won over these women and gave them courage. By April 2020, they started working on some pieces and formed an ad hoc troupe of ten grandmothers. Even thought they had long since given up performing their Lakhon Chatri art, they decided to gather, rehearse, and prepare a performance of some scenes that they knew well for a planned live-streamed event.

Mr Senamontri organised the performance with the help of the musician Anant Buasuwan, first performing in May 2020 on Facebook Live as the *Anant Rungswangsilapa*, or "the Brilliant Art Troupe of [Music Master] Anant" ("Chara Chatri" Facebook, 2020). It became a viral hit. Amid peak social distancing that spring, when people were stuck at home with little else to do, these elderly women dancers picked up their courage and prepared long-lost dance scenes and characters from the local Lakhon Chatri tradition for invisible and unknown online viewers. They transcended space and time through new social and mass media channels to become a surprise sensation in the region and across Thailand, gaining thousands of Facebook views, receiving surprise online paid sponsorships as "garlands" given from their admirers. (Chara Chatri Documentary, 2020; Super Active show on "Chara Chatri", 2020).

This surprise social media interest led them to get mass media attention from Bangkok and to prepare more online performances for June. Many people stuck in their homes were interested in their performances, and through their "likes" and "shares" and buying virtual "garlands," the grannies' troupe entered the mass media spotlight. The popularity of their performance surprised homebound audiences and showed people how older people could turn their dance knowledge into a vital embodied sign of resilient cultural power during the pandemic. Audiences admired their energetic and beautiful art form appearing on their screens. It provided a bold vitality that dared them to show what the elderly could do in a pandemic. Their new passion to perform gathered and grew in their minds after they prepared and streamed their first piece, and became something they wanted to build on and continue with more pieces and in more venues. They first performed as a group in an open-air space, at an old rice mill near their community. Their performances, both supported by and supporting their families, became a vital part of community life during the pandemic. They brought the old style and form of this hybrid folk dance drama presented again in a contemporary platform.

The live-streamed performances on social media platforms got the attention of a large public who shared it via mass media. They appeared on morning and afternoon television news shows, on educational channels, and on programmes for seniors, and then on YouTube channels. Eventually, they were asked to perform again, and this led to more viewers and more national attention, with the Thai PBS Arts and Culture Media Center filming them and their preparation, showing how these ladies also got more jobs performing thanksgiving dances for the spirits (NBT news report on Chara Chatri, 2020; WOW! Thailand Show on Chara Chatri, 2020; Thai PBS News Clip on Chara Chatri, 2021). They also became famous and were interviewed and seen as resource persons by scholars and performers in many university dance and theatre programmes.

The social and mass media successes of the troupe surprised viewers during the time of uncertainty and made the dancing grannies wonder about how they could show to others the courage they had with their art under pandemic conditions. Dancers and musicians aged from 60–90 years old performed at their best and cast a bright light of hope in the time of pandemic fear, worry and sadness.

By August 2020, the elderly women formed a more formal troupe called "Chara Chatri" (Courageous or Brave Elderly [Dancers]). Since then, interest in the troupe has grown from its base in Thachang village on the western edge of the Angthong province into an integral part of regional culture, while also providing the dancing grannies with a sense of mission for themselves, their friends and their dance tradition. Many of the dancing grannies once ran their own Lakhon Chatri troupes, and some of their children and grandchildren still performed, whether at Lakhon Chatri or using their knowledge in more popular forms like Likay.

Through their performances and the attention they received, staff of the United Nations Educational, Scientific and Cultural Organization (UNESCO) in Bangkok also became interested in them, along with other local styles of Lakhon Chatri (UNESCO, 2020a, 2020b). The Angthong province saw a new value in these old ladies, their performances, and their old tradition, acknowledging that they could bring happiness to their audiences and recognition to their community. Each of them has a fan club and they have helped to revive their form of Lakhon Chatri, which seemed to be on the verge of disappearing.

FIGURE 3.3A The Chara Chatri Troupe (2021)

Source: Photograph by Monkrit Thammapiyasin

Their fame attracted young people from Angthong to the art and made them interested in learning and practising these arts with their grandmothers and great-grandmothers. I have seen this in my visits with the elderly Lakhon Chatri dancers at their homes in Angthong. They spoke of how several of their grandchildren and great-grandchildren had taken up Lakhon Chatri. On one visit in June 2022, I saw how one young girl in the family wanted to showcase her talents in the art by performing for her elderly teachers (as well as for me as a guest). This cross-generational interest generated pride in the elderly dancers for their art and their ability, and helped them to arrange for more performances to fill the growing demand for their work. Their performances brought joy and happiness to diverse audiences, and it has made them stronger and more agile, providing good health and social connections tied to their art among good friends, neighbours and outside visitors. Since late 2020, they have performed in many places, often as part of cultural festivals, seminars, and conferences. This made these ladies idols and symbols of artists who work to show their best, despite their age. The "dancing grannies" have become known and become an idol for their grandchildren, who look upon them and are proud of them and also proud of their art.

Chara Chatri troupe members still maintain their everyday life much the same, but now their dance is more prominent in their lives than before COVID-19 struck. All the Lakhon Chatri dancing grannies who started performing in

FIGURE 3.3B   The Chara Chatri Troupe working with young people (2022)

Source: Photograph by Monkrit Thammapiyasin

2020 were still dancing in 2022. Thachang village in mid-2022 looked like other towns and has more opportunities now that people are back to work. Two younger members of the troupe who are in their 60s also have found more work dancing Kaebon. They are booked for several annual performances on an ongoing basis in Angthong city and in the nearby old capital of Ayutthaya. Besides teaching their grandkids and doing Kaebon, they have a regular set of performances 3–4 times a year as the large Chara Chatri troupe for local and regional communities.

Preparing and performing these pieces nurtures the dancers' minds and bodies and shows there are still places that value their knowledge, elegance and energy, even if they are more than 60 years old.

These ageing performers showed people in Thailand how to live during a trying time, and in doing so, they developed a sense of confidence and pride in their dance, performing with grace under the great uncertainties and anxiety at the time. The energetic vitality of each Chara Chatri performer blended complex movement with rhythmic singing, acting, and storytelling, bringing joy and happiness to both performers themselves and their audiences who have seen them perform whoever they are and wherever they live. The vitality generated among these elderly women was bold and genuine, and each artist saw the singing and dancing in the scenes they performed as their gift to their audiences.

FIGURES 3.3C–D Granny Thong-arb Tosawadi (aged 86); Chara Chatri troupe member

Source: Photograph by Monkrit Thammapiyasin

What is unique about these dancing grannies?

The dancing grannies of Angthong are unique for several reasons. They know and can perform rarely seen stories and scenes from the Lakhon Chatri tradition. They also perform in a distinctive style of Lakhon Chatri in Angthong that is no longer widely seen. Finally, they revived and reworked unfamiliar pieces from the Lakhon Chatri repertoire for new audiences and media channels. This inspired those in and around their community – in the country and beyond – by highlighting the neglected value of being able to dance at any age.

Ms Pathum Praesuwan, now aged 83, who played the lead male role in the troupe she ran, has taken a leading role in the newly formed Chara Chatri troupe, creating new scripts from little-known plots and verses from her own memory, both editing them for the stage and adjusting them to suit each performance. Saying the scripts are drawn from her "blood and bones," they consist of many wonderful but neglected episodes, including those involving "Kaew Na Ma" (the Horse-Faced Lady), with a scene disguising herself as a warrior who goes out to fight a powerful giant demon, and who delivers twins as she fought on the battlefield. A woman warrior defeating the most powerful demon is a universal theme, but the additional image of her giving birth to twins in the heat of battle adds more power to it.

Besides the neglected episodes, the Angthong troupe uses a unique style, often with practical and legendary links to court dance traditions and following an old style that unfolds slowly according to its own time. While perhaps not well-suited to the fast-paced rhythms of today's world, the troupe struck a chord during in the socially distanced lockdown time of COVID-19 and viewers who could recognise their simple and direct beauty in the strong dance moves and the witty verses sung by the main performer and the dancers in chorus in a recitative style.

FIGURE 3.3E   A solo dance battle with music master

Source: Photograph by Monkrit Thammapiyasin

Finally, the troupe also revived other little-known dance pieces, such as those by Granny Thong-arb Tosawad, aged 86, shown in the preceding photograph performing the famous "Horse-Faced Lady" teasing the Taphon (or big drum) played by music and ritual master, Master Anant Buasuwan. Viewers loved this piece since it first appeared on live stream, partly since this piece had not been performed for more than 30 years. It has become central to the repertoire of the troupe, performed again and again by Granny Thong-arb and Master Anant in many shows. Granny Thong-arb revived several dance pieces that had virtually disappeared from the Lakhon Chatri repertoire. Although she has problems carrying and holding things in her hands, when she dances, her hand gestures are clear, her legs are grounded, and her energy is strong as she moves smoothly and in sync with the rhythm using her muscle memory. Dancing helps to keep the grannies strong and active, and it helps to keep alive neglected parts of the Lakhon Chatri tradition.

My visits and interviews with the Chara Chatri grannies in the last two years (both on Zoom and in person) made it clear that they all still love to perform and enjoy their new role in lives as performers who still dance and who can share their knowledge with new audiences and with younger generations.

The dancing grannies talked about how they needed to put their bodies into better shape so they would be strong enough to do the energetic dance with controlled movement suiting the scenes they chose to perform. Although their legs are weaker than before and it is sometimes difficult to control them, all grannies worked to be able to do their best.

Conclusion

This chapter has considered the place of dance in an ageing society during the COVID-19 pandemic, focusing on the "dancing grannies" of Angthong, Thailand. By examining how these elderly women used their embodied knowledge of Lakhon Chatri to overcome the challenges of the pandemic lockdown and to reassert their individual and collective courage to dance in a time of danger, the chapter has shown how the new dance work, networking, and place-making with Lakhon Chatri has invigorated their roles in Thai society. This has opened new opportunities for them to dance for others in a world less bothered by COVID-19.

By gaining more recognition for their dance, the grannies' lives are now full of pride and courage for themselves and the unique, wonderful knowledge they carry in their bones, blood, and hearts. This pride helps highlight their lives and assures them of the value of their knowledge and the meaningful ability they have to move. What they learned and practised was valuable, and so is the wisdom and pride in each of them. Their knowledge has helped develop new educators and students to learn and collect dance moves, stories, and songs of a disappearing art form.

The dancing grannies also found new friends during their performances and in their lives. These grannies are siblings, mothers, daughters, in-laws or cousins to one another. They work together in dance as they grow old; some ageing people separate themselves although sharing the house, but some great-grannies like being alone. The performance spaces and events take part in making them and their families adjust. Performing again on stage, they learned to help and care for one another as they performed. Being together on stage, even though they are less agile and physically strong as they once were, allowed the grannies to find trusting partners and to be with their siblings and cousins.

Finally, the dancing grannies have (re)discovered and made new places for themselves and their art in their lives and in their local community and in Thai society. Their work since 2020 shows the importance of collective learning in Lakhon Chatri with masters to become a performer, a teacher, a master, and even a social media idol and people to look up to and admire their enthusiastic attitude to life, their fun and their devotion to doing their best and performing with all their hearts. They teach others by sharing, interacting, and performing. They have become living symbols of the power of their village and communities. They performed in important events and represented the unique Lakhon Chatri dance form in Central Thailand, forming an example of community wisdom that is intangible but living in them. This has won the attention of cultural experts in Bangkok and from UNESCO.

The embodied interests and abilities of the Chara Chatri troupe sketched in this chapter are important in their own right, but they also link up with several of the United Nations 2030 Sustainable Development Goals which are important for ageing societies and for the elderly. They show how dance can enable healthy ageing and wellbeing (SDG 3), keep up with lifelong learning (SDG 4), reduce gender inequality (SDG 5), promote work for the elderly who still want and are able to do so while also limiting inequalities later in life (SDG 8 and SDG 10), and build inclusive communities (SDG 11) (Rudge, 2020; Nakajima, 2011, 2019; Bolwell, 2017; Vinay, 2016).

In each of these ways, the dancing grannies perform not only for their families and local communities but also for the country and the world. They show one important way that dance can work to bring some vitality to an ageing society like Thailand and the Angthong province, and that dance has been an important sign of life among the elderly throughout the COVID-19 pandemic. This re-emergence has helped to provide them with pride in the knowledge and ability of Lakhon Chatri.

Notes

1   The best-known example of Lakhon Chatri are the short votive dances still performed at the Erawan Brahman Shrine by the Erawan Hotel in Central Bangkok, which were even performed through most of the COVID-19 pandemic.
2   Lakhon Chatri has also been included into the Thai Fine Arts Department's repertoire and curriculum. It was put into the national inventory of Thailand's "intangible cultural heritage" in 2009 by the Department of Cultural Promotion of the Thai Culture Ministry.

References

Bangkok Post Reporters. (2021, March 22). Uncertainty for the elderly. *Bangkok Post.* Retrieved from www.bangkokpost.com/business/2087527/uncertainty-for-the-elderly
Bangkok Post Reporters. (2022, April 23). Thailand to 'fully re-open'. *Bangkok Post.* Retrieved from www.bangkokpost.com/thailand/general/2298946/thailand-to-fully-re-open

Bolwell, J. (2017). Wellbeing and the aging dancer. In V. Karkou, S. Oliver, & S. Lycouris (Eds.), *The Oxford handbook of dance and wellbeing* (pp. 311–328). Oxford: Oxford University Press.

Damrhung, P., & Skar, L. (Eds.). (Forthcoming). *Thai lives in motion: Celebrating dance in Thailand*. Delhi: Routledge.

Department of Cultural Promotion, Thailand Ministry of Culture. (n.d.). *"Lakhon Chatri" designated a national Intangible Cultural Heritage element in 2009*. Retrieved from http://ich.culture.go.th/index.php/en/ich/performing-arts/238-stage/185-lakhon-chatri

Grow, M. L. (1992). Dancing for spirits: Lakhon Chatri performers from phetchaburi province. *Journal of the Siam Society, 80*, 105–112.

Karkou, V., Oliver, S., & Lycouris, S. (Eds.). (2017). *The Oxford handbook of dance and wellbeing*. Oxford: Oxford University Press.

Nakajima, N. (2011). De-aging dancerism? The aging body in contemporary and community dance. *Performance Research, 16*, 100–104.

Nakajima, N. (2019). This is (not) the ageing body in dance. *Performance Research, 24*(3), 55–65.

Nicolas, R. (1924). Le Lakhon Nora ou Lakhon Chatri et les origines du theatre Classique siamois. *Journal of the Siam Society, 14*, 84–110.

Rudge, M. (2020). *Ageing and the SDGs: Six steps to older people's inclusion*. London: HelpAge International.

Theparat, C. (2022, March 21). NESDC warns rapidly ageing society likely to hit economy. *Bangkok Post*. Retrieved June 10, 2022, from www.bangkokpost.com/business/2282375/nesdc-warns-rapidly-ageing-society-likely-to-hit-economy

UNESCO. (2020a, December 4). *Idea to digitize and publicize Lakhon Chatri of Nang Loeng Community, Bangkok, Thailand*. Retrieved May 10, 2022, from https://youtu.be/L5Bl-jdz80g

UNESCO. (2020b, December 7). *Idea to continue senior Lakhon Chatri performing art of Wisetchaicharn, Ang-thong Province, Thailand*. Retrieved May 10, 2022, from https://youtu.be/PGvkEKXRzME

Vinay, C. (2016). *Leave no one behind: Aging, gender and 2030 agenda*. UNDP Issue Brief.

The dancing grannies of Angthong performances in media on various TV programs, educational programs and community performances.

Chara Chatri Documentary (2020, July 20). Retrieved May 15, 2022, from www.youtube.com/watch?v=Rf1Hp1hISEo

"Chara Chatri" Facebook (2020, August 3). Retrieved June 10, 2022, from www.facebook.com/AgedChatri/

"Chara Chatri" Performance on RMUTT Channel (2020, October 31). Retrieved May 10, 2022, from www.youtube.com/watch?v=Yvo3HuIAguY

NBT news report on "Chara Chatri." (2020, June 29). Retrieved May 10, 2022, from www.youtube.com/watch?v=t4MwDHhwVBQ

Super Active show on "Chara Chatri." (2020, October 25). Thai PBS program for the elderly. Retrieved May 15, 2022, from www.youtube.com/watch?v=zTt8799qH00

Thai PBS News Clip on "Chara Chatri." (2021, March 22). Retrieved May 10, 2022, from www.youtube.com/watch?v=bVsWOOcoI0c&t=100s

WOW! Thailand Show on "Chara Chatri." (2020, November 18). Retrieved May 15, 2022, from www.youtube.com/watch?v=44hWki6G4d4

3.4

FINE LINES

A dance collective of mature artists – the story so far

Katrina Rank and Jenny Barnett

This study begins with the reflections of two of Fine Lines' founding members: director Katrina Rank and dancer Jenny Barnett. It concludes with a conversation between the two about the future of Fine Lines as it enters its tenth year.

Katrina

It began with intense frustration and a sense of alienation. In my 40s, with a chronic condition, the dance classes and projects I was interested in were no longer accessible or inclusive of my uncompliant body. There were fewer things I could do to my satisfaction. I spent a disproportionate amount of time adjusting the set material. I felt lacking, patronised and discouraged. Once, as a young dancer, I almost lost my dancer-self to injury and mental illness. Now I faced the danger of that erasure again.

As before, I persisted. Because the thing I missed the most in dance was sharing music, movement, artistic goals and the moment of creativity with other dancers, I decided to begin my own classes. Fine Lines began in 2013 at Dancehouse, Melbourne, Australia. Initially, there were very few people. In hindsight, this was a good thing, as it afforded me time to develop a new pedagogy responding to participants' backgrounds, interests and artistic goals.

Gradually, the Fine Lines collective grew. It drew people from diverse artistic backgrounds. It reunited Modern Dance Ensemble dancers after 20–30 years apart. It attracted ex-professional dancers and those who had enjoyed dance in their youth. It called to circus artists and those from allied movement approaches such as improvisation and somatic practices. The mix was eclectic and the skills wide ranging. Informed by these diverse individuals, an approach emerged that enabled growth, pride, purpose and attunement. The pedagogy worked to people's strengths. It led the way to a strongly connected group of women, ranging in age from mid-30s to 80s, a group built on trust and inclusion.

DOI: 10.4324/9781003307624-22

FIGURE 3.4A–C *The Right* (top); *Firebird* (middle); *JOY* (bottom)

Source: Photographs by Robert Wagner

In the early years, performance was peripheral to our practice, though the interest was there and some short pieces were developed with the entire group. In class, I introduced 'the long phrase' to build stamina and memory retention and provide an opportunity to engage as a performer. The choreographies were less about technical achievement than a focused movement intent. *The Right* (2019), Fine Lines' first large-scale work, grew from one such phrase. The experience itself – and the thrill of winning an award – stirred a hunger for more formal performance experiences. During the global pandemic, we developed and filmed *Firebird* (2020), a new experience for many dancers as they worked with camera and came to terms with the brutality of the editing process. *JOY* (2021) was in many ways a response to that brutality. Another dance film, it presented the other side of the COVID-19 coin: *JOY* on one side, *Firebird* on the other. *JOY* was Fine Lines' first international collaboration and its third major work, under my direction. It is a mature work by a mature company in its tenth year. The following images feature the dancers of five lines with choreography by Katrina Rank. The photographer is Robert Wagner.

Jenny

I've been with Fine Lines since day one: ten years of learning. Once, I would never have described myself as a dancer. My perception was that female dancers were young, lean and lithe, wore tutus, had expressionless faces and spun around on pointed toes. I'm an older woman, stocky, love to make faces and I hate net and frills. After a working life helping others to learn, I wanted to spend this final quarter digging deep inside myself to see what lay undiscovered.

I threw myself into myriad creative workshops before I spotted a new dance class, Fine Lines, for mature bodies with a dance/movement background. I turned up, uncertain of my dance credentials. There were few of us, but a warm welcome. I skulked around the back of the room; secretly, inside, I doubted myself. However, my sporty youth and lifetime of yoga served me well and I began – slowly – to learn this new movement language. Individual explorations and improvisations became all-absorbing. This resonated with my belief that singing, dancing and storytelling are for everyone, not just the professional and the trained.

Fine Lines evolved slowly: new people came; after-class coffee became a ritual; lives were shared; ideas tossed around. Experiments for informal performances began. I was thrilled when my dance pre-conceptions were smashed: a project creating a dance film with only feet in various guises; a duet within the confines of garden compost bags, exploring shelter, fear and breaking out; a small group creating a work using masks and reams of paper, fashioning a world outside time and space. My performance background had been limited to acting with words. I began to relish the possibilities of movement-led creativity.

Our first major work, *The Right*, was a real turning point for me. Here was a chance to capture and express with my whole body – face, gestures, movements, stance and even voice – the anger and frustration about the conduct of

FIGURE 3.4D *The Right*; dancers: Holly and Jenny; choreography: Katrina Rank

Source: Photograph by Robert Wagner

politics, with its power plays, aggression and negativity. I'd not only found a community of friends and creatives, but a way of making my voice as an older woman heard.

It's the tough times that test us. The pandemic found us apart physically and I was absent for months courtesy of a serious leg injury. The *JOY* project came along, its collaborative approach enabling me to return – albeit cautiously. So now I'm thinking about the future. Will I still be an active member of Fine Lines in ten years, when I will be in my mid-80s? I intend to be and I want my ageing body to contribute to original and exciting work. I wonder how this dream can become a reality.

FIGURE 3.4E   *JOY*; dancer: Jenny; choreography: Katrina Rank

Source: Photograph by Robert Wagner

Katrina

It starts with commitment to values, doesn't it? In our last whole-group conversation, Fine Liners identified inclusion as a central value. Whatever Fine Lines' creative trajectory, if we follow our values, there should be open access to all members of the group to contribute to and be challenged by exciting, original new work.

Jenny

I wonder, too, how Fine Lines will evolve as a collective. It has become a very close-knit and supportive group; can we guard this and be inclusive and welcoming to others? New blood is a great recharger, but I dread feeling squeezed out by those younger, more athletic bodies.

Katrina

I think about this a lot. The wide range of movement experience in the group leads to diverse ambitions and expectations. It forces me to be creative in class and in my approach to new projects. Currently, the biggest challenge to Fine Lines is its rapid growth in dancers attending weekly class and the search for a wheelchair-accessible space of the size we require at a cost we can afford. We may need to create two classes to provide sufficient space to move. But how to do that without establishing some sort of hierarchy? In class, I'll continue to push the pedagogy so that all options feel equally valid and exciting, so that each person can find satisfying outcomes and pride in their achievements. This pedagogical development isn't quick or easy, and the demands on it may change every few years as the Fine Lines cohort morphs and reframes itself.

In some ways, it's easier with the projects. We can offer a range of experiences. Some you say yes to, others you say, that's not for me. The approaches for new work will vary considerably but all projects should be innovative and stimulate unique, individual expression – all hallmarks of quality artwork.

Jenny

Directing a piece for performance is very demanding. I wonder how we might best tap into the wide range of skills within our collective, sharing the workload, without jeopardising the enjoyment we all have of simply dancing. If we invite in a guest choreographer, I wonder what impact that might have and how we might manage that opportunity.

Katrina

There's a plethora of talent and experience in Fine Lines, just waiting to be nudged. *JOY* showed us the importance of involving our community in early project design, developing processes for shared ownership and responsibility. In working with external artists, we'll ensure any new work reflects Fine Lines' values, aspirations and capacity. One thing I am adamant about, though, is that new Fine Lines' work must be inclusive. Imaginative choreographers and directors will find a way to develop work that is of high artistic merit while involving all who want to take part.

Who and what Fine Lines is, expects and wants will continue to change. In response, we will need to ask ourselves:

- What are the core values we must never lose sight of?
- What distinguishes a Fine Lines work?
- What are the criteria that shape it?
- Who can participate?

The responses to these questions frame who we are as a collective of mature dance artists and the sort of work we create. It's an ongoing story with no certainty – but much adventure.

3.5

DANCE MATTERS

Crows Feet Dance Collective

Jan Bolwell

> Griefs, at the moment they turn into ideas, lose some of their power to injure our hearts.
>
> *(Marcel Proust 1981)*

Proust's words helped to shape my life from the age of 48 when in 1998 I experienced two bouts of breast cancer followed by a double mastectomy. In order to rediscover my body and come to terms with its altered state, I returned to dance as a performer and choreographer, and I became a playwright. Something I did not anticipate happened in 1999. Following my dancing and spoken presence in Dame Gaylene Preston's 2001 film *Titless Wonders*, I was approached by women my age who asked me to teach them to dance. Crows Feet Dance Collective was born. This open entry community dance group for mature women began with four people and now numbers 45 dancers spread across four groups in the Wellington region of Aotearoa New Zealand. I asked five dancers of varying ages and dance backgrounds to describe their participation in Crows Feet and why dance matters to them at this stage of their lives.

Annie

Annie is 73, an ex-director of New Zealand's leading drama school, with a long and distinguished career as a drama educator, actor, director and administrator.

> I had promised myself that I would join Crows when I finished being director of Toi Whakaari: NZ Drama School. I had been really inspired by seeing these older women dance and the clear joy that shone out of them. The variety of backgrounds and ability made me aware that I had a chance of being able to do it, despite my lack of experience. My first show was *The Armed*

DOI: 10.4324/9781003307624-23

Man and it was a wonderful piece. Karl Jenkins music is sublime and it felt like a huge gift to dance it.

Women come to Crows Feet Dance Collective with many professional skills in a variety of fields. Annie's background as an actor was put to effective use in *The Armed Man* and in subsequent productions. However, being confident and skilful in one art form does not necessarily carry over to another, as Annie discovered.

> I was nowhere near confident and it was a huge struggle. I am not a natural mover and years of poor posture have created their own challenges. Another dancer called me "pure grit" because I was determined to at least not embarrass myself and the company and worked very hard at the routines. Lots of extra rehearsals and a very aching body. But how wonderful it was to be there.

Perhaps it is a characteristic of adult learners, especially when we are accustomed to easily demonstrating our skills in certain fields, that frustration can set in when dancing becomes a struggle.

> I hoped to be able to eventually *dance* the work rather than just hold on to the sequence of steps. That remains an ongoing struggle. There have been moments of success and that is such a delicious feeling but I continue to struggle.

COVID-19 brought our classes to a grinding halt, and Annie discovered how much she missed dancing and the company of the other women in the collective.

> I have been surprised how much I now need to dance, how much I look forward to class. I think I now own myself as a dancer as well as an actor and director and that surprises me. I love the humour of the other women and the grace with which they accept their ageing bodies. Crows Feet has taught me that dancing is a part of my birthright. I live, I breathe, I dance!

Trish

Trish is 67 and has a long and varied dance and physical exercise background since her childhood, one of eight kids growing up on a farm. She is a confident mover and practises yoga regularly. Trish has been with Crows Feet since 2013 after five years living in the UK.

> At first I found it slightly confronting seeing these wonderful dancers moving so freely and also having very lined faces. (It doesn't make sense to me now – perhaps to do with my own stereotypes about ageing) . . . Looking back, I had no real idea of what was possible at Crows but knew I loved to dance and here was an opportunity after all those years.

FIGURE 3.5   *The Witch Project* (2019), dancers: Helen, Trish and Annie in Crows Feet production

Source: Photograph by Annette Scullion

I asked the dancers if they found unexpected outcomes in joining Crows, and for Trish, there were

> physical and technical improvements and extension. I am way more flexible than I have ever been in my life . . . . It made sense of my yoga practice and social engagement and friendships have developed and are increasing . . . . Resilience! I've never stuck with a group for so long. I'm not really a great joiner and get bored pretty quickly. But I am really enjoying the benefits of being a committed member of a group and learning all the time. Fabulous!

Dorothea

Dorothea is 68, originally from South Africa, and our newest recruit to Crows Feet.

> I had polio as a small girl. To build muscles and enable me to walk, my dad, who was a very sporty person, bound my feet to a tricycle and walked with me for miles. He massaged me morning and evening and encouraged me to swim, run and play tennis. I always loved music and would move to everything I heard. As a music teacher, I am always doing movement with the children, too.

Dorothea finds aspects of Crows Feet challenging.

> I keep on reminding myself if I can't do something, I must persevere and be patient with myself.

Recently, the challenges have escalated.

> The joy is disappearing for me at the moment. Every week I have been feel-ing more and more disabled and less and less able to believe I can do this. I feel I am failing to meet external expectations and standards.

Dorothea's plight has put the onus back on myself as the teacher, to find a way to be inclusive in my choreography and to help her rediscover her joy in dancing.

Helen

Helen is 58 and the most highly educated dancer in Crows Feet. She has danced all her life, training at a tertiary level and as a dance company member. When Helen was asked why she decided to join Crows, she said,

> I liked the energy and the eclectic mix of women in the group and the opportunity to dance together. It was a new thing for me. I was apprehensive as to what I was getting into, but also open minded to join something new, just for me, rather than always being the leader/director as I have been in my role as a dance/drama teacher for the last 30 years.

The wide-ranging skill level in Crows Feet means that Helen's needs are not always met.

> I would like to work harder on choreography and be challenged more physi-cally with a broader physical exploration . . . of ideas to make dance. Also more opportunities to create new work that group devised/shaped by us alone.

Working with a group of opiniated, assertive women who are accustomed to being in leadership roles inevitably leads to friction at times.

> Some women are more challenging than others in regard to ego, especially during pre-performance/rehearsal times/stage management routines. This appears to be tolerated by others and for some reason not addressed . . . . Not good vibes at all.

Rachel

The last word is given to our oldest and most beloved dancer, 82-year old Rachel, who is a poet, fiction writer and retired IT (information technology) professional. She joined Crows Feet at age 65.

Rachel was extremely active as a child, and went through the sports, ballet, Scottish country dancing and ballroom dance phase – now she walks, does Pilates and every morning, tai chi. Why did she join Crows Feet?

> I had watched several performances, longed to join but was sure the skills required were way out of my reach. Then at one show I watched a dancer walk slowly across the back of the stage with a vase on her shoulder, while others were dancing "properly". That changed everything. At that moment I saw that even very limited dancers were accepted, and I joined.

Were there any unexpected outcomes in joining Crows?

> Friendships both casual and deep, opportunities to dance with other groups, and I have become more tolerant of different personalities.

Rachel's challenges are to do with age-related changes.

> At 82 balance is tricky, focus and concentration are strangely hard. But there is so much I can do . . . . I know I will be pushed to do new difficult things, and I embrace that. I also know I won't be pushed past my limits, and allowances will be made . . . . I know this can't go on forever but Crows is a core delight in my life.

The dancing body

I am a wrinkled apple
with an equator tied around
what used to be a waist.

Yet I am allowed to dance,
my darlings.
Turn away if you must.

My upper half is crumpled
but it works. Watch it stretch
and bend and flick and flow –
watch it go!

Down in the Southern Hemisphere
a committee intermittent
struggles to keep control.

A single pain commutes
from knee to arch of foot
to hip.

Warnings from the North Pole
travel slow in Morse code
and get diverted on the way.

The Southern body will not
bend or flip. It's all locked in
like old Gondwanaland.

It's not quite anarchy
here in the dancing body
more a quiet disagreement
with the plan.

Rachel McAlpine (2021)

Reference

Proust, M. (1981). *Remembrance of things past*. New York: Random House. Retrieved July 6, 2022, from https://gaylenepreston.co.nz/titless-wonders

SECTION 4

Pedagogy and recreational dance practice

FIGURE 4.0 Lucinda Sharp teaching an adult barre class for MADE dance company, Tasmania

Source: Photograph by MADE dance company, Tasmania (see case narrative in this section)

DOI: 10.4324/9781003307624-24

4.1

BECOMING AN AFFIRMATIVE COMMUNITY

Mature dancers' experiences in an age-aware contemporary dance class

Pirkko Markula, Allison Jeffrey, Jennifer Nikolai and Simrit Deol

In this chapter, we expand upon prior scholarship that investigates the idealisation of youthfulness in professional dance based on our research with a group of experienced mature women dancers. We first review the previous literature on experienced mature dancers and then engage Rosi Braidotti's (2018a, 2019a, 2019b) concept of affirmative ethics to consider dance classes as localised movement communities that can create change in the cultural construction of ageing. We then present findings from our study with seven mature, experienced dancers who participated in a dance class designed specifically for their needs. We conclude with a discussion of how these women's unique embodied relations support an affirmative ethics that enables mature dancers to subvert ageist assumptions.

Mature professional dancers: undervalued and underrepresented?

A growing body of literature demonstrates the health benefits of dance for the general population. However, in the case of professional dancers, research has revealed that these practitioners tend to retire early, often considering themselves to be no longer capable of meeting dance performance standards (without adversely compromising their health) (Coupland, 2013; Southcott & Joseph, 2020; Wainwright & Turner, 2004, 2006). As Hilde Rustad and Gunn Engelsrud (2022) observe, this leads to a paradox whereby everyone mature in their age is encouraged to dance, except professional dancers. Research with mature experienced dancers who continue to perform (i.e., Nakajima, 2011; Southcott & Joseph, 2020) reveals that mature dancing bodies remain extremely capable of captivating audiences. In addition, their performance presence challenges ageist assumptions of a youthful, agile, ageless dancer that remains dominant in many dance cultures.

DOI: 10.4324/9781003307624-25

As highlighted by research in various dance disciplines, mature dancers often consider themselves to be undervalued and underrepresented (Schwaiger, 2005; Southcott & Joseph, 2020). Such studies reveal tensions that mature women dancers experience while navigating "a cultural gaze that seeks to define older bodies as out of place" (Rustad & Engelsrud, 2022, p. 7) in dance cultures that often idealise youthfulness (Coupland, 2013, p. 3). Schwaiger (2005; Schwaiger, 2012) found that mature performers, in addition to being influenced by ageism, have simultaneously subverted it. When performing on stage, the ageing dancing body can become a site where self-realisation and wellbeing may be simultaneously explored alongside notions of the idealised feminine dancing body (Markula et al., 2022). Some research indicates that increased visibility for mature dance performers opens opportunities to subvert normative constructions of age and may "give rise to a revision of widely accepted conceptions of age(ing)" (Martin, 2017, p. 87).

In our research, we are also interested in the ways that a group of mature contemporary dancers called Initial 6 experience ageism in dance. Furthermore, we consider how their presence as experienced performers resists, subverts, challenges and exposes normative assumptions around ageing in dance. Beyond performances, participation in dance classes may also enable experienced dancers to subvert dominant ageist assumptions. Previous research has shown that classes for mature dancers can become sites of resistance whereby ageist limitations are explored and resisted (Ali-Haapala et al., 2020; Coupland, 2013; Krekula et al., 2017; Moe, 2014; Southcott & Joseph, 2020). For example, Jane Southcott and Dawn Joseph used a Bourdieusian framework to describe how women's prior dancer habitus, or socialised subjectivity, was supported through participation in a regular dance class that helped "create a different, masterful, mature, embodied dance practice" (Southcott & Joseph, 2020, p. 605).

In this chapter, we expand upon findings from dance and ageing research with experienced mature dancers, proposing that a regular dance class may act as a site of resistance whereby the admiration of youthfulness that dominates dance culture can be subverted and different possibilities for mature dancers can be cultivated. Through our research with Initial 6, we explore if affirmative ethical values that prioritise the knowledge, expertise and experiences of women mature dancers can emerge in class participation.

Affirmative ethics as *potentia*: transformation of ageism

The previous research on dance and ageing has tended to provide a critique of ageism by unmasking it as an ideological construction that oppresses ageing – particularly women – dancers. This approach positions the dancers through markers of their universal social identities (e.g., age, gender) within a system of oppression of dominant power formations (see also Mulcahy, 2022). Braidotti (2018a) also suggests, following Deleuze and Guattari (1987), that "we do need to start from identity" because identities are affected by power (p. 184). They capture, for example, individual women, to locations of such binary 'machines' of power as masculine–feminine. These binary identities then shape bodies and experiences, placing them into the appropriate categories (i.e., masculine or feminine). In her Deleuzian, 'post-identitarian' feminist approach, Braidotti first aims to expose the power-mechanism that structures identity to then move beyond it, thus advocating for different ways of thinking about experience that extend beyond reactive formation to power. Drawing on Braidotti's work, we are encouraged to move beyond identity-based critique to look for alternatives to the present cultural conditions that define femininity in dance; alternatives that can potentially actualise in local assemblages like a dance class. Braidotti (2019a) acknowledges that this is "hard work in cognitive capitalism" whereby "identity is the bloated signifier of compulsive consumerism and possessive individualism" (p. 473), but emphasises for searching the "new and different" (p. 470) as integral for finding freedom to create new, affirmative ethics that supports dancing through life in immanent local context. She summarises:

> An ethics that is constructed as the praxis of overturning negativity aims at achieving freedom through the understanding of the conditions that make us un-free, that is to say through the awareness of our limits, of our oppression. Ethics means faithfulness to this *potentia*, one's essence as joy, or the desire to become.
>
> *(Braidotti, 2019b, p. 13)*

Affirmative ethics emphasises the feminist politics of 'situational knowledges' that take embodiment and experience as central aspects of its empiricism (Braidotti, 2018a, 2019a). For Braidotti (2020), feminist thought "emphasizes the multiple perspectives that emerge from attention to embodiment and lived experience" that then act "as sources of counter knowledges, methods, and values" (p. 468). We frame our discussion of Initial 6 dancers' experiences in their class with Braidotti's (2018a, 2018b, 2019a) concept of affirmative ethics as a tool to consider how to overcome the negative effects of when captured by the machines of femininity and ageism. Braidotti further emphasises relationality as a cornerstone for creating affirmative values.

Braidotti (2018b) uses Deleuze's concept of assemblage to define the relational, local communities "bonded by affirmative ethics" (p. 33). Such local knowledge can "expose the repressive structures of dominant subject-formations (potestas)" (Braidotti, 2018b, p. 34). Therefore, in the localised context of Initial 6 dance classes, the women first had to become aware of what was limiting their freedom (e.g., ageist beliefs in dance). "By reworking together the negative experiences and affects that enclose us" (Braidotti, 2019b, p. 11), affirmative ethics facilitate alternative ways of thinking and questioning (i.e., what kind of humans/dancers can we be?). These imaginings establish "the affirmative and transformative visions," the *potentia* (transformative visions) embedded in the ethics (Braidotti, 2018b, p. 34). Consequently, creating affirmative ethics is based on positive pro-activism: the dancers' desire for freedom and change through "an ethics of joy and affirmation" (Braidotti, 2019b, p. 4) in dance.

The actualisation of freedom in a dance class provides an "expression of what embodied and embrained bodies can do and think and enact" (Braidotti, 2019b, p. 9). Affirmative ethics is, thus, grounded on bodies' 'power of acting' (Braidotti, 2019b), also in a physical sense. Thus, in a dance class, moving bodies provide their own forces that increase the power of acting and can actualise thinking differently of maturity in dance. Again, this embodied activity always takes place within the community; in this case, a community of dancers in a dance class. Creating affirmative ethics is a collective practice "aiming at empowerment. This means increasing one's ability to relate to multiple others, in a productive and mutually enforcing manner, and creating a community that actualises this ethical propensity" (Braidotti, 2019b, p. 9). In our work, we understand that such encounters take place in a specific dance community: in a dance class between the dancers, their movements, and the physical environment of the studio. These relations make it possible to affirm values different from the current cultural valorisation of ageing dancers as inevitably in decline and, as such, unsuitable to perform.

As feminist praxis, creating affirmative ethics is always a political, communal process of transformation by individuals committed to 'actualising' freedom (Braidotti, 2019b). Therefore, the emphasis on relationality in local contexts does not mean a focus on individual experiences or meanings per se, but how these may affirm different ethics from the current cultural conditions of, for example, dance. In this chapter, consequently, we analyse how one local community of mature women dancers, Initial 6, was exposed to the repressive power structures of ageism in dance, but also created affirmative and transformative visions of what mature dancers can do. We consider, thus, the force of their moving bodies as relations with other bodies to "collectively construct conditions that transform and empower our capacity to act ethically and produce social horizons of hope" (Braidotti, 2019b, p. 14). Our task is now to illuminate how affirmative ethics may materialise in a pragmatic engagement of dancing together in a class specifically designed for mature dancers.

Methods

As a collective, Initial 6 has been involved in previous research on ageing and dance (Nikolai & Markula, 2021; Markula et al., 2022). The women of the Initial 6 group are experienced contemporary dancers (when data was gathered: aged 45–68). They have been performing together since 2015 and each has a long history of training in a range of dance genres from a young age.[1]

In this chapter, we draw on a larger research creation study that included the dancers participating in a series of classes over the course of a five-month period (September 2019–January 2020) with the intention of preparing the group for a live performance in early 2020. Classes were led by one of the mature dancers in the group. Content of classes aimed at preparing the women's bodies for rigorous practices leading to performance. Sessions began with gentle warm-up sequences (e.g., floor work to increase mobility and range of motion), followed by a series of barre exercises (e.g., pliés, tendus, grand battements, port de bras), then moved to cross-floor combinations and jumps.

The seven dancers, including the teacher, were interviewed in January 2020, after the completion of all classes. Importantly, this extended process of interviewing and reflexivity was informed by our feminist research approach and prioritised safety, care and connection (Hesse-Biber, 2014). The semi-structured interviews (e.g., Markula & Silk, 2011; Reinharz & Davidman, 1992) were informed by previous research findings on dance and ageing, and developed based on themes such as: health and well-being, suitability of the time of day, length of class, frequency of classes, class composition, class pedagogy, and injury and fatigue prevention within the class. Dancers were provided with reflective prompts to prepare them for interviews, and a conversational style of questioning facilitated comfort and flexibility in the research environment (Hesse-Biber, 2014; Roulston, 2010). This prioritised the women's lead in conversations as experienced dancers with varied training and performance histories. Due to COVID-19, the interviews were conducted via telephone or Zoom. Further feminist collaborative thematic analysis was completed at a later date by all authors.

Affirmative ethics of mature women's dance class

Drawing on Braidotti's affirmative ethics, we focus on three main themes that developed during our analysis. First, we describe the women's awareness of ageism as a potential barrier to their desired freedom. Following this, we discuss how the women, recognising their perceived limitations, sought out and found *potentia* in dance classes (e.g., joy in movement). Finally, through their involvement in these classes, we note that the women cultivated a different set of values that were unique to this context. In what follows, we discuss each of these themes in relation with Braidotti's concept of affirmative ethics.

Awareness of ageism

The knowledge emerging from local contexts can "expose the repressive structures" (Braidotti, 2018b, p. 34) that limit freedom (e.g., ageist beliefs in dance). The women of Initial 6 often mentioned their ageing bodies as limitations. Many of them described the various aches and pains due to their age. Wanda described:

> If I didn't sleep well, or maybe my knee was bothering me . . . I'd have a feeling of inadequacy . . . but during these classes, I was always able to move through it. I'm willing to physically adapt. If I know something hurts I'm easier on myself, at least more than I used to be. Because things are okay for my age, I genetically have a body that moves, so I'm lucky.

Wanda was aware and appreciative of the ways that she is able to dance as she is ageing and attributes this to both her continued involvement in dance and her 'genetics.' Many of the women referred to ageing as a process that had the potential to limit their freedom, but also resisted ageism through their embodied experiences. They oscillated between worry for what the future may bring (in relation to their ageing bodies) and appreciation for their present capabilities. Teresa reflected on the ways that her experiences were similar to other older adults, then described how dance offered her the ability to resist decline:

> So I have arthritis in my back and it's caused me some problems . . . in this group, we all have some kind of ache and pain, or an old injury that continues to haunt us, but we're better off moving with it and through it than not moving at all. If we choose to avoid moving to stay away from arthritic pain, we would probably be much more hobbled and crippled. So I would say, moving keeps us younger.

Teresa was aware of her bodily limitations and not only engaged in dance as a way to resist what she determined to be an embodied indication of older age (i.e., hobbled, crippled) but also continued to move to stay 'young.'

Awareness of ageism in dance prompted some Initial 6 members to consider how their own ageist assumptions were influencing their experiences. In their reflections, some of the women mentioned how Initial 6, as a mature dance group, was challenging and subverting normative assumptions about age. Wanda reflected on this:

> So I'd like to think that the age just fell off. Like maybe they thought of it at first, but it was just initially, and then it was gone. And maybe I'm imagining an impossibility . . . but that's the way I think so that I can go on to dance another dance. If I thought they saw a bunch of old ladies up there dancing, I would never do this again. But I'm convinced that they saw dancers in good form, in full form, dancing a very interesting dance.

Throughout Wanda's description of her presence as a mature dancer, we illustrate how ageist assumptions and resistance can both exist simultaneously. For the women of Initial 6, participating in this dance class did not remove them from the ageism that persists in dance culture, but it did encourage them to reflect upon these limitations and resist by imagining alternative possibilities for ageing dancers (Braidotti, 2019a, 2019b).

Potentia in dance class

After becoming aware of the *potestas* (repressive structures influencing lived experience), it is possible to find embodied and embedded contexts whereby new *potentia* can transform limitations, making way for possibilities and affirmative ethics (Braidotti, 2018b). Drawing upon this definition, we recognised moments when Initial 6 dancers were moving beyond the social construction of the ageing dancing body. In this section, we discuss how the materiality of the dancing body and the movements themselves all contributed to thinking differently about ageing and dance. Further, we illustrate how dance classes with Initial 6 provided a local context where *potentia* could be cultivated through an embodied, embedded, movement community.

When reflecting on their experiences, many of the women of Initial 6 appreciated contemporary dance classes designed to their needs. As Teresa stated, "being able to individualise certain movements is part of why contemporary dance is so important." The women highlighted the class structure and described how the movements themselves were sequenced in a manner that enabled them to connect with (and observe) their embodied experiences. As Wanda and Teresa explained:

> We go on to the floor and we do some t sort of joint opening exercises, which is really good for me, rather than thinking about technique, it is just a matter of opening joints, in your hips, in particular, ankles, everything.
>
> *(Wanda)*

> The classes were progressive, they always started small . . . on the floor doing some movement that would open up . . . our feet, our backs, our chests, our ribs.
>
> *(Teresa)*

These women appreciated being given the opportunity to slow down, to observe and to connect with their embodied experiences. As follows, the teacher who led Initial 6's classes, Katie, explained the rationale behind choosing movements that could enable a gradual opening of the body and connected this with a consideration of ageing:

> It was good for older bodies because I didn't rush through things and get to exercises that were really strenuous too quickly. So it went slowly, methodically, deep, deeper into the body. You know, covering all the joints, all the muscles, carefully, thoroughly.

Considering that affirmative ethical practices are "deeply materialistic" (Braidotti, 2019a, p. 466), we acknowledge how the women's moving bodies enabled the Initial 6 group to be actively involved in the reflective, transformative and relational experience of cultivating *potentia*. Awareness to the diverse needs of older bodies in the class brought joy that enabled the dancers to find freedom from the limitations of ageism in dance culture.

The Initial 6 dancers' freedom was derived not only from performing the movement sequences, but also the pedagogical approach of their teacher. Their teacher, as a fellow Initial 6 member, was a uniquely positioned mature dancer who had a longstanding relationship with the women. The extent that these women felt comfortable with exploring their embodied experiences in classes was often attributed to the relation they shared with their teacher. Jane recalled her impression of the dance class teacher, and Katie (the teacher) reflected how this class differed from directive dance pedagogy:

> I think she has a real sensitivity, maybe just because she has watched us age . . . but still it was very similar to what I think she would teach in a regular class. Just teaching dancers to take care of themselves.
>
> *(Jane)*

> It's a different kind of approach than it would be in a traditional dance class, where . . . I would demonstrate, and then they repeat and I'd maybe go around giving a lot of corrections or feedback. So it is different for this class, because I'm moving with them and trusting that they can monitor and correct themselves.
>
> *(Katie)*

The dancers enjoyed being led by someone they trust, and appreciated an environment of mutual respect and collaboration. Similar to Southcott and Joseph's (2020) research with Fine Lines (see case narrative 3.4 by Katrina Rank and Jenny Barnett in Section 3), having an experienced and mature teacher who encouraged collaboration, danced alongside the women, and could accommodate for the needs of ageing dancers enhanced feelings of enjoyment. Unique to this local context, dancers were given the opportunity to communicate "affective components – social, emotional, physical, feeling, being" (Meredith), and were valued for their input as experienced dancers. This balance between care and respect was described further by Katie:

> They've been dancing most of their life, and they have their experience . . . obviously, if there's something very specific that they're not doing well, I will say something. But, I trust that they can manage because I didn't see any problems through the process with anyone.

The mutual trust that Katie described was shared between the women and blurred the boundaries of teacher/student. The women were supported in this space through the careful tutelage of their teacher and the encouragement of their fellow dancers. They were empowered to adapt and adjust movements for their own needs. Jane and Phoebe described the enjoyment they found when dancing in this context:

> I was happy, I was engaged, I was supported by my friends and peers, I felt meaning and purpose and I saw direct results from regular classes . . . some moments in the warm-up, I'd feel myself glowing, or laughing or smiling, totally stimulated and content.
>
> *(Jane)*

The class atmosphere was very, very supportive. We knew each other very well and also had similar level dance training. Depending on the level of current physical activity and on our injuries, we were encouraged to modify our movements. This enabled me to feel good.

(Phoebe)

Like the Fine Lines dance group, the Initial 6 dancers found joy and solace in sharing similar life stories and a passion for dance in a community that enabled them to continue doing what they love.

Drawing on Braidotti's (2018b, 2019a, 2019b) affirmative ethics, we further emphasise how the women's moving bodies, through sharing space and time, were becoming an assemblage in which it was possible to create alternative values to ageism. As a relational movement community with emotional and social support, this dance class provided a unique energy that created *potentia*, the desire for freedom from the limitations of the ageist dance culture. Teresa described this as a magic dance:

I enjoy our energy, I enjoy the process. It's like this cohesive little bubble that we start to build and there are all these cool things that happen between us. And that energy in the bubble feeds into the movement. And then it just becomes this thing of its own, it becomes this little magic dance of our own.

For these women, the movements contributed to a dance assemblage that was unique to this group and this enhanced feelings of joy and connection.

In summary, moving with the Initial 6 group was a source of enjoyment. The connection to one another through shared values as dancers with moving bodies changing over time influenced the women's experiences in these classes. These dance classes provided a localised, embodied and embedded context that made it possible for these women to experience joy and to experience moments of transcending ageist limitations. The movements, pedagogy, and relationships influencing this dance assemblage cultivated a context where the women could imagine new *potentia*. In our final analysis section, we illuminate the different values – the affirmative ethics – that emerged through this unique dance environment.

Affirmative values in dance community

For Braidotti (2018b), affirmative ethics are developed through relational communities that come together in a local context and create new *potentia* through embodied action. Initial 6, as a dance group of mature women provided a unique relational context. Having danced together as a group, the women shared relationships developed over many years. Jane and Meredith commented:

I feel so supported by this community of women with so much history crossing over, that the similar age, similar histories, similar interests and similar

> values in dancing, moving, being creative and staying current with dance as
> our bodies change.
>
> *(Jane)*

> We all have our own restrictions or limitations, and there was total accept-
> ance in the group. There were never any judgements, or expectations . . .
> I think it had something to do with the fact that we've known each other
> for so long, so mentally I felt safe, rejuvenated, encouraged. It was a good
> experience.
>
> *(Meredith)*

We propose that these women's shared relations, cultivated while moving
together and experiencing joy, further created an affirmative ethics. We consider
the joy from embodied freedom to move as increasing the dancers' *potentia*, their
power of acting (Braidotti, 2019a, 2019b), towards different values from youthfulness in dance.

Teresa found that moving with a community of women who shared a common
love of dance intensified her relationships and she was able to foster rich connections with the women who were "trying to find deeper meaning in the way that"
they "move together." For many of the members of Initial 6, the experience of
sharing space with other women's material moving bodies enabled different forms
of connection, and these resulted in the formation of affirmative values. Wanda
described these unique connections as "communicating physically" and expands
on this:

> I enjoyed dancing with these ladies and feeling the energy that we all create
> together, the way we communicate. And sometimes we weren't saying any-
> thing, it was just how our energy focused on that other person, and was able
> to communicate, 'OK, now's the time to go, now's the time to react, now's
> the time to really move this.' It's just something special, sometimes I can't
> explain it completely . . . . It's all a part of that physical communication,
> understanding how we each move and feel.

Notably, there was an embodied relationality being felt by the Initial 6 dancers
during their experiences of moving together, and these moments of connection
inspired different values. One of the most frequently mentioned was safety. Wanda
recalled that physically, she "always felt safe" with the other dancers, and Meredith
mentioned that "it was a really safe group of people." Through reflections like
these, we recognised that the women were able to find freedom when they could
rely on the safety of their dance environment.

For all of the women, moving with bodies of similar age and experience level
greatly influenced their enjoyment, their confidence, and their commitment to
dance. Jane added that "the impact" of dancing with this particular group of women
"continues to be enormous." Moving with mature dancers reminded her to value

the "accumulated knowledge, the physical, physiological but also social-emotional knowledge that comes with all of these years of knowing and experiencing through dance." Experience, care, safety, and mutual respect were all emerging as important values for the affirmative ethics for these mature dancers. Notably, these differ from dominant values of technical expertise and physical mastery that often influence experiences of young(er) dancers – and indeed, the dance culture broadly.

Jane's comments illustrate how affirmative relationships created locally also produce knowledge (Braidotti, 2019b). This knowledge was cultivated through the dancers' desire for freedom to move in a dance class specifically designed for them. The class then functioned as "an ethics of joy and affirmation" to transform the negatives of ageing into positive passion to dance (Braidotti, 2019b, p. 4). The local dance community that was integral to the emergence of affirmative ethics was deeply material as the relationships were built through bodies dancing together: the key was the chance to move together in a studio space large enough to enable a variety of practices. The dance movement had to be appropriate for the mature, experienced dancers' bodies for the affirmative community to emerge.

Conclusion

Through our analysis, we revealed how women who continue to practise contemporary dance in classes created an embodied/embedded community within which to subvert normative constructions of the dancing body. Based on Braidotti's (2018a, 2018b, 2019a, 2019b) work, we argue that the dancers participated in creating affirmative ethics that can be seen as positive pro-activism: dancing together inspired critical age awareness and different understandings of what the dancers' bodies can do. This, nevertheless, required an awareness of the limitations of the ageism that still shaped the dancers' responses.

When carefully considered, dance class environments where the mature dancers can move in ways that exceed their own – and societal – expectations have the potential to generate affirmative ethics. We emphasised that creating an affirmative ethics is deeply materialistic (Braidotti, 2019a) and described how the dancers' bodies – and the dance movement – were central to the affirmative ethics that was created in the local context of a dance class. A weekly regular class fostered embodied relationships with other dancers that then enabled an articulation of collective political transformative ethics, despite the women's somewhat negative reflections on their ageing physicality.

While our participants were clearly aware how ageism limited their potential as women dancers, we also wanted to move beyond a critique of ageism to consider how transformation can be initiated from a local context. This required a more careful focus on the materiality of dancing bodies in motion. Therefore, engaging in actual dance movement was essential for facilitating possibilities for thinking differently about maturity in dance. Following Braidotti (2019b), these micro-movements literally affected change by creating embodied, affirmative relationships for different ethics from the idealisation of youthfulness in dance. While providing awareness of limits of the mature body, Initial 6 demonstrated that a dance class can act as a location for *potentia*, transforming visions of what mature dancing bodies can do, think and enact to create affirmative ethics for dancing through life.

Note

1 Before beginning this research project with the women, we applied for and received ethical approval from the University of Alberta research ethics board.

References

Ali-Haapala, A., Moyle, G., & Kerr, G. (2020). Pleasurable challenges: Competing with the ageing body and mind through Ballet for Seniors. *Leisure Studies, 39*(4), 532–544.

Braidotti, R. (2018a). Affirmative ethics, posthuman subjectivity, and intimate scholarship: A conversation with Rosi Braidotti. In K. Strom, T. Mills, & A. Ovens (Eds.), *Decentering the researcher in intimate scholarship* (pp. 179–188). Bingley: Emerald Publishing.

Braidotti, R. (2018b). A theoretical framework for the critical posthumanities. *Theory, Culture & Society, 36*(6), 31–61.

Braidotti, R. (2019a). Affirmative ethics and generative life. *Deleuze and Guattari Studies, 13*(4), 463–481.

Braidotti, R. (2019b). *Posthuman knowledge.* Cambridge: Polity Press.

Braidotti, R. (2020). "We" are in this together, but we are not one and the same. *Bioethical Inquiry Journal of Bioethical Inquiry, 17*(4), 465–469.

Coupland, J. (2013). Dance, ageing and the mirror: Negotiating watchability. *Discourse & Communication, 7*(1), 3–24.

Deleuze, G., & Guattari, F. (1987). *A thousand plateaus: Capitalism and schizophrenia* (B. Massumi, Trans.). London and New York, NY: Continuum.

Hesse-Biber, S. (2014). Feminist approaches to in-depth interviewing. In S. Hesse-Biber (Ed.), *Feminist research practice: A primer* (2nd ed., pp. 182–232). Thousand Oaks, CA: Sage.

Krekula, C., Arvidson, M., Heikkinen, S., Henriksson, A., & Olsson, E. (2017). On gray dancing: Constructions of age-normality through choreography and temporal codes. *Journal of Aging Studies, 42*, 38–45.

Markula, P., Metzger, K., Bliss, T., Gervais, W., Rintoul, M. A., & Vandekerkhove, J. (2022). "It can be magic": Creating age awareness through contemporary dance. *Frontiers in Sports and Active Living, 4*, 1–12. https://doi.org/10.3389/fspor.2022.795541

Markula, P., & Silk, M. (2011). *Qualitative research for physical activity.* London: Routledge.

Martin, S. (2017). *Dancing age(ing): Rethinking age(ing) in and through improvisation practice and performance.* Bielefeld: Transcript Verlag.

Moe, A. (2014). Sequins, sass, and sisterhood: An exploration of older women's belly dancing. *Journal of Women & Aging, 26*(1), 39–65. doi:10.1080/08952841.2014.854574

Mulcahy, D. (2022). Enacting affirmative ethics in education: A materialist/posthumanist framing. *Educational Philosophy and Theory, 54*(7), 1003–1013. doi:10.1080/00131857.2021.1907744

Nakajima, N. (2011). De-aging dancerism? The aging body in contemporary and community dance. *Performance Research, 16*(3), 100–104.

Nikolai, J., & Markula, P. (2021). Aging, memory, and camera: Immersive choreography between live and digital improvisation and performance with the camera-dancer dyad.

In D. Owen (Ed.), *Digital performance in Canada, New essays on Canadian theatre* (Vol. 11, pp. 110–135). Toronto, ON: Playwrights Canada Press.

Reinharz, S., & Davidman, L. (1992). *Feminist methods in social research.* Oxford: Oxford University Press.

Roulston, K. (2010). *Reflective interviewing: A guide to theory and practice.* Thousand Oaks, CA: Sage.

Rustad, H., & Engelsrud, G. H. (2022). Everybody can dance – except aging professional dancers! A discussion of the construction of the aging dancing body in four dance texts. *Frontiers in Sports and Active Living, 4,* 1–9. doi:10.3389/fspor.2022.819572

Schwaiger, E. (2012). *Ageing, gender, embodiment and dance: Finding a balance.* New York, NY: Springer.

Schwaiger, L. (2005). Performing one's age: Cultural constructions of aging and embodiment in western theatrical dancers. *Dance Research Journal, 37,* 107–120. doi:10.1017/S014976770000838X

Southcott, J., & Joseph, D. (2020). "If you can breathe, you can dance": Fine lines contemporary dance for mature bodies in Melbourne, Australia. *Journal of Women & Aging, 32*(6), 591–610.

Wainwright, S. P., & Turner, B. S. (2004). Narratives of embodiment: Body, aging and career in Royal Ballet dancers. In H. Thomas & J. Ahmed (Eds.), *Cultural bodies: Ethnography and theory* (pp. 98–120). Hoboken, NJ: Wiley-Blackwell.

Wainwright, S. P., & Turner, B. S. (2006). 'Just crumbling to bits'? An exploration of the body, ageing, injury and career in classical ballet dancers. *Sociology, 40,* 237–255. doi:10.1177/0038038506062031.

4.2

FROM THE STAGE TO THE NEXT STAGE

Transitioning from a learner to a teacher – Amala Shankar's journey

Urmimala Sarkar Munsi

Introduction

Guru-shishya parampara is a system of teaching/knowledge-transfer from master teachers to the apprentice/student, popularly associated with the categories of dance and music that are known as classical or neo-classical. This chapter begins with a discussion on the structure and functions of the *guru-shishya parampara*, to understand the progression of a *shishya* (apprentice) into an expert while aspiring to transition into a *guru* (master teacher) as s/he goes through life. The chapter is as much about knowledge management as it is about age management and expertise management.

In the first part of the chapter, I think through the knowledge system in dance in the Indian context as a commodity that has to be managed differently at different times of life. All dancers know and navigate these different stages throughout their lives for dance to provide a means of survival.

In the second part of the chapter, I use the case study of Smt Amala Shankar (1919–2020), known to me as my teacher, mentor and guide, and an expert on Uday Shankar style of modern dance. Amala Shankar was by no means a *guru* in the traditional Sanskritic sense of the word, nor was she a teacher of any of the neo-classical dances. Her transition from being a dancer/student to becoming a troupe member/wife of the famous danseuse Uday Shankar to finally becoming an exceptional teacher would be seen as her journey from one stage to the next – in dance, and in life.

The *guru* and the *parampara*

Guru-shishya parampara has been written about within the context of music and dance in India by many scholars. According to Amanda Weidman, in the context

DOI: 10.4324/9781003307624-26

of Karnatik music traditions in South India *gurukulavasam*[1] "refers to a method of teaching and learning in which the *shishya*, or the disciple, lives with the guru, learning music by a process of slow absorption and serving the *guru* as a member of his household" (Weidman, 2008, p. 226). She further is of the opinion that this system is "a centuries-long oral tradition and a system of teaching that technology cannot duplicate" (Weidman, 2008, p. 226).

The debate goes on regarding the almost forced template of learning through the hierarchical process of the *parampara*, in the name of a specialised and non-standardised learning/teaching tradition, whereby the *guru* remains the ultimate judge of the *shishya's* progress (Vatsyayan, 1982). In the times when performing arts has also been formalised into a structured system of learning, no longer are a *guru's* words accepted as the proof of learning for any apprentice. Institutional affiliation is always preferred in comparison to a *guru's* assurance. The traditional dancer of today needs to be seen as a product of the in-between world of aspiration. On one hand, there is a formal entry into the proscenium by way of an *arangetrum* or a *mancha- pravesh*,[2] when the dancer proves his/her ability as a solo artist in the presence of the guru and an audience. The other way is to get specific training from an institution that ensures standardised teaching for each of the trainees enrolled, under a specific formal certification. Institutional certification also protects the parents from spending hundreds of thousands of rupees as per the *guru's* wishes, in order to organise the *arangetrum* which entails paying a formal *guru-dakshina*,[3] and all other expenses for the auditorium, musicians and other required arrangements. But even today for many dancers, the submission to a *guru's* teaching process is the way to transition to a phase of being recognised and certified as an expert who the *guru* then introduces to the world as a performer. For the performers, this opens the door to the next phase – i.e., that of claiming the space of a *guru* for himself or herself. If this is not a case of building an occupational trajectory, what is? More than critiquing the system or the remnants of *guru-shishya parampara*, I would like to posit this as the way the students learn to plan for the future as they transition from one stage to another with age.

As previously mentioned, the references to the *guru* and the *Gurukul* are inevitable and essential for a performer trained in any form of classical dance, when s/he ventures into the competitive world of proscenium performance. For a female performer, the auto-progression to the platform of a teacher, occupied by her own aging male/female *guru*, is many a time the ideal aspiration and the goal, but in that process, unfortunately, the aging *guru* is (often unknowingly or inadvertently) a competitor. Thus begins the progression of the dancer – transitioning from a student to a performer and then a *guru*. This progression is often a way to secure a lifelong profession, with or without institutional backing.

In a recently published conversation, five scholars from the Euro-American space of dance studies asked an important question – "How do we engage the common inheritance of the guru – shishya parampara, or the teacher – disciple mentorship model? – the context for collective training in various South Asian movement forms" (Banerji et al., 2020, p. 221). The important questions from that conversation are: (1) what does this system do for *gurus* in the current times; and (2) why do the *gurus* still find this system relevant? In my opinion, this reaffirmation of the positive utility of the *guru-shishya parampara* has to do with an economic implication of this particular tradition, whereby the career trajectories in dance in India ensure a chance at continuing with a (however fragile and marginal) occupational possibility of using one's expertise by transitioning from a performer to a *guru*.

Placing the context of ageing within the culturally managed fortification of *guru-shishya parampara*

In the systemic structure of *guru-shishya parampara*, the hyphenated link could be read as either a reciprocal relationship, or an indicative construct formalising a flow of knowledge, from the teacher (the *guru*) to the student (the *shishya*). The hyphen, however, may be critically interpreted as indicative of a deep hierarchy and power relation – where the *guru* controls the *shishya's* future as a performer. Anubhuti Sharma in her recent article wrote:

> The guru – shishya parampara is a case in point where certain unjust values, actions, behaviors, and doctrines are unquestioningly and unhesitatingly accepted by teachers and students. It commands values of subservience, duty, and unquestioned devotion on the part of the shishya while exalting the guru to the pedestal of a "master" who is divine and infallible.
>
> *(Sharma, 2020, p. 63)*

Sharma wrote these lines to discuss the scenario in the classical music community that also has deep-rooted systems of *guru-shishya parampara*. In her article, she implicated patriarchy and Brahminical monopoly over the bonded form of dedication that passed as a just and reciprocal system of understanding in the name of paying through service in return for receiving expertise in music (Sharma, 2020, p. 63). Sharma's words draw our attention to the misuse of power in the regressive structures of our patriarchal and Brahminical society:

> These feudal practices, values and mystification that surround the arts are nurtured and cherished by musicians, students, patrons and listeners who find any rationality dangerous to the mystical pursuit and appreciation of the art.
>
> *(Sharma, 2020, p. 63)*

Reading between Sharma's lines also alerts us to the precarity of the occupational space for the self-employed and ageing master teacher who is perpetually unsure of patronage, and whose insecurity about the future makes him/her fend for him/herself – defending and asserting his/her power and legitimacy (even by unfair means).

While the classical dance ecology within and outside India is full of teachers who are accepted or projected as *gurus*, the non-classical world also has master teachers, specially designated within their own communities with due respect and recognition of the traditional knowledge they have and can teach. Anthropologist Kalpana Ram writes in her article "Perspectives from apprentices of skilled practices: performing arts and scholarship":

> All of these forms of knowing value the importance of practice over time, lengthy periods of time, in coming to understand something about the art form. Apprenticeship is in one sense regarded as lifelong, but it takes several years of rigorous practice before a student can be said to have acquired *gnanam* . . . which entails far more than a theoretical understanding, although is usually a part of the training.
>
> *(Ram, 2008, p. 2)*

Ram's reference to acquiring of *gnanam* or knowledge is inevitably linked to the receiver remaining open to the possibility of this acquiring of knowledge never ever being complete. Thus, the subservience produced by the *parampara* keeps open the possibility of exerting control by the *guru* at any point in life.

Validated as well as maligned often – but consistently persistent in classical dance teaching – the roles of the *guru* and the *shishya* become two points in the cyclic order of a chain of perpetuity.

Smt Amala Shankar – a life in/on dance stage

Amala Shankar – the late dance maestro Uday Shankar's wife and our teacher, passed away in 2020 when she was 101 years old. She was unable to walk without assistance for her last five years, but her mind and her instincts responded to our voices. She recognised us without opening her eyes, immediately instructed us to set up a rehearsal and asked for the resumption of regular activities of the dance troupe of Uday Shankar India Culture Centre (USICC). The school was her life; the troupe in the same name was her pride and her space for experimentation. Her life in the years after she opened her school in 1965 was a mixture of two driving ambitions – to see USICC flourish as a modern institution of dance of very high standards, and to see the establishment of Uday Shankar's style of dance as a recognised technique. She sometimes called the style a Gharana,[4] but would refute the concept of the word herself by actively taking pride in training individuals as responsible and socially conscious members of the community who actively engage not only through dance but through a multitude of awareness built and developed through formal as well as arts-based education.

Amala Shankar was an innovative teacher. She also was a keen observer with an astute sense of choreography, stagecraft and scenography. She worked hard to restage, revive and rechoreograph several of Uday Shankar's original choreographies, but also created a number of her own choreographies. Her own choreographed work was showcased in the post-1965 performances of USICC troupe worldwide, as well as in the annual programmes of USICC, where she presented her own and our choreographies created around the year with the students of the institution. In the annual shows, she would present these performances as showcases or the progress reports for the parents of the students to figure out their children's progress over the last year of their time at the USICC. For the troupe, there were several full-length choreographies by her, where she was assisted by P. Raghavan, the Kathakali master teacher who was with Uday and Amala Shankar since the late 1940s.

To understand the system of learning she so passionately taught us, a bit of her own background is necessary. Amala Nandi (She married Uday Shankar at the age of 19) was born was born in a village named Batajore, in the erstwhile undivided Bengal. Her father, a well-known jeweller by profession, took her to Paris with him when she was only 11 years old, to set up a display of his jewellry shop Economic Jewelry Works as a part of the Hindoostan Pavilion for India for showcasing and selling Indian gems and jewellry at the Colonial Exposition of Paris in 1931. Amala Shankar's Bengali book *Sat Sagarer Pare* (Shankar, 2007) – describing the magical experiences of the next two years – is a first-hand document of the times she spent looking at the site of one of the biggest magical exhibitions of all times in Paris, where the colonial show brought all the colonised together in a choreographed display.

The experience of her tour of Europe with Shankar and his troupe was published after her return to India, once she went back to a regular education and her life back at home. Amala Shankar's writing mentions that she danced as one of the Indian dancers at the Indian pavilion of the exposition with Nyota Iniyoka,[5] although she was not a trained dancer. During the exposition, she and her father were invited to dinner by Uday Shankar – who was in Paris, preparing for his European tour with the famous Swiss sculptor Alice Boner[6] as his manager (Boner, 1993). There she met the family[7] of Uday Shankar – including his mother, his brothers and other troupe members. Uday Shankar asked Akshay Nandi to permit his daughter to become a part of the touring company named Uday Shankar's Hindoo Ballet Troupe. This was the beginning of Amala Shankar's life in dance.

Sat Sagarer Pare records the trip – from November 1931 to October 1933 – in great detail. Amala Shankar was soon rehearsing for the trip and sharing proscenium space with seasoned dancers such as Simkie,[8] Kanaklata,[9] Uday Shankar and others in performances across Europe, in the best of auditorium spaces, such as city halls and opera houses. She was being mentioned in newspaper reviews as the young dancer with great promise for her duet performance in *Kaliya Daman*.[10] According to her writing, the training for the troupe was very strict. Discipline figured as a very important aspect of that training. So did the idea and practice, concentration and dedication. One thing Amala Shankar mentioned again and again in her reminiscences in our classes was the importance of ensemble practice and the spirit of sharing mind and body space with all other co-participants (dancers and musicians) within the choreographic process, as well as on stage. While preparing us for our roles in the dance troupe of USICC, she often talked about the emphasis Shankar accorded to being willing to practice, co-create and take joint responsibility through the complete performance.

Amala Shankar had transitioned from the role of a learner to a troupe member – and she acknowledged a certain sustained form of training that made her understand her role as a part of the troupe. She carried these learnings close to heart as important elements that she would mention and impose later at the USICC on her trainees, troupe members and apprentice teachers under training.

Amala Shankar mentioned that she returned home after the two-year tour of Europe to India with Shankar's mother and Ravi Shankar, and completed her matriculation examination as well as an undergraduate degree. She was now ready again to join the troupe that Uday Shankar had created by then in the mountains. She travelled to Ranidhara in Almora, where Uday Shankar had started his academy of artistic excellence and dance. It was the first Indian academy for creative dance-based experiments and training, Uday Shankar India Culture Centre.[11] The institution had a performing troupe and Amala Shankar became a part of that. She simultaneously trained in specific classical forms (much before these forms were declared as classical dances). Her body and movements retained the knowledge of that training, in Kathakali and Manipuri, from the master teachers at USICC, Guru Shankaran Nambudri (Kathakali), Guru Kandappa Pillai (Bharatanatyam) and Guru Amobi Singh (Manipuri).

The teaching was based on a non-Gharana construct of knowledge dissemination. In a system of teaching that aspired to keep references to the older *guru-shishya parampara* alive but yet was driven by modern needs of creating an internationally relevant dissemination system, all the expert master teachers were referred to as *gurus* while they were teachers at USICC. Shankar was very clear that all the traditional regional forms (Manipuri, Kathakali and Bharatanatyam) needed to retain their traditional movement systems. The movement systems framed the body aesthetics, as well as expanded capacities for moving for the trainees. The class on creativity then pushed the students to improvise and experiment with these movement bases in the classes on creative dance conducted by Shankar himself, which the regular students, as well as the troupe members, had to join every day. Shankar was expanding the vocabulary that could be available to the dancers.

In the next 20 years from 1940, Amala and Uday Shankar got married; until 1944, they performed in a series of national and international spaces regularly with their troupe based in USICC Almora; in 1944 USICC at Almora closed down. Amala was 25 years old, and Uday Shankar was 44. The couple moved to Madras (now known as Chennai), and the next three years were spent by Uday Shankar in making the now-famous film *Kalpana*.[12] The film was a time for experimentation with the new medium of film-making and a lot of unlearning, relearning and stress due to lack of funds and support. *Kalpana* – the sole film written, directed, choreographed by Uday Shankar – had him and Amala Shankar in the main roles. In this film,[13] Amala Shankar's training in ensemble practice comes through in all dance sequences, even though she remains different from all others in her distinctive role.

The years of performing and choreographing continued for the couple, until the mid-1960s. The Shankars then opened the USICC again in Kolkata in 1965 with Uday Shankar as the founder director and Amala Shankar as the director-in-charge. Uday Shankar was 65 then, and Amala Shankar was 46.

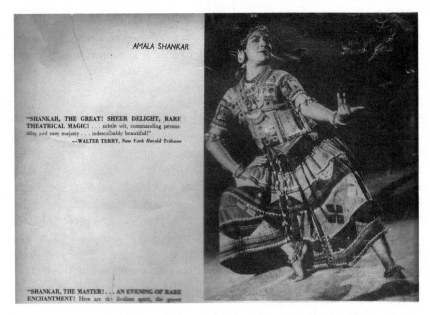

FIGURE 4.2A Publicity material (Uday Shankar and his Hindu Ballet Troupe) featuring Amala Shankar (top) and Uday and Amala Shankar (bottom)

Source: © Author's personal collection

Around the time when the school was opened in Kolkata, Uday Shankar began working with a different team of dancers. The school became the space where Amala Shankar created new generations of young dancers, asserting on building a group of dancers who would not only be trained in dance but would also be groomed to become active, conscious, responsible, intelligent and capable members of their community. For the parents who admitted their daughters into this institution, it was a second family they were creating for their daughters. But this was not a Gharana. There was no promise of "belonging" to the lineage. Learning to improvise and create was somewhat like learning to fly for young birds. It was setting us free. Amala Shankar was our teacher, our mentor and our guide in many ways. She never called herself the *guru*, at least I have not heard her do so in the 50-plus years of being with her as a student, as a dancer/performing troupe member, as a teacher and as an administrator at USICC.

Ageing as a journey through stages of different relationship with the skill sets

Many dance vocabularies are taught to extremely young learners. Young bodies are pliable, easy to sculpt and fashion, as per the requirement of a dance grammar. Ballet classes specify the age of entry as 4–5 years in the specialised international academies. The young learners memorise easily, and with practice, achieve perfection with ease. The kinaesthetic journey for each dancer is different. It is shaped by the different experiences and world views and also the stages that the dancer goes through as s/he ages. Amala Shankar stopped dancing on stage, for a period of time, after opening her school. She prepared her students and brought them to a stage where they could perform as fully trained dance artists. It is only after then that she began creating her new choreographies, i.e. *Chidambara* (A choreography based on a number of poems written by the famous Gyanpith Award–winning Indian poet Sumitra Nandan Panth), *Vasavadutta* (a dance drama based on a poem by Tagore), *Sita Swayambara* (a part of the story of Ramayana), *Yuga-Chhanda* (*The Rhythms of the Changing Times* – with music composed by Ananda Shankar) and many others. She also re-entered the proscenium with her senior students and danced prominent roles once again. Looking back, one sees this as renewed beginning for her, entering the stage once again without her extraordinarily talented and masterful partner for years, Uday Shankar, who passed away soon after, in 1977. Amala Shankar was then 58 years old. Her institution was in its prime popularity, and Kolkata was in awe of her as a teacher. She had made the transition a successful one, without becoming a *guru*.

Restaging a number of Shankar's choreographies was the next phase in Amala Shankar's life as she began to think of the legacy and of long-term recognition for Shankar's creative process.

FIGURE 4.2B   Amala Shankar (front row – second from the left) with her students (including the author, last row, fifth from the left) at the Uday Shankar India Culture Centre (USICC) Kolkata (1970–1972)

Source: Author's personal collection

National and international tours

The USICC troupe travelled frequently, within and outside India. Within India, we would travel by train or bus. Travelling with us on overnight buses, staying with us and using the same facilities – i.e., shared bedrooms and bathrooms – Amala Shankar shaped our ideas of how to be a teacher.

In trains, she would be traveling with us, in the same compartments, sharing food, seats and time for as long as 40 hours. She accompanied us all, a group of young male and female dancers, four or five musicians and singers, technical assistants, stage-hands and one manager. She often shared stories of her earlier travels and also kept us all strictly under control, as well as safe.

In her own ways, she imparted intercultural/intersectional understandings. Talking about cultural differences, geographical distances and socio-political implications of gender, class, caste and religion, she pushed us to experience different places, food and histories, maximising our possibilities of experiencing during the free time of each tour. She was an avid learner, and she wanted us to become enabled and interested in absorbing experiences from all journeys near and far. She could not have faked her interest in our development for the long time we were with her. She really loved being the teacher, not only training us in dance but as social and intelligent beings.

The unfinished stage

In her academy of dance, Amala Shankar chose to highlight Uday Shankar's process of dance creation through the modern system of learning, preferring to establish an open experimental/experiential learning system over the unilinear learning system of the *guru-shishya parampara*. In my understanding, she was aware of the impossibility of claiming a creative process of dance-making as a *parampara* in the Indian dance ecology, where there is always an over-emphasis on presentational products (dance repertoires) as proof of tradition or the long root of *parampara*. In her reminiscences, her dilemma about the best way to keep Uday Shankar's dance that she referred to as "Uday Shankar style" was clear. The contradiction remained confusing and unclear – on one hand encouraging creativity, enabling students to create new movements from everyday actions and encounters, while asking them to bind and hold their imaginations under strict control through references of a fixed and slightly confusing aesthetics of Uday Shankar style, remained an unfinished but dedicated journey for her.

Amala Shankar was 94 years old when she was forced to close down her beloved dance academy, Uday Shankar India Culture Centre (USICC), Kolkata in its 50th year, due to age-related poor health. Any hope she may have had of creating a family legacy through her institution did not materialise. She was still very fit and nostalgic of the heydays of USICC. She remained hopeful of restarting the activities. For her, dancing or conducting rehearsals was a means of being alive. Being with dance was a proof/experience of liveness. It is through her journey through the stages of training, accomplishments, national and international recognition, and finally the institution she so lovingly built and nurtured that she herself became a part of the dance history in the post-independence times. Without insisting on claiming the space of a *guru* through a Gharana or a family legacy, she is remembered as a master teacher whose pedagogical success is clearly measurable through the modern institution of creative and classical dances that she continued to run for 50 years.

Acknowledging ageing and vulnerability

As stated earlier, the *guru* needs to be seen as a vulnerable being, insecure in terms of continuing his/her professional achievements while he or she teaches the new generation of learners to become good performers. On the other hand, the ever-present threat to the unstable income that is dependent on getting a steady stream of students also continues to loom large. As a result, systems of control emerge and clamp down on the processes of teaching. This is true in the case of those who name themselves as *gurus* or otherwise. A recent essay in *Pulse* talks about individual enterprises such as institutions headed by single-teacher (celebrity) being prone to many exploitative systems, including the disturbingly common sexual violations reported in the recent #MeToo movement, that proves that "the rhetoric of complete obedience and service can leave a student open to still worse kinds of abuse" (Gorringe, 2019, p. 7). Gorringe asks:

> In the light of this and given that the most distinctive feature of the tradition (gurukulavasam) has largely died out, there is obviously a question about whether the term should continue to be used at all. And yet, all institutions and traditions are liable to corruption because they are embodied in people, and should such instances of exploitation and corruption mean a wholesale abandoning of the spirit of the tradition?
>
> *(Gorringe, 2019, p. 7)*

The answer is not a simple one and it will continue to be debated. But what I propose is a way of pulling the idea of the *guru* and the *shishya* and the *parampara* firmly into the realistic realms of survival of the skilled dancer/teacher. So long as the dance ecology allows exoticisation of the persona and the role of the *guru* or the teacher, who is supposedly the godly enabler of the *shishyas*, the *guru* is never going to be able to truly express his/her vulnerability and dependence on the earning from his/her labour of teaching. Maybe the institutional space of professional teaching that Amala Shankar could create through her institution made her different from traditional *gurus* in the Indian dance scene.

Notes

1 *Guru-shishya parampara* is explained by Anubhuti Sharma as,

> The guru – shishya parampara is a case in point where certain unjust values, actions, behaviours, and doctrines are unquestioningly and unhesitatingly accepted by teachers and students. It commands values of subservience, duty, and unquestioned devotion

on the part of the shishya while exalting the guru to the pedestal of a "master" who is divine and infallible. There is a deep Brahminical as well as patriarchal logic to this – the guru stands for the figure of knowledge, and, by extension, the Brahmin who monopolises knowledge. Inherent to this relationship is a feudal service to the guru that shrouds the implicit violence that such a hierarchical structure entails.

(Sharma, 2020)

2 *Arangetram* or *mancha-pravesh* is the first experience of performing alone on stage after completing training in Bharatanatyam, Odissi and other forms of classical dances. It is a formal certification ceremony whereby the *guru* publicly acknowledges the end of training for an apprentice dancer.

3 *Guru-dakshina* is a way of repaying the *guru*/teacher at the end of the training period in traditional learning systems. This was meant to be a way of thanking the *guru*, but has been criticised at times as a system of exploitation and extortion.

4 Gharana is a familial system of knowledge perpetuation in artistic practices. Hindustani classical music, as well as Kathak dance, has depended largely on a few such familial transmission of knowledge.

5 Nyota Inyoka's actual identity always remained a mystery. She made her name as a oriental dancer, and was known as a vaudeville dancer born of a French mother and an Indian father in Pondicherry and settled in Paris.

6 Alice Boner was a Swiss Sculptor who got to know Uday Shankar in the mid-1920s. She travelled to India with Shankar in 1930 and they established a limited liability company for promotion of Indian culture. Uday Shankar's first European tour was funded and arranged by Boner, and she travelled with the troupe as its manager.

7 Uday Shankar had travelled to Paris with his mother, his brothers and other members of his troupe. Alice Boner had organised a house for the Shankar family to reside in with the members of the troupe as they all prepared for the tour.

8 Simkie (originally named Simone Barbiere) was a French pianist who became Uday Shankar's dance partner in the late 1920s.

9 Kanaklata was Uday Shankar's cousin and had joined his troupe in its earliest days.

10 *Kaliya Daman* was a story of the killing of snake Kaliya (performed by Amala) by the god Krishna (danced by Uday Shankar).

11 Uday Shankar India Culture Centre, Almora (USICC), was opened formally in 1939 and closed down in 1944, as per records.

12 Uday Shankar made a single film named *Kalpana*, which was released in 1948.

13 *Kalpana* can be accessed at www.youtube.com/watch?v=dl-rPuRq90w, accessed on 29 June 2022.

References

Banerji, A. Kedhar, A., Mitra, R., O'Shea, J., Pillai, Shanti. (2020). Postcolonial pedagogies: Recasting the Guru – Shishya Parampara. *Dance Research Journal*, 221–230.

Boner, A. (1993). *Alice Boner Diaries: India 1934–1967.* Delhi: Motilal Banarsidass.

Gorringe, M. (2019, May 5). Does the guru-shishya model of dance teaching hold out the best prospect of creating a performer? *Pulse: Asian Music and Dance*, 1–18.

Ram, K. (2008). *Perspectives from apprentices of skill practices: Performing Arts and Scholarship.* Retrieved from Guru Shishya Parampara: Elephant House Project @ Macquarie University: www.criticalpath.org.au

Shankar (Nandi), A. (2007). *Sat Sagarer Pare [Bengali].* Kolkata: A Mukherjee & Co. Pvt Ltd. (Original work published 1934)

Sharma, A. (2020, November 7). Beyond a culture of debt: Reflections on the Guru – Shishya Parampara. *Economic and Political Weekly*, 63–64.

Vatsyayan, K. E. (1982). *Guru – Shishya Parampara: The Master – Disciple Tradition in Indian Classical Dance*. London: Arts Council of Britain.

Weidman, A. (2008). In search of the guru: Technology and authenticity in Karnatak music. In I. V. Peterson & D. Soneji (Eds.), *Performing pasts: Reinventing the arts in modern South India* (pp. 225–251). Delhi: Oxford University Press.

4.3

LEARNING IN CREATIVE DANCE

Adults and children share the space

Ann Kipling Brown

Introduction

Recently, I have been asked to present my thoughts at various symposia about my experiences in the teaching of creative dance. I was asked questions about how I became involved, what did it mean to me, had I encountered any resistance, who did I teach? The preparations for these commitments required me to delve into my own past with creative dance, as well as the history and value of creative dance. It was important to recognise the publications and teaching of Rudolf Laban and his devotees who were celebrated and supported, particularly in Britain, where I received most of my education. This chapter has empowered me to review more closely some of the projects where I assist different age groups to experience and learn through creative dance, find ways to express themselves and understand and implement pedagogical practices that are relevant and meaningful to the individual or group.

My story

There were several events in my formal dance training that set me on the pathway of teaching dance in a different way. My first formal experience of dance was in primary school in Britain, where our classroom teacher taught country dances. The steps were simple walking, running, galloping and skipping, and I loved the intricate patterns of their characteristic formations for partners and groups. It was *The Syllabus of Physical Exercises for Public Elementary Schools* (Great Britain Board of Education, 1909) published by the Great Britain Board of Education which associated dance with physical training. Such country dances that our classroom teacher taught connected with the study of technical skill knowledge and the organization of games, gymnastics and swimming. There was an emphasis on physical health and drill procedures.

DOI: 10.4324/9781003307624-27

At the same time, I also had formal dance classes at a studio in ballet, tap and acrobatics. At the age of 11, I moved with my family to live in India, where I continued with those Western dance forms, as well as classes in Manipuri and Bharatanatyam dance forms with a young professional dancer. I admit that I loved my dance classes, but I felt there was something missing. I have written and talked about how I was losing interest in my ballet classes. It did not seem to be dancing at all but a series of exercises that said very little to me about dance and expression. Midway through the year, a new teacher came to our class and taught the standard ballet class. However, at the end of the class, she asked if we knew the story of the Dying Swan (which we did). She reviewed it with us and played the music and asked us to dance our own version. I was in heaven, transported in my story of the Dying Swan. I loved ballet again. I was inspired and believe I understood implicitly why the class was organized in the way it was. I waited every class for that time to improvise (Author's journal, July, 1999).

It was in my high school programme back in Britain where I was introduced to modern and modern educational dance, later called creative dance. Our young and forward-thinking physical education teacher introduced our class to modern educational dance and gymnastics, First, I believe, she wanted to introduce more modern approaches; and second, she believed that it would engage more students in physical activity. At this time, she also arranged for a group of us to attend a workshop organized by the Manchester Dance Circle where we participated in a dance session led by Lisa Ullmann. The session was transformative for me, a profound sense of expression and freedom in dance that I remembered from my improvisation in the ballet class. I was inspired by these revelations about what dance could be – which, I believe, influenced my studies and teaching in dance.

Looking back

In Britain during the period (1950–1980), many significant changes occurred in children's education, including dance. In general education, there was less teacher direction and less formal methodology. Children sat in open settings and groups instead of formal rows and were involved in project-based learning. While teachers and administrators were initiating new ideas in the general classroom, the pioneering theatre dance professionals were exploring the idea that the essence of dance was separate although linked to other physical pursuits. Dance professionals – such as Isadora Duncan and Ruth St Denis in United States, Michel Fokine in Russia and Rudolf Laban and Mary Wigman in Central Europe – were all working independently to change established dance forms. The work of these pioneers in modern dance had much impact on both professional and educational dance. For instance, Rudolf Laban – one of the founders of European modern dance with his collaborators Mary Wigman, Sigurd Leeder and Kurt Jooss – questioned the traditional constraints against showing feeling and opened the way for a freeing of the body. Additionally, Laban's theories of universal movement principles inherent in all structural movement included theatrical dance and were communicated through his writings and publications. World War II forced Laban out of Nazi Germany to take refuge in Britain, causing the redirection of his work and influencing emergent movement and dance in education in Britain.

Laban's theories presented a new perspective on the basic elements of human movement referred to as "movement training" or "movement education", which influenced how dance, gymnastics and games were taught in schools in Britain. There were two important publications from the Ministry of Education that recognized the importance of this new focus on movement education, *Moving and Growing* (British Department of Education and Science, 1952) and *Planning the Program* (British Department of Education and Science, 1953). Laban was also the first person to develop community dance, and he set out to reform the role of dance education, emphasizing his belief that dance should be made available to everyone. He presented a revolutionary idea of "modern educational dance" or "creative dance".

In his book *Modern Educational Dance* (1948), Laban offered a dance technique that aimed to foster and promote children's unconscious dance-like movements, preserve their spontaneity and foster artistic expression and provide an inclusive, creative and affordable dance programme for all ages. The pedagogy is teacher-led, not teacher-directed; it is open-ended, with tasks set for students to explore and create. Creative dance was seen as a means of education of the whole person and was supported and taught in many training colleges and secondary schools, as well as primary schools. Later noteworthy publications in modern educational dance, then named creative dance, appeared from educators and scholars such as Valerie Preston-Dunlop, Betty Redfern and Joan Russell, who reference Laban's contribution in their texts for teaching creative dance. Also of significance was the Gulbenkian Foundation's *Dance Education and Training in Britain* (Brinson, 1980) which separated dance from the physical education programme to a strong arts educational focus.

Creative dance in the 1980s in Britain was accepted by dance educators in schools, as it offered not only an analysis of movement and the elements of dance that provide a framework for understanding and building dance, but also a pedagogy. However, there were certain myths and concerns about the content and teaching of creative dance. Many dance educators of traditional forms felt that anyone could teach the creative dance form and that there were no guiding principles or clear dance vocabulary. Additionally, the introduction of the London School of Contemporary Dance (LSCD, 1968) and The London Contemporary Dance Theatre (1969) by philanthropist Robin Howard and under the artistic direction of Robert Cohan had immense impact on both professional and educational dance. The LSCD training and style were based on the training and style of Martha Graham's work, led by Cohan and demonstrated in his choreography class (1975). Cohan's teaching and choreography influenced both Britain's professional artists and educators. In schools, we began to see the dance content and pedagogy change to teacher-directed and Graham-style technique taught to both primary and secondary students. Of course, this was not the case in every school and, in some cases, the introduction of the Graham style was very successful at involving students in dance, for instance, Nadine Senior, founder of Northern School of Contemporary Dance at Harehills Middle School. These changes promoted debate and several workshops were held, initiated by the UK dance organization at that time to examine the role of dance in education, particularly dance is public schools. The focus of Laban's dance education continues to contrast with the dance taught in dance studios or academies that accept students based on audition for preprofessional training. However, I have witnessed that many dance studios and academies that have dance classes for young children adopted creative dance as an appropriate introduction to dance; for example, the Royal Academy of Dance.

There were also criticisms of how creative dance was being taught. There was a tendency to work through the elements of dance, a somewhat instrumental approach and similar in contexts where technique is the focus, rather than work with children from their innate ways of moving and personal ideas. It was recommended that a dance programme should encourage students to explore and discover dance in a meaningful way and enable them to express themselves through nonverbal means of communication. It was considered that Laban's work confirmed the importance of the symbolic form of representation in dance, the absence of which would deprive the child of a particular way of expressing ideas and feelings. It is also understood that before the child – particularly the very young child – can experience or be introduced to those adult forms such as ballet, tap, jazz or contemporary dance, there was a need to master the "language of dance" and experience those processes of selection and organization of the movement material for the child's own ideas and feelings. The adult forms of dance have a highly structured and specialized vocabulary which determine the type and extent of ideas and feelings that can be conveyed – and therefore, the meaning of symbolic representation that can be achieved by the child is constrained by the dance form in which he or she is working.

Judith Lynne Hanna's comprehensive article, "A Nonverbal Language for Imagining and Learning: Dance Education in K – 12 Curriculum" (Hanna, 2008, p. 491), outlines the importance of dance education in the public school settings, provides evidence of success and "addresses cognition, emotion, language, learning styles, assessment, and new research directions in the field of education" (p. 491). She explains that the dance curriculum today in most public schools focus on an "interdisciplinary reach" or a more liberal arts approach.

> The substance of K–12 dance encompasses a palette of building blocks that students think about and experientially and symbolically embody. In addition to gaining intermodal declarative and procedural dance knowledge, students acquire various skills as they exercise multiple intelligences that are applicable in non-dance realms.
>
> *(Hanna, 2008, p. 498)*

Hanna's words are supported by the many examples of dance curricula shared at the "Curriculum in motion – Special event" held at the daCi/WDA Global Dance

Summit in 2012.[1] Two significant educational goals were outlined: the Laban-derived model provides the diverse educational values of dance and also provides support for dance to be considered an art form rather than a physical education activity (p. 5). Shu-Lien Huang (2011) supports creative dance, as it uses "the body as a learning tool, employing elements of movement as mediums, and recognizing individual differences – can enrich students' learning in different aspects of sensory intelligence, develop their physical and motor abilities, and spur their creativity" (p. 112). Sherrie Barr's (2016) insightful paper helps us to examine the pedagogical knowledge within Laban studies through examining "shared ideas between Laban Studies and critical pedagogy" (p. 4). Through his work, Laban raised the status of dance as an art form, and his explorations into the theory and practice of dance and movement transformed dance scholarship. Valerie Preston-Dunlop (1998) said of Laban's contribution that it is well-known that his "initiating ideas in dance theatre, dance scholarship, dance therapy, choreology, ethnochoreology, dance literacy, dance notation, dance as recreation, drama, movement profiling and dance education" reveals a breadth of influence" (p. 270).

In my introduction, I mentioned various experiences that I initiated with different age groups. One focus was on different age groups dancing together – dancing with students, parents and children dancing together, senior students dancing with younger children, preservice education students dancing with different age groups, and learning Motif Notation in creative dance lessons. My study of Laban's theories and experiences teaching various ages influenced how I continued to teach and choreograph dance and shape experiences. I was not formally conducting research – I wish I had been – but thankfully, I do have my journals that describe the activities and responses. It is through the lens of critical pedagogy that calls for a fair education for all and identifies the teacher as facilitator that I share the following examples.

Parent and child classes

I often danced with my students. I remember clearly being told in a dance pedagogy class that a teacher should not do this, as the child(ren) will copy you. Yes, some did – those struggling with an idea – but maybe what they see will spark an idea: the sheer joy of dancing together when all the exploration has been undertaken and the ideas generated, and everyone knows their dance. I didn't do this all the time! I realized that having an adult dance with you can be energizing, comforting (not being watched) and confirming. It led me to reconsider the traditional sharing days we held when parents were invited into the dance class to witness their child's progress. I was aware that parents may not always know what is appropriate for their child's age level and, therefore, I would preface a showing with what we had been working on and what to look for. However, I witnessed situations when a parent was disappointed in the child's performance or urged the child to do better. Thus, I introduced the parent and child dancing together; at times, learning something together and at other times the child teaching the parent a dance phrase or complete dance.

There were more encounters with parents and young children; first, in after-school programmes provided by the local education authority in London and then later with the work of Joyce Boorman and Jan Vallance at the University of Alberta, Edmonton, Canada. Joyce Boorman taught dance education courses in the Faculty of Sports Studies and created the Alberta Children's Creative Dance Theatre (ACCDT), and her colleague Jan Vallance taught in the Faculty of Education. Both had attended the Art of Movement Studio in Addlestone, Surrey and studied Laban's theories of movement and dance education. The sharing sessions where parents were invited to watch their children stimulated positive response from parents who stated that "the children have required activities in groups and recognize others in sharing and giving different ideas, in listening and responding to sounds; to the teacher and their peers" (Vallance, 1989, p. 81). Parents further explained that they witnessed what was being learned: the child's coordination, balance, strength and good memory, the clarity in presenting the dance movement and the ability to collaborate and explain the dance. The parent and child experiences were family focused and often involved both parents and siblings.

The idea rests on experiential learning where the learners' experiences are central and valued as a pedagogical tool. Helen Payne and Barry Costas (2021, p. 281) state "[K]nowledge from creating dance, viewed as experiential learning, can be constituted in phenomenological terms involving feeling, thought, imagination, sensation, sensitivity, corporal, and relational experiences in a bidirectional process between body, brain, and mind". While many sessions are not always focused on learning specific dance forms, some do and result in profound benefits, such as the parent and child "Tap to Togetherness" programme that was described by Katie M. Heinrich et al. (2021). The parents' feedback confirmed the physical, social, and emotional benefits they felt their child(ren) gained from programme participation. Luke Muscat's (2021) study of a parent–toddler class revealed that dancing with a parent can be a joyous activity but more importantly, if the parent is able to relinquish control over decisions, it will support the toddler's growing autonomy and desire to be in control. A further study reported by Edward C. Warburton et al. (2014) was conducted in the family community dance classes held by the Luna: A Dance World studio-based programme in Oakland, California, USA. The three-year study of teacher practice and parent–child interaction focused on "relational engagement" in dance, an investment in building interpersonal skills. Through the conceptual approach to dance whereby everyone is a dancer and choreographer, there have been many successful stories for families whose relationships have floundered or who have encountered injustice and lack of respect while struggling to access services for their children.

Teaching in schools

The experiences with parents and children dancing together encouraged me to look further into these shared experiences, and in the public school setting, I introduced dancing between schools, inviting a class of high school students to dance with a class of elementary students. Each class prepared a dance and then students taught and learned the other's dance. What excitement there was in the room as they watched, learned and performed! As a result of this, a principal invited me to her school to work with parents of preschool-age children who had recently arrived in London from India. Language was a barrier, and the principal believed that through exploring dance movement, this would help language development for all. We selected body and movement words that they would encounter in daily life: body parts, moving those parts such as wiggling fingers; actions such as run, sit, jump, turn, big, small, fast, slow, etc.; and we danced. It was difficult at first for the mothers who seemed uncomfortable to move, but the enthusiasm and energy of their children relaxed them and there was joy in the room.

Teaching preservice dance education students

While teaching in schools for nine years, my role at times was to help primary classroom teachers present their own dance classes. I came to realize that many were resistant to teach not because they could not learn the movement vocabulary or find ideas for dance but because they were embarrassed or uncomfortable about moving. In consequence, we implemented dance workshops and focused on experiencing dance, which they told me helped their confidence. This experience inspired me to create experiences for ballet students who would be required to teach creative dance to primary students. I approached teachers who I knew would be interested in having us in their classroom. I would lead the class with a warm-up and exploration of specific movements, then the preservice students and primary students would pair up, introduce themselves and dance together, experimenting with the movements I had introduced and finding further movements. Following this, the preservice students would teach a dance idea that we had prepared in previous classes. The final part of the class was sharing time, when groups watched and talked about each other's dances. There was lots of chatter and excitement in each part of the class, and there was an eagerness to meet again.

In the debriefing session, the preservice students commented on the ease with which the primary students absorbed and practised the dance content and the excitement demonstrated when sharing with others. The preservice students also reflected on their trepidation that they would not be able to manage the situation and that the primary students may not respond to them or like their ideas. A study conducted by Trine Ørbæk and Gunn Engelsrud (2021) confirmed that physical education students in Norway found the experience of teaching dance challenging as did the preservice dance students discussed previously. Four themes emerged – fear of unconnectedness, creating trust, giving time and space, and unfolding freely – and demonstrated "how concepts introduced in Laban's (1948) effort theory contributed by providing a language that helped pupils and teaching students both to explore various movements and put various movements together in a composition" (Ørbæk & Engelsrud, 2021, p. 331). Mary Jane Warner (2012) echoes these concerns in her report of preservice teachers working with older adults. She notes,

> Generally, the student teachers developed patience, an increased sensitivity to individuals, a greater versatility in designing classes for a wide range of levels, an increased flexibility in modifying a class in progress, and the ability to adapt core movement concepts to offer instruction to a diverse population.
>
> *(p. 5)*

Teaching Motif Notation

In many of my dance education classes for children and university students, I introduced Motif Notation to assist in the understanding of movement. Several educators have talked about the relevance of notation within the dance education of the child. For instance, Rose Hill, Ann Hutchinson Guest and Betty Redfern in their individual writings have stated that the creator and performer of dances, involved in a creative process, need a language in which the creative aspects of movement can be analyzed and recorded. Some consider that one all-important function of notation is to provide an objective record of movement and a common denominator for thinking and communication, independent of any theory, style or technique – in fact, a universal language. The Laban system of notation offers two ways of recording movement: Motif Notation depicts movement in a general way, providing possibilities and allowing for a personal version. Structured Notation[2] records the specific details of movement, recording a specific version that is to be reconstructed definitively. As Teresa L. Heiland (2016) identifies, "Notation is a tool that generates ways of moving and provides inspiration for unique ways of devising new ways of knowing, expressing, and discussing movement" (p. 5). I admit that I began teaching notation as a subject but found that students did not see the relevance. Consequently, I embedded notation, whether Motif Notation or Structured Notation, in dance courses rather than teaching notation as a separate topic. As Heiland believes:

> Empowering students through engagement with notation and pedagogical approaches can be the work of the current notation users, and returning to Laban's tenets of community and reflexivity toward personal meaning making may provide some stability and mobility with these aims.
>
> *(p. 3)*

In my teaching, I would use Motif Notation in choreography or dance pedagogy classes to engage students in exploring and recognizing possibilities in categories of movement by changing timing, spatial or dynamic features, etc., and shaping ideas for their own or children's choreography. The use of Structured Notation allowed for the study of different dance forms and works of choreographers in dance history or technique classes providing a visual representation of the choreographer's manipulation of movement and choreographic devices.

In the research for my master's degree, some years ago now, I addressed whether children between the ages of 8 and 14 were able to learn and use Motif Notation within their creative dance classes. The children's responses and attitudes were positive, and the testing sessions revealed their ability in both reading and writing dance, confirming for me the importance of using a notation system in the dance class. In further teaching, I witnessed the ease with which children embraced the notation and were eager to learn more. Together with my research and teaching practice of embedding notation within the dance class, colleagues and I created and presented Motif Notation workshops for teachers. Each morning of a week-long workshop, primary-age children joined the teachers in creative dance using Motif Notation. A teacher and child paired to work together and through the pedagogical practices of presenting the notation through dance tasks in systematic and relevant ways they danced, created dances and learned the symbols and scoring. There was lots of learning taking place by both teachers and students. The students loved the mystery of the symbols and dancing with the adults, and some teachers lost the intimidation they had felt learning system in their own training but could now see how useful it could be within the dance class.

Conclusion

Today's educational context has many challenges, not only from the COVID-19 pandemic that the world has experienced, but from the socio-economic and psychological needs of families and children. The choices and restrictions of what is being taught in schools is also a dilemma and, in many countries, dance is not included in the curriculum. The responsibility for providing experiences where children can learn and succeed rests with all of us. In creating encounters with adults and children in creative dance, I have seen – as also many dance colleagues have also reported – the benefits of these dance encounters to be positive and, at times, life changing.

Notes

1 Dance and the Child international (daCi); World Dance Alliance (WDA), Proceedings of the daCi and WDA Global Dance Summit. Ausdance. URL https://ausdance.org.au/publications/details/dance-young-people-and-change
2 Kinetography Laban or Labanotation.

References

Barr, S. (2016). Mining Laban studies as a critical pedagogical praxis. *Journal of Movement Arts Literacy*, *3*, 1–17. Retrieved from http://digitalcommons.uncg.edu/jmal/vol3/iss1/2

Brinson, P. (1980). *Gulbenkian report. Dance education and training in Britain*. London: Calouste and Gulbenkian Foundation.

British Department of Education and Science. (1952). *Moving and growing*. London.

British Department of Education and Science. (1953). *Planning the program*. London.

Great Britain Board of Education. (1909). *The syllabus of physical exercises for public elementary schools*. Retrieved from http://books.google.com

Hanna, J. L. (2008). A nonverbal language for imagining and learning: Dance education in K – 12 curriculum. *Educational Researcher, 37*(8), 491–506. doi:10.3102/0013189X08326032

Heiland, T. L. (2016). Special issue: Pedagogy in theory and practice in Laban studies. *Journal of Movement Arts Literacy Archive (2013–2019), 3*(1). Retrieved from https://digitalcommons.lmu.edu/jmal/vol3/iss1/1

Heinrich, K. M., Pentz, J. L., Goodman, B. L., Casey, K., & Rosenkranz, S. K. (2021). Tap to togetherness: A program for parents and children together. *Journal of Dance Education, 22*, 199–205. doi:10.1080/15290824.2020.1854456

Huang, S. (2011). Action research on the integration of creative dance and dance forms. *The International Journal of Arts Education, 1*, 109–139.

Laban, R. (1948). *Modern educational dance*. London: Macdonald & Evans.

Muscat, L. (2021). Moving together: Supporting attachment in parent-toddler dance classes. *Journal of Dance Education*. doi:10.1080/15290824.2021.1897128

Ørbæk, T., & Engelsrud, G. (2021). Teaching creative dance in school – a case study from physical education in Norway. *Research in Dance Education, 22*(3), 321–335. doi:10.1080/14647893.2020.1798396

Payne, H., & Costas, B. (2021). Creative dance as experiential learning in state primary education: The potential benefits for children. *Journal of Experiential Education, 44*(3), 277–292. doi:10.1177/1053825920968587

Preston-Dunlop, V. (1998). *Rudolf Laban: An extraordinary life*. London: Dance Books Ltd.

Vallance, J. M. (1989). *Collegial conversation: A search for meaning in children's creative dance*. [Doctoral dissertation]. University of Alberta.

Warburton, E. C., Reedy, P., & Ng, N. (2014). Engaging families in dance: An investigation of moving parents and children together. *International Journal of Education & the Arts, 15*(1), 1–26. Retrieved from www.ijea.org/v15n1/

Warner, M. J. (2012). Intergenerational dance: Changing perceptions of student teachers through teaching older adults. In *Proceedings of the daCi and WDA Global Dance Summit*. Taiwan: Taipei National University of the Arts. Ausdance. Retrieved from www.ausdance.org

4.4

MANAGING EXPECTATIONS

Teaching mature dancers in lutrawita/Tasmania

Lesley Graham

Introduction

In nipaluna/Hobart, several experienced teaching artists specialise in working with mature dancers. Three of them were interviewed for this chapter, their common link being a strong formal ballet training, a professional career as a performer, well over 20 years of dance teaching experience and their age being older than 65. Their perceptions of their dance teaching practice is the focus in the interviews, with each teaching artist asked to reflect on a recent experience of teaching a particular group of dancers, within a formal weekly one-hour class structure.

The article presents results of a qualitative analysis of the interviews, giving insights into the pedagogy of teaching mature dancers. Five key areas were investigated covering the motivation and experience of the teaching artists to work in this context; the characteristics, needs and motivations participants; the pedagogy and the practice (including the key components of the classes, how they plan for a sequence of sessions, adapt their approach and maintain participant engagement, mitigate risk (Lesley Graham, 2005), create a safe space and cater for the needs of mature bodies); and their reflections on what stimulates teaching artists to continue working with mature people.

The teaching artists

Wendy Morrow is a performance artist, mentor and arts consultant. After training at the Australian Ballet School in the 1970s, she pursued a career as a professional dancer and further training nationally and internationally in contemporary dance, improvisation, various alignments and somatic practices. Morrow has taught all ages and abilities in a broad range of settings, environments and contexts for more than five decades.

DOI: 10.4324/9781003307624-28

Judith Ker has taught ballet classes in Hobart for 70 years after a career between 1949 and 1958 performing in Europe with the International Ballet Company, and Australia and New Zealand with the Borovansky Company. Her initial training in Sydney with Francis Scully and Kathleen Danetree was followed by a Royal Academy of Dance scholarship to study in London.

Lucinda Sharp joined The Australian Ballet as a dancer in the early 1970s. After the end of her own stage career, Sharp helped many young dancers achieve their performing arts dreams – either as a rehearsal director or as a Clinical Psychologist. In 2016, she left her position as Student Health and Welfare Director at The Australian Ballet School and now runs Forty South Publishing and teaches for Mature Artists Dance Experience (MADE).

Motivation

As an older person, Morrow wanted to explore ideas of moving the body with people of a similar age; particularly concepts and ideas of dance and writing with others who have had different life experiences.

> I assume that other people have their own history . . . and one of the things that I think is missing [for] mature people in a dance environment is that it could offer insights into themselves in terms of sensorial [experience] because most of those people haven't had that invitation.
>
> *(Morrow)*

After her performance career, Ker took over teaching children in an established ballet school. In the early 1960s, she moved into teaching ballet for adults through pre-existing adult education classes.

> Well, I never wanted to be a teacher. I never envisaged being a teacher. It was just a progression that happens. [You teach] when you have to. You'll find that most dancers that have been in ballet companies, automatically drift into teaching.
>
> *(Ker)*

For Sharp, teaching mature dancers is an opportunity to share her experiences. She has

> a lot of knowledge about a fairly direct, sort of harsh and negative style of ballet, and then [during] my professional career as a dancer, learning from [international] teachers coming into the Australian Ballet to teach not just different styles but different methods of teaching. I want people to enjoy

what they do and have fun, but I want them to learn . . . . I like to have fun and I like to learn . . . not just do it.

(Sharp)

When asked to teach classes for mature dancers, Sharp needed several months to think about it.

I'm still the perfectionistic ballet dancer type and I wanted to be prepared . . . . I hadn't taught for a long time, and I think when I'd stopped teaching, I was bit over it . . . this was a completely new challenge and I actually really enjoy working with that age group . . . . They were there to do a class, but they liked the fact that I was giving them lots of corrections and teaching.

(Sharp)

The participants

Morrow's 'mature' class is made up of women older than 50, who are interested in moving, mostly with background in social dancing, yoga, ballroom and/or foundational ballet. During the time of the interview, the group was limited to eight due to the COVID-19 pandemic.

Most of Ker's participants are women from about 18 to their 80s. They are people past thinking about a professional career – people who come to keep fit. Some have a background in ballet, and some have 'bits that can't move well'.

I don't have very large classes. Some might just want it for the exercise. Some might want it to keep flexibility going. Someone might want it to remind them of when they first learned . . . and would like the feel of it again, like to feel that they're still capable of doing the work.

(Ker)

There is a mixed cohort in Sharp's classes. There are some who have never danced before, some who learned ballet as a child and some who have strong body knowledge through their own training through yoga, Pilates or ballroom dancing. Sharp's classes are between 18 and 24 students.

Sometimes you might think that mature [dancers] are just people who have got to a point with their dancing and decided they don't want to do it anymore, and they might be 20, but they want to still do some adult classes . . . . I think one of the things [that makes us mature] is that our bodies won't do what they used to.

(Sharp)

Morrow cites the need for exercise, socialising and personal expression as motivators for participation. There are also those who seem to feel that they missed out on the dream of ballet in their childhood and a strong sense of familiarity with the structure of a ballet class. In contrast, Morrow sees her classes contributing to lifelong learning by

> opening older age people to continue to approach new things and ideas with curiosity and inquiry and placing themselves into challenging unfamiliar environments. Many have physical restrictions that are age related. A few have quite limited physical capacities. They bring their own perceptions and experiences of what dance is.
>
> *(Morrow)*

Morrow reflects that she found working with peoples' understanding and expectations a challenge, particularly differences in ideas of aesthetics, expression and understanding of performance and what constituted dancing and movement. She claims that the mindset of many older people is not one of 'ownership' of their learning. For many, learning is still all about skill gaining, knowledge and fact, whereas younger generations have grown up with a greater focus on inquiry. When working with mature aged people, Morrow observes that there's

> a big wall where the mature dancers either pretend that [ageing] is not happening, and we'll be young and gay and free and put the old music on and do what we used to do when we were in our 20s, or there is an aspirational thing of looking at young bodies and going: Wouldn't that be nice to be able to do that? There's something missing in between, which is about working with what you have, really being in that body and really working with what that body is; in accepting that body in the state that it's in, and how it feels . . . . [There is] a bigger question of emotional, psychological the physical body mind stuff that isn't really talked about.
>
> *(Morrow)*

Ker claims to teach 'the individual' in the class and has students who are not as physically able as other people. She teaches what she feels her students need for improving. There are two quite different cohorts in the same class: those who want to do something for exercise and chose ballet because they remembered and enjoyed it as a child. Then there are the adult beginners.

> The discipline is the important thing . . . but it's not just the physical, it's also the emotional connection with the music.
>
> *(Ker)*

For Sharp, the dancers are:

> someone whose body will not do what it used to but still wants to really get maximum enjoyment or fitness or whatever they're looking for out of it.

> You have to work around people's body's capabilities, restrictions, more than I probably was ever working with when I was working with pre-professionals and professionals . . . . That is really challenging as a teacher, to really try and explain this concept to people who can't do it to the degree I'm looking for. I find that one of the most enjoyable things about it.
>
> *(Sharp)*

Sharp believes that her dancers really like learning, receiving corrections through specific feedback and feeling their technique improving. Her experience as a psychologist has exposed her to research that people will stay at things if they are having fun. She also acknowledges there's a social element to attending.

> I know some of them do socialise outside, but when they come there, they belong to that group. They feel a sense of belonging. I'm approaching them as a group and as individuals. It's very important to know your students and when they walk in the door to welcome them in by name and [to ask them] 'How are you this week, Susie?' 'Mary, how's your back?'
>
> *(Sharp)*

Sharp also offers corrections to the whole group: 'I want you to try this. Let's all do this'. She will also ask how something feels and encourages them to share their reflections with a touch of humour, even if it is, 'Oh, we were so hopeless'.

Pedagogy

A teacher's first impressions of working with a group and the need to change previous approaches are often a clue to pedagogy.

> I was really challenged by their assumptions and expectations. I found them quite rigid and intimidating. I spent a lot of time trying to gauge how best to engage them into what was obviously new territory that extended beyond their previous experiences.
>
> *(Morrow)*

> Nothing has changed because it's always been a case of teaching according to the person in front of me.
>
> *(Ker)*

> When I first went in, I tried to make it less technical, but I've realised they do like the technique of it. The beginners like technique too but balanced with something that feels more 'dance-y' such as a 'port de bras' because they get a sense of movement by moving the head and coordinating the arms. The more experienced class like a good balance of strong technique and

then some centre where they really get to move. They prefer to really fit a lot into the class.

(Sharp)

Morrow refers to her dance teaching pedagogy as

open and inviting for people to discover their bodies through movement. I try to read and adapt according to the group and abilities and encourage a level of autonomy and personal inquiry. Throughout the class I encourage an imaginative approach to the body by providing a lot of anatomical and image-based information alongside experiential exercises.

(Morrow)

Ker states that nothing prepared her for teaching, except the fact that she had two very good teachers and followed their example.

I didn't learn to be a teacher. What I do is simply encourage each pupil to achieve their personal best to improve on their own capabilities; whatever the age group and whatever their capabilities. You're finding different ways to communicate with them so that you can get the best out of them.

(Ker)

Sharp's focus is on people feeling a sense of achievement.

I'll structure something that week, even just for one person in the class, without them knowing. Then, when they get it, [it is wonderful] be able to go 'It worked!' I think we all like to achieve. I think that's why mature aged people go to these classes . . . people want something to happen for themselves. No matter how small the achievement, I want to celebrate that.

(Sharp)

Morrow introduces new foci that accumulate and build over time under larger physical movement concepts and explorations. She also repeats and develops exercises that strengthen and prepare the body.

For Ker, it doesn't matter whether you are teaching beginners, or soloists or the top ballerina; the class always goes the same way: the warm-up, the barre work then the centre.

Sharp tries to give her more experienced students exercises at the barre that feel like they're dancing, combinations that are not too static but that use heads, arms and coordination using different dynamics. She moves around the room, giving personal corrections. Sharp then gets them to try some things in the centre, facing a single front where there is a wall of mirror which she faces for a better view of the class, and promotes a sense of togetherness.

Sharp's beginners' class is a slow progression,

> I started off the beginner class just sitting on the floor and going through how to point your feet, how the ankle works and things like that and they loved it. We weren't even moving, but they said it was fascinating. To break that up a bit I would do something really simple like a 'port de bras' with nice arms, nice head, nice little waltz and some walks down the room. They liked that balance. It surprised me how much of the technique they want.
>
> *(Sharp)*

Each session of Morrow's lesson sequence has a specific focus and exploring that through a variety of ways. Her recent teaching was set up as a block of ten weekly daytime classes. Being employed to teach a pre-existing class created a different teacher/student relationship for those who are usually attracted to Morrow's work.

> I have been more used to teaching workshops where I've totally designed a controlled context and environment. It might be a walk, it might be a workshop inside a studio, but the material and the setup of everything around that was within my remit.
>
> *(Morrow)*

For Morrow, the teacher student relationship is reciprocal. If she were to arrive each week and give them what they had expected,

> then I wouldn't be teaching because I would be providing them and keeping them within the bubble of what they already know. If somebody's interested in my kind of knowledge and inquiry, my job is to invite people to extend themselves into something that they don't know, safely.
>
> *(Morrow)*

Morrow reflects that her sessions are offered within the context of doing something and producing something. She believes her sessions are about enabling people to own their experience of whatever is guided within that framework.

> I see it very much as working with and alongside people, and not necessarily about teaching.
>
> *(Morrow)*

Ker's barre work is usually set, but she may change aspects of it each lesson. She adapts the centre work and enchainment to different pieces of music.

> You use the steps as the alphabet, and you do your own sentence . . . . I never change [the enchainment] every week because I don't have professional dancers. If I [did], someone in the class wouldn't be able to cope.
>
> *(Ker)*

Ker also gives her pupils an opportunity to improvise at the end of the class.

> I give them what to do and then the music will keep on going and I just let
> them do what they want, and they enjoy that. I've watched them and they
> just do what they feel, like they dance like children, like when children just
> hadn't learned anything.
>
> *(Ker)*

For the beginners, Sharp starts the term breaking things down, and then building on that each week. They learn a certain number of new steps, building on what
they've learned and moving a bit faster.

> I might have an idea [to focus on] in that term, say, the proper use of a plié,
> for example. By the end of the term, they really understand what a plié is, or
> it could be posture and plié. Then I might add posture and plié and pointe
> work.
>
> *(Sharp)*

For the more experienced dancers, Sharp usually focuses for two or three weeks
on a concept. This may not necessarily be one they're always aware of, but she
might point out later that they have worked on various things and now they are at
a new place without thinking about it.

> A concept might be something like preparing for pirouettes. Over the term,
> each of the activities such as plié in fourth, working their hip flexors, feeling
> where that retire position is, balance on a flexed foot, coordination of arms,
> strength of supporting leg, strength of upper back, contributes to a pirou-
> ette, but I don't say . . . we're preparing for pirouettes. We just build it up.
> There are those key movements [pirouettes], along with an arabésque and
> jeté, which are absolutely part of the seduction of ballet.
>
> *(Sharp)*

In an effort to satisfy her students' expectations, Morrow increased the movement and dynamics.

> I became really aware that most older people have a preconditioned under-
> standing of passive learning. They want someone to lead and tell them what
> to do, to instruct them. A contemporary approach of allowing people to
> determine and meet the learning situation is something new for them. I was
> interested in how to feed into something that people are already doing so
> they have a greater experience of it, rather than the one that they've already
> been having.
>
> *(Morrow)*

Her challenge was how to structure something within what would be a class but within the mode of learning that she was hoping for.

> The experience of it is structured just like it would be in a normal class except that its focus is not necessarily on skill development, but more aware-ness, eliciting some sensitising and kinaesthetic awareness.
>
> *(Morrow)*

She acknowledged the importance of music and created a playlist with a broad range of musical styles ranging across popular, culturally specific, contemporary, experimental, ambient and classical.

Ker has not changed her approach although she does use different music depend-ing on her mood and her pupils.

> I simply moved on from having these super good teachers [to] just passing on the experience. I don't do it intellectually at all. I'm not a pedagogue. No, absolutely not.
>
> *(Ker)*

In the past, Ker would have employed a pianist to accompany her class but no longer does due to cost. While often using recordings from existing ballets, she will choose the music that is suitable to what she needs. The advantage of recordings is that the tempo will be the same every time, but she misses communication, because a good pianist very often learned what each individual dancer needed if they were doing a solo. The pianist and the teacher were a team.

Sharp, for example, uses improvised piano music by Neil McNeil, specifically recorded for use in dance classes. She notes that there is more of a balance between talking, explaining and doing.

> I use a lot less [explanation] now in that class because they're capable of doing it. I set a very basic, simply choreographed piece so that they can really just concentrate on doing it right without me doing much talking. Every now and then I'll do a class where I do a lot more.
>
> *(Sharp)*

In order to keep students interested, Morrow seeks to offer a variety of modes of learning and exploring, personalising the information specific to the individual. She likes to focus on why the participants are there, aside from the social and a little bit of adrenalised moving.

For Ker, the level of ongoing interest depends on what each individual wants to get from the class. The more comfortable they are with the technical part of the enchainment, they then can put the feeling into it, the emotion into it, the interpreta-tion of the music into it. If they need a challenge, she gives them a new enchainment.

Sharp believes that it is important for participants to get a sense of achievement and have some fun. The social aspect of coming every week and meeting same people is important, along with a strong sense of commitment to seeing through a term and seeing their bodies benefiting.

Practice: working with mature bodies

Morrow's approach is to go gently and with a solid understanding of the implications of physical restrictions and health conditions. It is important to read the situation and energy of the group.

> A ballet class for older people has to be taught really carefully and the person that's teaching has to be really well trained in ballet, so that they understand, intimately, what rotation of the hip is, support of the knee and the ankle, the action of the foot and landing. All of those things have to be absolutely under their belt, to be able to observe in others and explain . . . and kind of train into an old body.
>
> *(Morrow)*

In this context, Morrow's preference is to teach contemporary rather than ballet. She reflects that the risk for someone who decides to learn ballet at 60 is much higher than for someone who trained as a child. It may be a childhood dream, but ballet is so codified and so formalised and requires mastery of certain steps, whereas Morrow's contemporary method has a looser feeling and offers a bigger 'frame' than that of ballet.

Younger teachers should be particularly careful when demonstrating those extreme moves. Morrow prefers to 'move with' and 'alongside' people while they are 'doing' rather than demonstrating, which has the potential to intimidate. Again, she emphasises the importance of being really explicit about the intention of this experience in the mature context.

> As they're moving, they [can say] what they're feeling and what they experience, because articulating and verbalising that is something that people can witness, they can see it. Then when you're teaching and you start using that same language, they've seen a visual of it, they've seen somebody else experience that, they can actually [verbalise] 'I'm feeling my feet push off the floor'. 'Now I'm feeling my spine swing over to the left, and now my arm is taking a big arc with my longest finger out through space'. So [they are] 'languaging' the body.
>
> *(Morrow)*

For Ker, it is important that you connect with each pupil individually and she believes that the barre is the most important preparation for the centre work.

Sharp believes in checking in with people with injuries before the class starts and giving people options of exercises during the class. She encourages people to tell her what they know and what's happening with their body. 'It's something that they take responsibility for, quite easily'. However, her focus is on teaching technique correctly, so that they don't injure themselves in her class. She is very careful to watch as much as she can, even when demonstrating.

At the beginning of the class, Morrow will enquire about existing injuries and the general mood of the group on the day, and she will remind them to work within their own ability – it's not a competition. She sets the premise and the expectations of the class at the outset and believes there should be a very clear description for people before they step into that arrangement. From there, she will encourage participants to go at their own pace.

Ker states that she teaches and caters for the individual in the class allowing for opportunities for interpretation and self-expression.

Sharp teaches her beginners' class from the middle, on the barre, within the group so they can all easily see her. Everything faces the front, and she asks them to swap sides on the barre rather than them turning around to reduce confusion. In the more experienced class, she moves around all the time. Emotional safety is really important for Sharp.

> If something funny happens, I try to laugh, not at them, but laugh at myself. It doesn't matter if anything goes wrong. I'm very clear that it's about enjoying it, having a go, doing the best at the time that you can; not the best that you can ever do but the best at that time.
>
> *(Sharp)*

Her focus is on always giving them a sense of achievement; that in every class there has to be a little achievement of something getting better. She gives a lot of verbal encouragement and 'permission' that they can laugh at themselves sometimes,

> but I also know you can't do that with everyone. So, the psychologist in me is very careful who I can say what to.
>
> *(Sharp)*

Reflections

Morrow teaches what interests her. She continues to explore and uses the class as a way of focusing on how to communicate that and of making public her personal investigations. She does not teach in lots of conventional settings.

> What's happened in dance is that that kind of lineage goes way back and inherent within that language is a disconnect between the people in the room and the person leading those people. Each participant has an experience of their own moving. It might be limited but it doesn't matter. [Teachers have]

got to find their own language about . . . and sense of exploration, of communicating. Do I communicate better with my hands? Do I communicate better with my voice? Do I communicate better bringing in visuals to aid our imagination? Sound? Primarily, it's about making it your own.

(Morrow)

Ker enjoys doing something that's of 'use to somebody'.

I teach because people need it. They come because they want it and need it and I've got the ability to teach and the experience. So that's what I do. You just hope that you're helping to improve on their own ability. Apart from it being ballet it's good for them physically.

(Ker)

For Sharp, who had basically given up teaching prior to taking on these classes, it is the sense of challenge that motivates her. She enjoys that she has to think every week about how she's going to develop a concept or where she's going to take them to next. She views clips of classes from around the world looking for ideas about trying to teach a concept, and she admits that she is learning about different ways of teaching different bodies – mature bodies.

For Morrow, this experience has highlighted the limited view that people carry of what dance is. It has reminded her of how assumptions prevail and the difficulty of changing perceptions.

It left me feeling like there is a mismatch between my professional experiences, specific deep study and understanding of movement that has alienated me from the mainstream. It made me realise how little has changed in the field, and that as an older person, I don't have the energy to convert. It has clarified my role as a mentor and teacher, and how and who I wish to work with in the future . . . outside of the convention of running classes. (Morrow)

Teaching mature dancers has kept Ker connected to dance.

Without teaching it would have been very difficult, because what else would you do? Also, I believe the music always has to come first. The dancer has to interpret the music. The other way around is hopeless.

(Ker)

For Sharp, the major thing that has come up is the importance of understanding the bodies that are in front of you and not going in with your own expectations.

I have learned that flexibility is really important. To teach mature dancers don't go in with expectations of what you think they can do . . . because you might be disappointed and then you'll be lost as to where to go and what to do with them. They want to learn, they want to have fun, they want to feel like a dancer.

(Sharp)

Conclusion

nipaluna/Hobart has developed a reputation for offering mature dance practice, but even amongst the three teaching artists interviewed, there is a wide range of practice. Wendy Morrow, Judith Ker and Lucinda Sharp have generously offered insights into their wealth of experience in this area. These are three different teachers with diverse interests and approaches, yet their students seem to fall into familiar cohorts. Those who find themselves working in this increasingly growing area and want to know best practices, safe dance approaches and creative methods for working with older dancers will find a wealth of knowledge in their words. For a new teacher, coming into a situation with a set format of a class, there is an opportunity to bring something fresh and of yourself to inform a class situation emerging from knowledge and engagement with your body that could be useful to other people.

Reference

Graham, L. (2005). The risks we take – Investigating a model for risk stratification and recognition of competency in dance teaching. In K. Vincs (Ed.), *Proceedings of dance rebooted: Initializing the grid* (pp. 1–9). Canberra: Ausdance National on behalf of the Tertiary Dance Council of Australia.

Notes

Wendy Morrow, face to face interview, recorded and transcribed using Otter.ai, Bellerive, Tasmania, 09/06/2022

Judith Ker, face to face interview, recorded and transcribed using Otter.ai, Battery Point, Tasmania, 09/06/2022

Lucinda Sharp, face to face interview, recorded and transcribed using Otter.ai, Bellerive, Tasmania, 09/06/2022

4.5

TRADITIONAL APPRENTICESHIP IN CONTEMPORARY TIMES

Lim Fei Shen

Caren Cariño

> A teacher is a sculptor . . . . She starts out with a lump of clay and works away
> at it to reveal something spectacular within.
>
> *(Dance student, Nanyang Academy of Fine Arts, Singapore)*

Traditional apprenticeship is evidenced in teaching and learning throughout history when the tasks or skills are "externally visible, and thus readily available to both student and teacher for observation, comment, refinement, and correction, and the process bears relatively transparent relationship to concrete products" (Collins, 2005, p. 48). Traditional apprenticeship not only includes "meaningful real world tasks . . . in a social or functional context" (Collins, 2005, p. 48), such as sewing and carpentry, but also comprises the performing arts such as music, theatre and dance making. A teacher is deemed to be a master, a confirmed expert or a renowned practitioner, and is usually an adult family, guardian or member of the community (Collins, 2005). A student, also called an apprentice, is chosen by a master and is privileged to the master's profound and personal knowledge, including "secrets" of the form (Brandon, 1967). In return, the apprentice is often obligated to the master for this honour (Brandon, 1967; Kirschner & Hendrick, 2020).

Traditional apprenticeship eventually evolved into instruction by practitioners with formal qualifications to teach. Students select and pay a teacher or organisation to be trained or educated. In this context, Anthony Grasha, a cognitive and social psychologist, describes three teaching styles, or patterns of beliefs and behaviours, that can be associated with traditional apprenticeship. The "expert" teacher possesses, displays and transmits knowledge and expertise, as well as expects students to be well-prepared and proficient. The "formal authoritative" teacher determines the learning outcomes, expectations and rules of conduct, and provides feedback concerning the correct, standard and acceptable way to do things. The "personal model" teacher establishes how to think and behave, and expects students to observe and emulate him/her (Grasha, 1994).

DOI: 10.4324/9781003307624-29

Additionally, psychologist Raymond Cattell describes "crystallised intelligence", another characteristic associated with traditional apprenticeship. A teacher with crystallised intelligence is typically an elderly person. This person has the wisdom to transmit his/her immense knowledge gained by many years of acculturation and learning (Cattell, 1971).

In the late 20th century, as educational systems developed, the relevance of teacher-centred education was scrutinised vis-à-vis student-centred education. Teacher-centred education focuses on the teacher and teaching. Teachers transmit their knowledge and expertise, and they direct learners' practice. On the other hand, student-centred education places emphasis on the learner and learning. Teachers consider the abilities, interests and needs of students, as well as their learning styles, to facilitate learning, and students are encouraged to actively participate and experience (Brown, 2008) through collaboration and problem-solving. In spite of the advancement of institutionalised education, traditional apprenticeship is still regarded as an effective means of knowledge and skills transmission and acquisition. Howard Gardner, an American cognitive psychologist, reasoned that the "judicious introduction and integration of apprenticeship methods within a scholastic setting should yield students whose potential for understanding is engaged and enhanced" (Gardner, 1991, p. 181).

This case narrative is about Lim Fei Shen (born 1945), considered one of Singapore's early doyens of contemporary dance. A well-respected choreographer and a veteran dance educator in Singapore, Lim obtained a dance degree in 1969 from Folkwang Hochshule Music, Theatre and Dance, Essen, Germany, where she was a student of Kurt Joos, regarded as the founder of Tanz Theater, also known as an expressionist dance form. Lim went on to obtain a Master of Fine Arts in Dance (1992) from Tisch School of the Arts, New York University, USA, where she studied with Phyllis Lamhut, a revered American artist-educator. Lim has choreographed several contemporary works and taught dance exploration and creation at Nanyang Academy of Fine Arts, a tertiary arts institution, for more than 15 years. Her teaching style and personal attributes, as perceived by her dance improvisation students from 2020–2021, depict her as a master and describe her approach to teaching and learning as traditional apprenticeship. Hence, Lim exemplifies the practice of traditional apprenticeship in contemporary times.

Grasha's expert and personal models, characteristic of traditional apprenticeship, would see Lim as a reputable dance practitioner and an enigma of dance creation and teaching. James Brandon, an American academic specialising in Asian theatre maintains that "almost without exception the best performers are considered the best teachers . . . . Famous performers are besieged by eager youngsters who wish to learn from them" (Brandon, 1967, p. 155). Lim also exemplifies Raymond Cattell's notion of crystallised intelligence, whereby her senior age is acknowledged and respected by her students. One of Lim's students describe her as "a very well known dance artist in Singapore, and very rare for teachers to teach in her age. Her class shows the experience that she went through throughout the years". Other comments included that when she

> shared her life stories with us, when she told us all about her dance journey and how she started dancing, I found it to be very inspiring and it made me see her as an amazing artist and choreographer.

> What impressed me most was the day we told her that she showed us the dance she had choreographed before, as well as some wonderful dance photos. She also shared her choreography experience with us, and I really saw in her what an artist should be like.

> She is filled with enthusiasm and passion and it is definitely shown through her years of dancing and teaching. She is also very creative and has many ideas which can be seen through her choreographies. Despite her age, she is always energetic and passionate about the things she teaches in every class.

> I value Lim Fei Shen's experiences. She has a lot of experience as a choreographer, dancer, and leader. It's always nice to listen to her advice as they are very insightful and coming from someone who has spent many years in the field.

Lim's students also describe her as a teacher who is very much in control of their learning. This "formal authoritative" role saw Lim as providing "step-by-step instructions on how to complete the activity of that day"; "very particular and strict on what she wants us to do during class and she will make sure that she repeated the instruction a few times so we know what we are supposed to do"; "extremely clear in what she's looking for when we are given tasks"; and "she also does not like it if we do not follow exactly as she said". As a "formal authority", Lim also guided students to accomplish exemplary creative outcomes. Her students reflected that Lim would "give us comments and critics to our improvisation on what is right and wrong"; "She is very fundamental and develops our thinking from many angles"; "She is very focused when doing all things. She gives students a lot of suggestions to let them know how to do better"; and she "sets high expectations of us".

Although student-centredness has been promoted in education today, teacher-centredness – characteristic of traditional apprenticeship – is still relevant. This is evidenced in the master–apprentice teaching style of Lim Fei Shen. The reflections by her students reveal that she is an expert and formal authority fortified by being a personal model privileged with crystallised intelligence (Grasha, 1994; Cattell, 1971).

> Lim Fei Shen is like a compass, she points in a direction . . . to navigate our own learning journey. She provides the true north, and helps us find a worthy course – one that will challenge our skills in the open learning seas.
> *(Dance student, Nanyang Academy of Fine Arts, Singapore)*

Traditional apprenticeship will still have a place in education, provided that teachers continue to be valued as experts and authorities who have the ability to apply knowledge and lead with personal experience and wisdom (Cattell, 1971). However, the relevance of "cognitive apprenticeship" associated with student-centred education should not be discounted. Therefore, this author is interested in the possible convergence of the physical and explicit aspects of traditional apprenticeship and the cerebral and implicit aspects of cognitive apprenticeship in the context of dance education. Perhaps looking more closely, teachers like Lim Fei Shen may already be at the crossroads of traditional and cognitive apprenticeships.

References

Brandon, J. (1967). *Theatre in Southeast Asia*. Cambridge, MA: Harvard University Press.

Brown, J. K. (2008). Student-centered instruction: Involving students in their own education. *Music Educators Journal, 94*(5).

Cattell, R. B. (1971). *Abilities: Their structure, growth, and action*. Boston, MA: Houghton Mifflin.

Collins, A. (2005). Cognitive apprenticeship (Chapter 4). In *The Cambridge handbook of the learning sciences*. Cambridge: Cambridge University Press.

Gardner, H. (1991). *The unschooled mind. How children think and how schools should teach*. New York: Basic Books.

Grasha, A. (1994). A matter of style: The teacher as expert, formal authority, personal model, facilitator, and delegator. In *College teaching* (Vol. 42). Washington, DC: Heldref.

Kirschner, P., & Hendrick, C. (2020). Cognitive apprenticeship revisited. *American Educator, 44*(3), 37–40.

SECTION 5

Dance therapy and well-being

FIGURE 5.0 Dancer: Ella, the *WINGSPAN* project

Source: Photograph by Michael Bond

DOI: 10.4324/9781003307624-30

5.1

AN EXAMINATION OF THE FACILITATION OF DANCE PRACTICE FOR OLDER ADULTS

A focus group discussion between practitioners working in community settings across New Zealand, Australia and England

Francine Hills and Barbara Snook

Introduction

New Zealand and Australia are both facing the challenges associated with ageing populations. Older people are expected to make up approximately a quarter of New Zealand's total population by 2051 (Lavery, 2007). "Increasing longevity is an historic triumph and population ageing is emerging as one of the major global issues of the 21st century" (Kendig et al., 2016, p. 3). Within an ageing population, a need for creative ageing is important, with evidence that creative arts improve personal feelings of wellbeing (Cann, 2016). Health and social care intervention programmes with older adults have acknowledged the importance of dance as an avenue of exercise that introduces expression, communication and socialisation, contributing to improved emotional, mental and physical health (Amans, 2013). Dance for older adults is a developing field of creative practice in which the experiences of dance provide artistic opportunity and support the health and wellbeing of those aged older than 65. According to People Dancing's (2016) report on older people's dance practice, "dance and older people, just like any other kind of participatory dance, is diverse in its manifestation and driven by a multiplicity of purposes and ambitions" (p. 6).

Grounded in the conviction that people who have lived with similar experiences are often the best source of expert knowledge about these experiences (Thorne et al., 1997), we used a focus group discussion to explore the art of facilitation as described by seven dance practitioners in their older adults' dance practice. Spanning New Zealand, Australia and the United Kingdom, where we had contacts working in this specialised field, we approached the following group of dance practitioners whose practices focus on teaching, researching, and

DOI: 10.4324/9781003307624-31

training future dance artists. We collaborated to explore what, how and why we do what we do. Francine facilitated the focus group discussion and Barbara participated as a practitioner. The practitioners involved are each well known in their field and have agreed to be identified within the chapter. They are as follows:

Diane Amans	U.K.
Julie Chenery	Australia
Gail Hewton	Australia
Carlene Newall de Jesus	New Zealand
Suzanne Renner	New Zealand
Barbara Snook	New Zealand
Kerry-Ann Stanton	New Zealand

The research aim of this chapter gives voice to the processes and creative choices that shape practice and pedagogy whilst "framing the implicit knowledge emerging from craft practices" (Fortin et al., 2021, p. 14). Beyond recognising that dance provides a range of benefits, we seek to address a distinct under-representation in both qualitative and quantitative research that attends to the specifics of facilitation (Fortin et al., 2021).

Definition of dance for older adults

Dance for older adults can refer to groups with participants aged 65 and older. Carlene commented that this "is false simplification of what is a *really* diverse group of participants and types of sessions". As she pointed out, we would never consider a 20-year-old and a 50-year-old within the same classification, and yet within older people's dance, these age differences are not uncommon. "Relevant terminology for those aged 50–105+ years is lacking, and they are not one cohort but individuals and groups with different life-styles and needs" (Jacqueline Richards, 2018, p. 10). Richards (2018) extends her observation proposing that ageism is an unchallenged societal issue. Whilst this is beyond the remit of this chapter, it is raised here in acknowledgement that the stereotyping and bracketing of older people and older people's dance as a homogenous group does not serve the dance sector nor the participants. When conversing around the factors shaping artistic practice in this field, we are speaking to specific groups of older adults, delivered in specific contexts. As such, the professional make-up of this group of practitioners is a blend of dance educators and academics, community dance artists and programme leaders. Table 5.1 provides an outline of the groups that are taught by the artists involved in this chapter.

TABLE 5.1 A Summary of the Focus Group's Professional Practice

Name	Diane Amans	Julie Chenery	Gail Hewton	Suzanne Renner	Barbara Snook	Kerry-Ann Stanton	Carlene Newall de Jesus
Based in	UK	Australia	Australia	New Zealand	New Zealand	New Zealand	New Zealand
Type of dance	Creative activities	Contemporary and jazz, modified to suit the participants	Contemporary and jazz-based, includes a variety of dance genres and styles, modified to suit the participants. A mix of seated and standing movement	Technique based. Variety of dance genre. Performance oriented	Creative activities	Creative activities in a contemporary style modified to suit the participants. Movement meditation	Seated creative dance. Choreographic dance projects
Group	One-to-one and small groups. Mature movers. Dance artists and activity leaders	Over 50s. People living with dementia	All classes for over-60s with a health and wellbeing focus, particularly falls prevention, emotional wellbeing and social connection	Over 50s	People living with dementia. Tertiary students. Teachers	Over 60s	People living with dementia. Over 60s. Tertiary students. People with mild cognitive impairment. Young people, children and teenagers
Delivery context	Hospitals. Care homes. Community-based halls and centres	Local gym. Community halls. Senior citizens centres	Community-based (local hall, leisure centre, retirement villages)	Community-based local studio	Retirement villages. Universities	Community-based halls and centres	Retirement village and community-based dance companies

The focus group provides reflections on practice which are then viewed through an interpretive lens. Fortin et al. (2021) use the analogy of opening a "black box" (p. 2) in reference to making explicit the "inner components and the logic of action" (p. 2) of those leading sessions. Although speaking within the context of dance and health, Fortin has published two articles, both drawing attention to the distinct lack of pedagogical detail within dance and health studies. We liken/extend the black box analogy to the separate but often overlapping field of dance for older adults and in particular, dance for dementia and dance for those with limited mobility. We concur with Fortin et al. (2021), that: "As long as the dance classes themselves remain a mystery, any evidence of their impact will fail to provide a solid contribution to research" (p. 3).

Methodology

An interpretive methodology was selected as a framework for analysing and organising the experiences and reflections of the seven facilitators (Vaismoradi et al., 2013). We have documented our discussions around themes that emerged, beginning with quotes from the participants, followed by a discussion and interpretation.

Dance as a fun and joyful practice

DIANE: I've got to create the right conditions for people to have fun and enjoy themselves. The top of the list is fun.

KERRY-ANN: She is experiencing exquisite joy, she is turning up every week, she is already noticing after four or five weeks that her inner being is loosening, as well as her shoulders. And for me, that's it. Whatever you call that experience. That's it.

SUZANNE: The classes must be enjoyable for me to teach, as well as enjoyable for the participants.

KERRY-ANN: I do this work because it is a complete sense of joy in my own life – so in that sense, it's completely selfish. I offer dance because I'm dance passionate.

BARB: I love doing this. I love teaching. I think I bring my best self to dance classes.

All focus group attendees agreed that fun was at the top of their list of outcomes. The classes are about fun and enjoyment, for without it, we believe that the attendees would no longer attend the sessions. The articulation of joy was expressed directly as a driving goal for participants, and equally important for the practitioners themselves. Perrin et al. (2008) theorise that "there is a certain disposition, a certain personality type" (p. 118) that is better equipped to enact fun and enjoyment.

Whilst not necessarily what we expected to uncover in our focus group discussion, the implications of 'joy' through pedagogical approaches in this field suggest that those leading sessions find ways to nurture the playful spirit of their participants.

This would seem an essential part of any training programme. Indeed, playfulness has been argued to be crucial to developing coping strategies (Guitard et al., 2005), arguably a necessary resource for any dance practitioner.

Intrinsic personality: how we teach

Following on from the discussion around being able to be a playful person, the participants turned their attention to their own personalities and how this informs their teaching.

JULIE: Because I'm quite introverted, I have to turn into the extrovert – so that's a constant switch that I have to make when I'm facilitating.

KERRY-ANN: Sometimes that means being really real myself. I might have a wobble. But we do often talk at the end that however we've arrived, we leave differently because of the experience of dancing together. I try to stay present with the group and be able to spin on a diamond or do something different.

GAIL: There have been times when it can be a struggle when I've got serious stuff going on in life, and what I find is that I've got to switch into my performer mode. Leaving stuff out in the wings, coming onto the stage. It's an honest performance, but I see it like that sometimes. I need to go to a different place in order to be the best facilitator for the people I'm working with.

CARLENE: I can really listen and watch and get as many clues as possible about that group and what the energy is and what the vibe is and what they're feeling into . . . or not feeling.

BARB: I go by intuition and look at what's happening, whether people are enjoying it and if I need to insert something or say something that might just lift the moment, well, then I do that.

Intuition was mentioned by Barb and Carlene as a fundamental principle of this practice, an element of facilitation that grows and develops over time as facilitators learn to trust their intuition and read how the group are feeling on any one day. In an interview with Brierley (2014), David Leventhal describes the connection between the practitioner and participants: "It's deep empathy and intuition, I hope, and the thing that's the hardest to explain to a new teacher" (p. 15).

Dance as artistic practice

As we focussed on the 'what' of dance practice for older adults, creativity as an integral part of any dance class was referenced by all. Creativity in this instance refers to the creation of movement, expression and artistry. Fortin et al. (2021) noted, "It is one thing for a facilitator to deploy artistry, but another to nurture the artistry of the participants, while being attentive to the participants' own initiatives in that regard" (p. 11). The following attends to how the practitioners in this study bring artistry into the older adult's dance arena.

DIANE: It might just be a structure like opening and closing . . . they could just open and close hands, whole bodies, eyes, mouths, whatever.

GAIL: So, you know, we've done a lovely little, 'uncaptured moments' where we talk about a moment in your life that you wish you had a photo of, what would be that moment . . . so it's all about them, their stories.

BARB: After the warm-up, they might do little tasks to do with memory and feelings and things like that. They might work in groups and create some wonderful freeze frames, as an example.

The engagement of imagination and creative impetus initiates movement from an internal place, allowing each person "to offer their own dance to the group" (Brierley, 2014, p. 6). As a pedagogical example, the Dance for Parkinson's model strongly emphasises the use of gesture and metaphor, with the use of image as a fundamental starting point (Brierley, 2014). Related to the 'what' of the session is the noted difference in perspective when practice stems from a creative root as opposed to a functional root. There is a difference between giving a movement instruction and setting up movement instruction as imagery. The former causes a cognitive response through following instructions that explain what and how to do the movement, whilst the latter can offer the opportunity to create and interpret movement (Chappell & Craft, 2011).

For Diane, working one-to-one in hospital environments, creativity serves as "something totally different from medical interventions. It's an opportunity to share something creative which distracts her from the other things". Diane speaks here to an artistic process, separate and existing alongside the medical disciplines.

Several facilitators illustrated how movement tasks are set up in response to a theme. For Suzanne, the well-known genre of steampunk had been the starting point for devising a waltz. Importantly, it was acknowledged that devising opportunities for creative expression are not necessarily a given in any one class and neither is it always a sought-after outcome for their participants. In line with our interpretivist lens, we raise further acknowledgement that there is no one way to dance with older adults.

Shaping the delivery

DIANE: I get feedback about how it is for them. And that helps me plan next week's session. I'll go around in a circle and I'm aiming with my manner to make it clear that I'm happy to hear negative stuff, as well as positive stuff, and I will listen to what they're saying.

GAIL: I haven't done any formal feedback from filling out forms for a while, but I am constantly asking what they like, what they don't like, how they're feeling – you know: new learnings and they often now share things before I even ask which is great.

KERRY-ANN: I do an informal "what are we noticing today?"; "what have you observed or what have you noticed between when you arrived and when you are about to leave?". Often, there's some unexpected gold in those comments about what has or hasn't worked that informs the next session.

The checking in and checking out process is helpful in catering for the participants' specific physical needs, but also in understanding what is most enjoyable for them. The issue of appropriate methodological tools for evaluating practice has been raised by Fortin (2018): "research in dance for health cannot escape a space of indeterminacy, troubling to traditional medical research protocols" (p. 161). Carlene put it well: "it's a meeting of complexities. We can know that things are happening at the same time, things are addressing multiple things and yet not know exactly how, and that's the beauty of playing in this space". Whilst Fortin is keen for us to unpack the contents of 'the black box', we wonder whether this assumes that the contents can be separated one by one as a suitcase would be unpacked, or whether the contents can only be viewed as an outfit, each item layered and worn simultaneously.

Challenges and new experiences

JULIE: One session is at my local gym, so mostly they're very active and agile people who have found the main challenge comparing their gym experience with the dance experience. And they're just stunned about, "oh my goodness, my memory". I've seen such a difference over the last year, that now they're getting more interested in learning longer sequences.

CARLENE: We don't suddenly stop enjoying new experiences, and we don't suddenly stop enjoying a beautiful song that feels like the kind of music you just want to move to. So, kind of figuring out what's going to challenge the group in a nice way. So possibly creatively, or if it's a group that I've been working with long term like what are the next kinds of things in the task that's going to bring a new experience . . . just unravel the possibilities.

SUZANNE: I made up a line dance. But we don't repeat front, side, back . . . . I try to make the choreography a bit more challenging than that.

Inclusion/person-centred/adaptability

SUZANNE: Because of the people I am teaching, I have to always be aware that they might not be able to get into that space that I think of spontaneously.

GAIL: I look at where people are at and what their experience is. Age is not really the thing. It's where they're at and where they feel comfortable about placing themselves. We work out what type of class or session will suit them.

CARLENE: A 90-year-old with severe dementia is not going to have the same capacity to communicate or convey an emotional journey or what they're bringing to class that day in the same way that a younger participant might. We know that dance is that thing that's guiding. Recognise all the differences.

KERRY-ANN: Often, we have to have different ways of speaking about it to be an invitation to different people for the same outcomes. Some people will come for social reasons. Some people will come for exercise, albeit dance. I think there's something about staying very open about how we speak to and invite people to the sessions.

Practitioners were keen to emphasise how important it was to adjust to who was in the space, and what was known about their medical history or contra-indication for exercise, and being alert to the responsibility of keeping bodies safe.

The facilitators offer different classes aimed at different interests and abilities. Classes ranged from instructional to much more improvisational. Suzanne's classes appeared to be much more instructive: "I will call out instruction. And I'm in there with them. I will demonstrate movements such as 16–24 counts, on the spot work, three or four sequences with arms, shoulders, hips, foot work. Points, flexes, pliés or travelling across the floor in waves"; whereas Diane speaks from a different point on the continuum: "I don't want them to copy Diane for an hour".

We observed a range of social – as well as physical and emotional – factors at play within the sessions as discussed by the focus group participants with comments revealing their developed ability to determine when and how to introduce extra complexity and challenge to the group. Within many classes, as mentioned by Gail, some sections will see some participants standing, some sitting and some will work between two rows of chairs so that they can hold on and maintain their balance whilst still offering the opportunity for safe challenge. A facilitator's capacity to adapt to the needs of the class participants is crucial (Fortin et al., 2021, p. 13). This is not only to gently challenge as previously discussed, but to ensure continued interest in new and enjoyable content. Sarah Gregor et al. (2020) raise "the critical importance of having a dance instructor who is encouraging, adaptive, and mindful in the way they conduct their class" (p. 2628). As in any type of teaching, the focus is on facilitating for individual learning and enjoyment. Choice needs to be at the heart of participatory arts processes. For many people, choices diminish in older age.

Music

Music is an important consideration in community dance classes. The participants in this study use a variety of music styles from ABBA to classical. Sometimes music is chosen as a meditative background, but most often the music is chosen for its ability to encourage people to dance. Music can be chosen to stimulate memories for older adults, or to introduce something new.

BARB: They are enjoying the music alongside the dance – and together, they make art.

CARLENE: Music for me is a big anchor to feeling like I've got things to draw from. My older participants see me as very young. I'm probably not as young as they think I am, but I embrace that in the music that I use. I find it's a really nice bridge to come in with something that is unfamiliar . . . it builds a nice bridge of conversation and really thinking into the music.

SUZANNE: I have to like the music that I've chosen, and if the participants really don't like a piece of music, they show me that. I try to make whatever sequence I'm giving them really link to the music I've chosen.

KERRY-ANN: Often my musical choices are determined by what's going on in the world, reflective of the seasons or an event in our community, or something that I know people will have a relationship with or interest to explore.

DIANE: I sometimes make conscious decisions whether to use music that is familiar to them, bringing memories and it will have an association. Sometimes, I deliberately use music they won't have heard with no associations for them – right things for them at that moment, responding in a way that is not cluttered up with any memories. There's not any right or wrong way.

Research exists regarding the positive benefits of music in the lives of older adults, specifically for those with dementia or conditions associated with a lack of memory (Elliot & Gardner, 2016). There has been wide interest in the application of reminiscence processes for health and wellbeing, with connections being found between reminiscence and the alleviation of depression in old age. Lauren Istvandity (2017) has researched the area of music and reminiscence therapy and posits that, "music can trigger autobiographical memories with strong emotional content, and that an individual's personal memories are closely tied to their self-identity" (p. 19).

It was clear from these practitioners' comments that reminiscence is often a part of the mix of arts practice by and with older people. What is pertinent to conversation surrounding the 'what' of practice is the considered choice that facilitators make in their musical choices. We found from this focus group that those working in the dementia field were employing music that the participants were likely to know from their past. Those working with different groups and catering for different needs, used a variety of music, ranging from known to unknown, but always chosen for a reason. Music choices within this focus group highlight the potency and potentiality of music for supporting specific purpose, as well as setting the mood and tone of any session.

Conclusion

We recognise that dance within an older adults' context is often framed as an intervention or a means of alleviating, reducing or attending to the problems associated with ageing. We do not consider what we do as therapy, as there are specialists who do this work. A focus on health and wellness outcomes are, however, applicable to this study. The main focus of this work appears centred on the values of the dance practice. We concur with the People Dancing (n.d.) website (2020) that states these values as:

- Placing the participant at the centre of the activity
- Respecting differences

- Establishing dance as an empowering tool for participants in the dance and the rest of their lives
- Being inclusive rather than exclusive.

Dance for older adults within a community dance context is about the guiding and encouraging of participants though the process of engaging with the dance, regardless of age or associated health conditions.

The focus group mirrored the diversity of life in its varied pedagogies and practice. From our conversations, we interpreted that the practitioners were not entering the space with a lesson plan with problems of old age to be solved, or deficits to be addressed. Dance was not spoken of as a solution to the 'problems' of the ageing self, centred rather around how dance can facilitate Kerry-Ann's expression of "exquisite joy" and create opportunities for newness. The joy and love that practitioners have for their work is ultimately linked to their personalities, their own personal growth as humans as well as professional artists.

This articulation of pedagogy raises further questions for knowledge transfer for this growing sector. How do we teach the intrinsic qualities of joy, intuition and creativity so clearly iterated within this group? There is an increasing need within the dance sector to address issues of teacher training and professional development. Drawing authoritative conclusions about 'best practice' in dance for older people seems almost impossible when considering the diversity in all variables. Such variables include – but are not limited to – the personality of the facilitator, the processes that shape content, the genre of dance, and the context in which they deliver.

References

Amans, D. (2013). *Age and dancing: Older people and community dance practice*. London: Palgrave Macmillan.

Brierley, M. (2014) Gathering practitioner and participant perceptions of dance for people with Parkinson's. *Winston Churchill Memorial Trust*, 1–32. Retrieved from www.wcmt.org.uk/fellows/reports/gathering-practitioner-and participant perceptions-dance-people-parkinson

Cann, P. (2016). Something to get out of bed for: Creative arts for a happily ageing population. *Working with Older People*, *20*(4), 190–194.

Chappell, K., & Craft, A. (2011). Creative learning conversations: producing living dialogic spaces. *Educational Research*, *53*(3), 363–385.

Elliot, M., & Gardner, P. (2016). The role of music in the lives of older adults with dementia ageing in place: A scoping review. *Dementia*, *17*(2), 199–213.

Fortin, S. (2018). Tomorrow's dance and health partnership: The need for a holistic view. *Research in Dance Education*, *19*(2), 152–166. doi:10.1080/14647893.2018.1463360

Fortin, S., Beaudry, L., Caroline, R., Hélène, D., McKinley, P., Trudelle, S., & Swaine, B. (2021). All dancing bodies matter: Six facilitators aiming for inclusion and wellbeing for people with special needs. *Research in Dance Education*, 1–18.

Gregor, S., Vaughan-Graham, J., Wallace, A., Walsh, H., & Patterson, K. K. (2020). Structuring community-based adapted dance programs for persons post-stroke: A qualitative study. *Disability and Rehabilitation*, *43*(18), 2621–2631. doi:10.1080/09638288.2019.1708978

Guitard, P., Ferland, F., & Dutil, E. (2005). Toward a better understanding of playfulness in adults. *OTJR: Occupation, Participation and Health, 25,* 9–22. doi:10.1177/153944920502500103

Istvandity, L. (2017). Combing music and reminiscence therapy interventions for wellbeing in elderly populations: A systematic review. *Complementary Therapies in Clinical Practice, 28,* 18–25.

Kendig, H., McDonald, P., & Piggott, J. (Eds.). (2016). Introduction: A multidisciplinary approach to ageing. In *Population ageing and Australia's future.* Canberra: Australian National University Press.

Lavery, N. (2007). *New Zealanders: Getting older, doing more.* Wellington: Office for Senior Citizens, Ministry of Social Development.

People Dancing (2016). *Older people's dance activities: The first UK survey.* Leicester: People Dancing.

People Dancing (n.d.) Professional code of conduct. Retrieved January 16, 2020, from https://www.communitydance.org.uk/membership-services-and-join/professional-code-of-conduct

Perrin, T., May, H., & Anderson, E. (2008). *Wellbeing in dementia an occupational approach for therapists and carers* (2nd ed.). Edinburgh; New York: Churchill Livingstone/Elsevier.

Richards, J. (2018). *Active older people participating in creative dance-challenging perceptions* [Doctoral dissertation], Middlesex University.

Thorne, S., Kirkham, S. R., & MacDonald-Emes, J. (1997). Focus on qualitative methods. Interpretive description: A non-categorical qualitative alternative for developing nursing knowledge. *Research in Nursing & Health, 20*(2), 169–177.

Vaismoradi, M., Turunen, H., & Bondas, T. (2013). Content analysis and thematic analysis: Implications for conducting a qualitative descriptive study. *Nursing & Health Sciences, 15*(3), 398–405.

5.2

THE HAPPIEST HOUR IN THE WEEK

Memory Dance and Dance Movement Therapy for elderly people living with dementia

Helle Winther

Introduction

People living with dementia often experience memory problems, mood swings, loss of independence, and difficulties in communication (Karkou & Meekums, 2017). They may have difficulties in conversation and perhaps also with even recognizing their own families. Thus, they risk becoming lonely, depressed, passive, and isolated. Often their close relatives are also very affected when their mothers, fathers, grandparents, or spouses quietly disappear into the landscape of forgetfulness. Many individuals with dementia live in care centers all over the world. There it can feel as though time stands still. But feelings do not get dementia, and the living language of the body is accessible all through life. Therefore, dance can create contact and awaken the joy of movement and positive memories. This chapter focuses on why and how *Dance Movement Therapy* (DMT) and the dance form *Memory Dance* can be used with individuals with dementia. DMT is a multidimensional arts-based therapy form, which in its practice must be guided by dance movement therapists with an internationally recognized qualification. Memory Dance is a simply designed recall-inspired movement method that can be facilitated by the caregiving staff. Here dance, music, song, and warm-hearted caregivers, together with the elderly, have the possibility to create what in many places is termed "the happiest hour in the week."

This chapter illustrates DMT through examples from international research, and Memory Dance through research, experiences from practice, stories from caregiving staff, and cooperation spanning many years with the Danish Alzheimer Association.

Dementia: an illness with a negative spiral

There are more than 200 different illnesses which entail dementia, the most common of which is Alzheimers. People living with dementia may have symptoms

DOI: 10.4324/9781003307624-32

such as memory loss and mood swings (Karkou & Meekums, 2017). This may also involve personality changes, neuropsychiatric symptoms, and increased use of medication (Bergh et al., 2011; Bonde & Ridder, 2017). Due to these symptoms, individuals suffering from dementia often withdraw into themselves and thus risk becoming lonely, depressed, and isolated. Therefore, it is often difficult for them to involve in social engagement and maintain experiencing moments in everyday life that give them pleasure and enjoyment (Bonde & Ridder, 2017; Nyström & Lauritzen, 2005). Thus, a negative spiral may easily arise which affects the progression of the illness in an unfortunate way. However, bodily awareness, motor functions, and centers for feelings in the brain are often not affected by the illness. Thus, it is in these areas where movement and emotional stimulation have possibilities to create experiences of connection and continuity (Nyström & Lauritzen, 2005; Palo-Bengtsson & Ekman, 2002; Baumgarten & Winther, 2023).

Even though most dementia illnesses damage memory function, research shows that musical memory remains surprisingly intact (Bonde & Ridder, 2017). Therefore, dance, song, and music can recall movement patterns from much earlier times in life. International studies show that dance can awaken joy, mirroring, and positive behavior (Palo-Bengtsson & Ekman, 2002).

In many countries, DMT is also used to work with individuals with serious illnesses, including those with psychiatric diagnoses and dementia (Karkou & Meekums, 2017; Kowarzik, 2006; Coaten & Williams, 2016; Newman-Bluestein, 2021). As DMT is a multimodal and sensual therapy form, there are many possibilities for working with DMT with elderly people with dementia (Bräuninger, 2014; Hamill et al., 2012; Newman-Bluestein; 2021; Nyström & Lauritzen, 2005; Payne et al., 2017). Throughout the world, there are 35.6 million people who suffer from dementia (Karkou & Meekums, 2017). Even though there is a growing body of literature that highlights the value of the arts and embodied practices to address the complexity of dementia, international sources point to the lack of research on both dance and DMT (Guzman-Garzia et al., 2013; Karkou & Meekums, 2017). Nevertheless, dance and DMT appear to have an especially positive potential to increase the quality of life for people with dementia – physically, psychologically, emotionally, and socially. Therefore, the connection between dance and dementia is particularly interesting.

Phenomenological inspiration and methods

> I look at this man who is my father and who has now become so unusually quiet. He almost seems like a stranger. "Hi Dad," I say, to push off that thought, "Good to see you!" He nods but does not speak. How fragile he seems! With a shudder, it strikes me that I no longer really understand my father as I always thought I did. It is as if his forgetfulness of me becomes my forgetting of who he is. Yet I feel closer to him than ever.
>
> *(van Manen, 2014, p. 254)*

This is an anecdote from a book by Max van Manen (2014). Anecdotes may be constructed from lived experience descriptions or gathered through interviews, personal experiences, and observations (van Manen, 2014). The anecdote touched me deeply, as I have had similar experiences with my own father who suffered from dementia. While his forgetfulness increased, the sound of his voice and the feeling of sitting close beside him and holding his hand became more and more meaningful – because in this way, we could still reach each other across the sea of forgetfulness. My father did not dance, as this was not possible at his care home. But we sang together. By heart.

The aim of this chapter is to illustrate the potential in working with DMT and Memory Dance for individuals with dementia. Thus, it is relevant to draw inspiration from phenomenology. Phenomenology is basically characterized by an openness for the importance of the body and movement, and for *what is experienced* (van Manen, 2014; Merleau-Ponty, 1945/2006). Within phenomenology, the body is considered to be the basis for human existence. The body is both *living* and *lived* and connected with our being in the world. We are continuously connected with each other from our earliest contact with the world. The lived body carries our experiences anchored as body memories, which connect us with other people, actualize our past, and thereby make us feel home in various situations. According to Maxine Sheets-Johnstone (2012), these memories are not an implicit knowing but rather are actually kinesthetic memories that are initially grounded in the qualitative dynamics of movement, with distinctive energetic qualities.

This chapter illustrates DMT through examples from international research. The study about Memory Dance presented in this chapter is based on earlier research and writings (Rishøj & Eckermann, 2015; Bonde & Ridder, 2017). It also builds on my own observations and experiences of participating in Memory Dance, as well as a longtime cooperation with Danish Alzheimer Association (from 2015–2021). Caregiving professionals told stories from practice, especially "Ulla," a care assistant at a nursing home who guided the Memory Dance sessions. After one of our meetings, she began to write down short stories from her practice and gave them to me. These stories may be seen as phenomenologically inspired anecdotes, which can have methodological power as they express unique stories that bring out the particular in or singularity of a certain phenomenon (van Manen, 2014). Anecdotes are very short, simple stories with a narrative structure. An anecdote usually describes a single incident with important details. It may contain several quotes about what was said and done, and it closes quickly with an effective "punch" in its last line (van Manen, 2014).

Dance Movement Therapy

Dance has played a role in human life since prehistory. Here, dance rituals accompanied major life changes. Working with movement, especially dance, as a form of healing or an early form of psychotherapy is thus perhaps as old as dance itself (Levy, 1988).

DMT, also known as Dance Therapy in the US or Dance Movement Psychotherapy (DMP) in the UK, is – like music, voice, art and drama therapy – an arts-based form of therapy. DMT is an internationally recognized therapy form defined by the European Association of Dance Movement Therapy (EADMT) as "the therapeutic use of movement to further the emotional, cognitive, physical, spiritual and social integration of the individual" (EADMT.com).

DMT is rooted in the idea that the body and the mind are inseparable (Levy, 1988). The body is basically regarded as an anchor for experiences, memories, and comprehension, and is thus related to a holistic view of the body (Koch & Harvey, 2012; Wengrover & Chaiklin, 2021; Winther, 2023). Here "relationship to 'lived-body' experience is fundamental and underpins every aspect of who we are, how we feel in ourselves and our relationship to others and the world" (Coaten & Williams, 2016, p. 163). Therefore, movement is also simultaneously connected to the present moment, the past, and the future, as well as to individuals' existential processes from birth to death (Wengrover & Chaiklin, 2021; Winther, 2023). When DMT is used with individuals with dementia, this is often in individual sessions or through artistic, creative, and improvised movement sequences in small groups. Here, it is possible to create a community and awaken joy and mirroring and diminish anxiety and depression in people with dementia (Bräuninger, 2014; Hamill et al., 2012; Nyström & Lauritzen, 2005).

For people experiencing challenges in verbal language, this can also eliminate their struggle to communicate, as they are being met by others on an embodied level (Coaten & Newmann Bluestein, 2013). DMT can thereby create space for the participants to express themselves and explore their existential processes through movement. Dance movement therapists create a resonant and trustful client-therapist relationship by attuning themselves creatively to the clients' movements, feelings and flow, supporting the client to get in touch with their resources and the embodied self (de Witte et al., 2021). This is especially important when the relationship to the self is threatened through neurodegeneration (Coaten & Williams, 2016).

In DMT, group sessions with people with dementia and other diagnoses, the circle is often used as the way the participants are placed in relation to one another. DMT researchers Elena Karampoula and Heidrun Panhofer (2018) write that the circle allows for the holding of the client's fears and anxieties through movement. The circle thereby creates a symbolic space and a physically embracing structure for the group. The synchronous movement itself, the rhythm, holding hands, and the ritual function of the circle can all help clients feel contained and held within the circle of the group.

> Holding hands in a circle may be the only active and nonthreatening way for withdrawn clients to touch and be touched in a safe and holding environment. It may be their only opportunity to be touched whatsoever.
>
> *(Karampoula & Panhofer 2018, p. 30)*

Holding hands and forming a circle are therefore common approaches especially suggested for older people in DMT. This can also be experienced as bodily emotional narratives, which unfold in rich life-giving present moments.

The present moment

The present moment is a holistically experienced moment that we often share with others (Stern, 2004). The present moment unfolds during a stretch of awareness. According to Stern, the present moment can be seen as a special kind of lived story, which is lived as it happens – not as it is told afterwards. It is of short duration and is made up mostly of feelings that unfold a sort of emotional narrative. The present moment entails also the possibility to *rewrite* what we experience as the past. Therefore, these moments are of great importance in therapeutic processes.

> The present moment can hold the past within its small grasp and the past is only 'alive' when on the stage of the present moment. The past plays a constant role in influencing what we experience from second to second. . . . Perhaps what is most important therapeutically is that one begins to see how the experience of the present moment can rewrite the past.
>
> *(Stern, 2004, p. 218)*

The sensitivity for present moments is also important in Memory Dance, which often takes place in the common living spaces or dining rooms of nursing homes.

Memory Dance

Memory Dance was originally developed by Susanne Rishøj in 2008 and is today part of the offers of Danish Alzheimer Association. Susanne Rishøj was a nurse for dementia patients, and for many years she danced herself at a local dance school. Thus, she began to wonder what would happen if music and dance were introduced at care homes. That became the start of her developing Memory Dance in close collaboration with the Alzheimer Association Foundation (Bonde & Ridder, 2017; Rishøj & Eckerman, 2015). Memory Dance is inspired by the reminiscence method (*reminisci*, to remember). It is not therapy, but a simply designed form of dance guided by specially educated dance instructors from the care personnel (Rishøj & Eckerman, 2015). Memory Dance is practiced at 700 care centers in 81 Danish municipalities. More than 1,000 employees have been educated as facilitators. The target group is primarily individuals with moderate to severe dementia (Bonde & Ridder, 2017; Rishøj & Eckerman, 2015). Memory Dance is intended to be a contact-creating and joyful space where relatives, elderly people with dementia, and the care staff dance together. Memory Dance seeks to meet the resident with dementia where she/he is, and let the dance bring what it may (Rishøj & Eckermann, 2015).

Even though many of the participants cannot remember from one week to the next that they have participated before, the dance leaves its traces and may be of great importance. The dance often takes place weekly in a light, pleasant, and familiar location, often in a dining room converted to a dance space.

The happiest hour in the week

When Memory Dance is on the daily schedule, best dresses, shirts, and ties are brought out; this goes for the residents, as well as for the care staff and relatives. In the dance, everyone is herself or himself on an equal footing. Before the dance starts, a circle of chairs and wheelchairs is formed. Here, all are included and can see all the others.

In this way, a circle is formed in which all participants may sense, notice, and move to the music, while at the same time, there is a dance space in the middle, as in ancient ritual dances. Then the care home residents, relatives, and staff dance and sing together. Everyone can participate when the music of his or her youth is played. Those with psychiatric diagnoses and dementia can also participate; the space is large enough so that they may sit to one side, but without being isolated. The dancing and music often awaken joy in movement and positive memories. When the music starts, the participants dance together in the middle of the circle in pairs. Hands are stretched out, and the dance steps of their youth, song, and play fill the room. Many older people also dance in their wheelchairs. In the embrace of the dance, a safe – and for many, a recognizable – sensory memory is created, and the caregiving staff tell in their stories that some of the elderly also begin to flirt a little with each other in the same way that they did when they were very young.

Time and time again, the facilitators have reported that music and dance invite all the participants to moving, surprising, and often very joy-filled sessions. They have also emphasized how important it is that they as caregiving staff dare to be *in* contact and bodily present in the dance. If they feel challenged by dancing, it easily affects the openness and the experiences of the elderly people with dementia.

At the end of almost every dance session, all the participants stand holding hands in a ring and sing "The Last Dance" from a film called *Meet Me on Cassiopeia* (1951).

> The very last dance before we go home,
> before the sun and a new day break forth.
> You are still close to me – the night is still ours,
> and the last waltz is delightful, before we go."

The elderly often suddenly sing along with this and other songs, even though in daily life they have lost the use of verbal language. It is not uncommon that some wheelchairs are left unused in the room when the dance is over – as who can remember sitting in one of those, when rhythms touch memories carried in bodies and minds? At the end of the season, everyone gathers for a ball. Such a ball was once portrayed in the news on a local TV channel. The journalist interviewed one of the participants, a 100-year-old woman with very serious dementia. "It was a fantastic ball," she said. "I will never forget it!"

The anecdotes of Ulla

The following anecdotes written by Ulla are presented as testimony of a caregiver as a base for an analysis of the value of Memory Dance.

Two ladies come haltingly to the dance. They do not have any desire to participate whatsoever. They demand pain medication, look very suffering – and will definitely not dance. However, when one of our gentlemen engages them – suddenly their pains have disappeared. They shake their hips like young girls – and reverse quickly when the session is over.

"Carl" has serious frontal temporal dementia. He has lost many words. He does not want help with personal hygiene. As a rule, Carl is dressed in several layers of clothing, gloves, knit hats, several jackets – regardless of the season. He is trying to protect himself – perhaps the last thing he has to lose. He seems very unkempt. But once a week, life is different for him. That's the day of the dance session. On that day, he cooperates. He consents to having a bath, getting shaved, putting on some aftershave, getting out some fine clothes and his dancing shoes. Then he appears as an attractive gentleman. When we dance, he is the man at the dance. He insists on being the one who engages a partner. He is transformed. His ex-wife usually comes on dance day to help with his personal care, but also to dance, too. He dances like a dream – and shows clear signs of this being his world.

Music and dance is all that "Philip" has left. It's very difficult for the staff to get him to take critically important medicine. Only a select few are allowed to come into his flat. When one of the nurses walked by the café, when we were dancing, she came in spontaneously, and danced – and she danced with Philip. The next morning when she knocked on his door, he opened as usual, but this time she was allowed to come into the flat without him being talked into it. He could recognize her from the dance.

"Frans" uses a wheelchair. He has had several strokes and is paralyzed on one side. For him, Memory Dance is the happiest hour in the week, as he himself says. He has undergone a big change: from being a recluse, interested only in his computer, he has become very interested in social contact, and is very positive after having participated in dance. He proudly tells about all the lovely girls who ask him to dance. "They didn't do that in my younger days," he says. When his legs are healed, he wants to learn to dance the salsa.

The power of the circle, the present moment, and the embrace

Attempting to understand the wonder of dance, and understanding why and how DMT and Memory Dance may be used with people with dementia, is a very complex undertaking. Here the circle and the holding hands play an important role. As the stories from Memory Dance and Ulla's anecdotes show, the contact created by holding hands, looking into one another's eyes, and singing together can create a sensory noticeable feeling of community. This is important, as individuals with dementia can often feel lost in the world of words. In the circle – also used in DMT – it is possible to be mirrored in a multidimensional way. The circle formation in both DMT and Memory Dance also may include synchronizing, echoing of emotional states, and touch through holding hands. Through these methods, people with dementia have the possibility of experiencing that they are "echoed by others" and therefore have a possibility to feel that they are seen, heard and accepted (Karampoula & Panhofer 2018, p. 30). The narrative of how the difficult relationship between Philip and the nurse opened up through dance shows that synchronizing, touch, and the "echo" in dance can also be meaningful for a later trusting professional relationship.

The story about Carl, who is often dressed in layers of clothing but dances like a dream and transforms himself into the man on the dance floor, also paints a picture of how dance can give a unique possibility for creating enriching present moments by awakening positive kinesthetic memories, including those of dance itself in social contexts. It gives Carl and his ex-wife the possibility to at once re-experience the embrace of dancing and sensual contact in a world that is and was his – and theirs. Carl's positive kinesthetic memories as a gentleman while dancing can bloom into what the dance, the music, and the sensual contact awaken to life. In Memory Dance, the stream of joyful life energy can bring the lived body in motion and be experienced, as Carl also says, the happiest hour in the week. The language of the body is our first, last and most important language (Winther, 2013). Memory Dance is about letting the dance bring forth whatever comes, and precisely because this form of dance is about eye contact, touch and embrace, it may awaken memories – not only about dancing in youth, but also about the meaning in childhood of noticing the joy of movement and the safe embrace of an adult. As Ulla's stories show, this applies to both individuals with dementia, their relatives, and the staff. Thus, they can dance together across the sea of forgetfulness and into the intense present moment, which simultaneously embraces both past, present and future.

In the fields of DMT guided by dance movement therapists, there is a possibility to go even deeper into resonance-creating therapeutic processes and thus open up for resources to face lived changes in both the group and the individual resident in a multidimensional way. Here there is also the possibility to embrace all of life's movements, kinesthetic memories, and feelings such as joy, sorrow, anxiety, anger and love.

Perhaps the practice both Memory Dance and Dance Movement Therapy within the field of dementia may even expand Daniel Stern's theory. As previously mentioned, he wrote that the "experience of the present moment can rewrite the past" (Stern, 2004, p. 2014). The stories from Ulla in this article might enhance the quote with this conclusion: "*and experiences of the past can rewrite the present moment.*"

Closure and future possibilities

Dementia is a complex global challenge affecting millions of people and their relatives around the world. Existential and holistic dance practices such as DMT and Memory Dance may have much potential as a physically, psychologically, emotionally, socially, culturally, and spiritually meaningful activity for many individuals living with dementia, as well as for their relatives. Therefore, it is also important that the caregiving staff or dance movement therapists are able to stay resonant, present and "in tune" with whatever comes – and this is not an easy task.

Indeed, dancing has no age limit, and even if time flies, forgetfulness arises, and life hurts, DMT has a possibility to embrace the existential processes of dementia through movement - and Memory Dance can create "the happiest hour of the week."

References

Baumgarten, L., & Winther H. (2023). Erindringsbevægelser for mennesker med demens [Memory movements for people living with dementia]. *TRØST: Nordic Journal*. I review.

Bergh, S., Engedal, K., Røen, I., & Selbæk, G. (2011). The course of neuropsychiatric symptoms in patients with dementia in Norwegian nursing homes. *International Psychogeriatrics/IPA, 23*, 1231–1239. doi:10.1017/S1041610211001177

Bonde, L. O., & Ridder, H. M. O. (2017). Erindringsdans og livets sange: Musik, sang og dans som oplevelse i demensomsorgen i Danmark [Memory Dance and the songs of life]. In: A. Jensen (Ed.), *Kultur og sundhedsfremme [Culture and Health promotion]* (pp. 191–214). Aarhus: Turbine forlaget.

Bräuninger, B. (2014). Dance movement therapy with the elderly: An international Internet-based survey undertaken with practitioners. *Body, Movement and Dance in Psychotherapy, 9*(3), 138.

Coaten, R., & Newman-Bluestein, D. (2013). Embodiment and dementia – Dance Movement Psychotherapists respond. *Dementia, 12*, 677–681. doi:10.1177/1471301213507033.

Coaten, R., & Williams, S. (2016). ' "Going far is returning": Dance Movement Psychotherapists find resilience and learning and call for more collaboration and dialogue. *Dance, Movement & Spiritualities, 3*(1–2), 161–75. doi:10.1386/dmas.3.1-2.161_1

de Witte, M., Orkibi, H., Zarate, R., Karkou, V., Sajnani, N., Malhotra, B., Ho, R. T. H., Kaimal, G., Baker, F. A., & Koch, S. C. (2021). From therapeutic factors to mechanisms of change in the creative arts therapies: A scoping review. *Frontiers in Psychology, 15*(12).

Hamill, M., Smith, L., & Rohricht, F. (2012). Dancing down memory lane: Circle dancing as a psychotherapeutic intervention in Dementia – A pilot study. *Dementia, 11*(6), 709–724.

Karampoula, E., & Panhofer, H. (2018). The circle in dance movement therapy: A literature review. *The Arts in Psychotherapy, 58*, S27–S32.

Karkou, V., & Meekums, B. (2017). Dance movement therapy for dementia. *Cochrane Database of Systematic Reviews, (2)*. Art. No.: CD011022.

Koch, S. C., & Harvey, S. (2012). Dance/movement therapy with traumatized dissociative patients. In S. C. Koch, T. Fuchs, M. Summa, & C. Müller (Eds.), *Body memory, metaphor and movement*. Amsterdam: John Benjamins Publishing Co.

Kowarzik, U. (2006). Opening doors: Dance movement therapy with people with dementia. In H. Payne (Ed.), *Dance movement therapy – theory, research and practice*. London: Routledge.

Levy, F. J. (1988). *Dance/movement therapy. A healing art. American Alliance for Health, Physical Education, Recreation and Dance*. Reston, VA: National Dance Association.

Merleau-Ponty, M. (1945/2006). *Phenomenology of perception*. London & New York: Routledge Classics (Original work published 1945).

Newman-Bluestein, D. (2021). Seeing with the heart: The aesthetics of dance/movement therapy with older adults and people with dementia. In H. Wengrover & S. Chaiklin (Ed.), *Dance and creativity within dance movement – International perspectives*. New York: Routledge.

Nyström, K., & Lauritzen, S. O. (2005). Expressive bodies: Demented persons' communication in a dance therapy context. *An Interdisciplinary Journal for the Social Study of Health, Illness and Medicine, 9*(3), 297–317.

Palo-Bengtsson, L., & Ekman, S.-L. (2002). Emotional response to social dancing and walks in persons with dementia. *American Journal of Alzheimer's Disease and Other Dementias, 17*(3).

Payne, H., Koch, S., & Tantia, J. (2017). *The Routledge international handbook of embodied perspectives in psychotherapy – approaches from dance movement and body psychotherapies*. London and New York: Taylor & Francis Ltd.

Rishøj, S., & Eckermann, A. (2015). Erindringsdans®- at snakke med kroppen [Memory Dance. To speak with the body]. *Demenskoordinatorer i Danmark, 19*, 9–12.

Sheets-Johnstone, M. (2012). Kinesthetic memory: Further critical reflections and constructive analyses. In S. C. Koch, T. Fuchs, M. Summa, & C. Müller (Eds.), *Body memory, metaphor and movement*. Amsterdam: John Benjamins Publishing Co.

Stern, D. (2004). *The present moment in psychotherapy and everyday life*. New York: W. W. Norton & Company.

Van Manen, M. (2014). *Phenomenology of practise. Meaning giving methods in phenomenological research and writing*. London and New York: Routledge.

Wengrover, H., & Chaiklin, S. (2021). *Dance and creativity within dance movement – International perspectives*. New York: Routledge.

Winther, H. (2013). Professionals are their bodies. The language of the body as sounding board in leadership and professional communication. In L. Melina, G. Burgess & L. Falkman (Eds.), *The embodiment of leadership: Building leadership bridges* (pp. 217–239). San Francisco, CA: Jossey Bass.

Winther, H. (2023). Danseterapi (DMT) – når livet er i bevægelse (Dance movement therapy (DMT) – When life is moving). In I. H. Winther, J. Toft, & S. Køppe (Eds.), *Kunst, Krop og Terapi [Art, embodiment and therapy]* (s. 51–82). Copenhagen: Hans Reitzels Forlag.

5.3

FEELING THE TOUCH

Integrating sensations into dance activities for the elderly with dementia

Szu-Ching Chang

Introduction

In recent years, with the rise of the elderly community in Taiwan, health-related physical fitness and health promotion activities have been emphasized to maintain physical health. However, except for traditional folk dance and square dance which are mostly practiced by middle-aged and older women in community parks, most of the physical activities designed for the elderly focus too much solely on training their physical fitness. While the major intention is to maintain muscular endurance to delay the process of aging, little attention is paid to the importance of mental expression for the elderly. Although some activities, such as aerobic dance, are practiced with music, the purpose of the fast tempo is still to increase exercise intensity and cardiorespiratory endurance. The importance of the mental aspects and the balance between the physical and the mental in the activities for the elderly are largely ignored.

Dance, as an elderly- and dementia-friendly activity, as well as a pleasant intervention, has been developed widely in Europe and the United States. Dance-related senior programs, such as the Royal Academy of Dance's Silver Swans Ballet classes in the UK, dance in expressive arts programs for the elderly, and Creative Dance for seniors, all intend to introduce dance, in a form that combines physical movements and expressive arts to the elderly, maintaining both mental and physical wellness. Similar programs and considerations for the elderly are in the initial stages in Taiwan, such as the National Theater and Concert Hall's "Performing Arts Project for Older Adults" and Cloud Gate Dance School's "Life Rhythm for Seniors." In addition to learning from the experiences of other countries, the planners are constantly adjusting and improving the contents and pedagogies of the courses for the elderly, from the perspectives of local culture and lifestyles.

DOI: 10.4324/9781003307624-33

Very few educational implementations and studies have focused on sensational awareness and practices for seniors, and those with dementia, especially on the theme of touch. Compared with the visual, such as the attention to colorful photos, and the aural, such as the accompaniment of music, both of which attract a large amount of interest, the tactile inspires less attention. Even though dance and physical activities involve the implementation of corporeal dynamics, the touching of the skin and its sensation has largely been ignored in discussions. Especially in the traditional culture of East Asia that considers the body as a locus of individual spirituality, touch is the least sensation that people here notice and practice in daily life and culture. Even though in Taiwan some dance mentors noticed that a welcoming hug between the teachers and the elderly members could break the distance both physically and mentally at the beginning of the class,[1] there is still minimal focus placed on the importance of touch itself as a major element to be integrated into activities for the elderly and those with dementia.

This chapter discusses an initial project[2] in which I advised dance-major students to design dance activities for the elderly and those with dementia. This project is intended to improve the contents and the pedagogy of this dance class by introducing the theme of touching and emphasizes the aspects of experiencing and practicing in sensation awareness. The purpose of this chapter is to analyze and discuss the designed contents of the class, named "Uncovering Your Veil." The target participants are the elderly and dementia people with mild to moderate impairment. Therefore, most of the dance movements involved are practiced while sitting and while standing without locomotion. A silk scarf is used in this class for building the interactive relationship and connection between human beings and the prop. For participants, it is the medium to increase the sensation of touching and also to express emotions and feelings.

The initial application of this project is to teach six mild to moderate dementia participants in a daycare center. The age range of these participants is approximately 50–70 years and all the members have been diagnosed with early-onset dementia. The teachers are two fourth-year dance-major students under my pretraining and advice; Cindy Tsai was the major teacher and Chia-Chi Chen was the assistant teacher for this class. This class "Uncovering Your Veil" was a 60-minute class taught on the morning of December 21, 2021. Before the implementation of this class, the two teachers had visited the daycare center twice a week regularly and spent at least one hour before the teaching accompanying members in their daily activities, such as watering the plants, on each visit. After teaching the dance activities, the two teachers also accompanied the members to re-cover the tables and other jobs until the preparation for their lunch. In other words, the two teachers built up a relationship of familiarity with these dementia participants when teaching this class.

From the perspectives of "Space" and "Shape" in Laban Movement Analysis (LMA), this chapter will analyze the movement elements incorporated and arranged in this dance lesson. I will also discuss the participants' reactions and movements in the process. By investigating both the lesson plan and the participants' movements,

I will discuss, for future reference, the possible improvement in designing dance activities that integrate the theme of touch.

This chapter discusses the sensational stimulation and feelings of dance as a form of performing arts that requires largely bodily involvement, which can be introduced into the lives of the elderly and those with dementia. With imagination and creativity in the extraordinary context of dancing, we can enjoy our body movements, playful props, and interaction with others by which we experience and practice the sensation of touch from both our inner-self and outer-expression aspects. All these could bring mental and physical wellness to the elderly and those with dementia. Although the course described in this research is still in the initial stage, without quantitative materials to support the results of the participants, the mental and physical delegations from the participants in their dance practices created valuable feedback for this initial exploration.

Sensation and expression: touching without physical touch under COVID-19

Aging and touch

With aging, the acuity of all the body's senses decreases. This decline of sensory perception not only causes the inconvenience to the elderly in their self-care and daily activities but also reduces or delays their response to surrounding environmental stimuli, which often makes them feel uneasy and depressed about aging. Among all the senses, tactile aging is less noticeable but has a huge impact on the lives of older adults. For example, the aging of fingertips, which provides sensory information for postural stability, may cause the uneasiness in control of movements. The elderly have to use higher force on the meeting ground between skin and the object in order to "overcome the age-related loss in tactile sensation" (Wickremaratchi & Llewelyn, 2006, p. 303).

In addition to the effects on body movement and weight balance, the importance of touch systems on the dimensions of social engagement, emotions, and expressions – ignored in the past – has recently been explored. While the ability of recognition on touching declines, the need and the awareness of gentle touch from loved ones increases and it is more important to a quality of life for the elderly. As Sarah McIntyre et al. (2021) suggests, "the pleasantness of being touched has been founded to increase with age above 60 years in sharp contrast to the decrease in perceived intensity of touch, and the decline in discriminative tactile functions" (p. 56). With aging, the sensibility on affective touching or being touched is enhanced, so the psychological needs of the elderly for a friendly touch are actually higher. Moreover, "interpersonal touch is also crucial for strengthening bonds and communicating emotions" (McIntyre et al., 2021, p. 53). Friendly touch can make the elderly feel more valuable and confident, and also improve the responsiveness of interpersonal interactions. Therefore, although the function of the tactile system declines with aging, the elderly need more opportunities to practice and experience pleasant touching, and being touched with affective support, to maintain their physical and mental health.

Dance for the elderly

Dance and other expressive arts activities are beneficial to balance the elderly's emotions and maintain their social well-being. Integrating arts-based, human-interactive activities increases social engagement and reduces memory loss in older adults. Among all kinds of dances, community dance is widely applied to older adults. These community dance activities often rearrange simple preset steps for the physical and mental conditions of the elderly. This "gets people moving who may not normally dance" (Amans, 2017, p. 44) and allows them to dance together in a short period of time.

In addition to community dance, dance in the expressive arts uses free dancing to allow all seniors to participate together and use their own bodies to create and to share their feelings and thoughts with each other. Dance, as participatory arts, offers the opportunity and the medium for the elderly to have good communications and interactions with others, both socially and emotionally. Moreover, dance is an eyes-opened and mind-opened artistic practice that involves being curious about others, imagining possibilities, and offering expression and responses kindly. In this kind of dancing activity, "participants get the chance to engage with each other's expressions, experiences, and ideas" (Andersson & Almqvist, 2020, p. 268) and, therefore, as "democracy among people 65+" (Andersson & Almqvist, 2020). From this perspective, providing opportunities for the elderly to participate in dance activities embodies the ideal of inclusive arts.

There have been a few discussions about how dance instructors transform their dance professional knowledge into elder-friendly class content, pedagogical skills, or practical implementations. Kai Lehikoinen (2019) discusses how the dance profession can form a holistic approach to contributing to social change in this context. He suggests for a "mindful attention in encountering the other" (p. 6) and argues it is "a knowledge of how to be present in the moment and have one's senses open to different forms of information-auditory, visual, kinesthetic, affective-as one interacts with the other" (p. 6). In other words, dance teachers should be able to appreciate the diversity of each elderly participant and to maintain a flexible attitude and guided teaching methods. By the implementation of dance knowledge and "mindful attention," the dance artists or dance instructors could help the elderly to build up social relationships with peers and encourage them to enjoy their dancing with others.

Touch, dance and the elderly

Touch, both physical and imaged, is an essential vehicle to express and to connect in dancing. By experiencing the ways of touching and being touched, dancers acquire information and organize their responses quickly for self-reference or to interact with others (Brandstetter et al., 2013). Dancers are able to precisely move and perform movements in space by the means of touch and, accordingly, kinesthetics, without totally relying on visual reference. When it comes to expressing and interpreting emotions, dancers often look inward to explore how they perceive their inner selves. As a result, "touch – the sense that connects 'sensing' and the emotional 'feeling'/being affected – is closely related to processes of kinesthetic perception and empathy" (Brandstetter et al., 2013, p. 7).

The essence of touch is responsiveness, which forms a set of active call-and-response relationships. The moment of the touching and being touched while dancing with others is full of possibilities and multiple combinations that carries the interactions forward. In this process, touching and being touched are not only sensual perceptions but emotional communication and feedback. In additional to physical touch, "non-touching and touching before the actual (tactile) touch" (Brandstetter et al., 2013, p. 9) also contribute to the responsivity in the interactions of dancing. These touch-related perceptions initiate and trigger interpersonal sensitivity, and therefore, motivate the physical and spiritual energies flowing between the dancer and the others.

From the perspective of dance for the elderly, the inevitable tactile practice in dance allows older adults to engage with their inner emotions inwardly and interact outwardly with others at the same time. Moreover, this process may offer the opportunity for the elderly to gradually change their self-image and self-evaluation from the responses of others. As Tuure Tammi and Riikka Hohti (2020) argued,

> Touch also necessarily affects and changes those involved in touching . . . . Touch is thus directed toward bodies and worlds yet to come, and its improvisational and responsive nature entails that the futures present in touch are never fully settled.
>
> *(p. 16)*

As discussed previously, touching and being touched contribute to a dynamic process of understanding in which participants carefully explore the possibility and adjust themselves according to the feedback from the partners and from the environment. For the elderly who participate in dance, they could enjoy the valuable encounters in the process of touching and being touched, which expands their views toward themselves, others, and other beings in the world. With the opportunity of reflecting and creating in body movements, touching as well as dancing is "worlding" (Tammi & Hohti, 2020, p. 24) that renews the elderly's life.

The forbidden touch under COVID-19

Dance activities which were expected to emphasize tactile exercises encountered the impact of the epidemic COVID-19. Touching soon became a prohibited and demonized action. After deciding to use the silk scarf as the medium of touch, the participants' active touch, especially on their own bodies, becomes the choice in this situation. Active touch, also called "*tactile scanning*," produces "variations in skin stimulation . . . caused by variation in his motor activity" (Gibson, 1962, p. 490). Through active touch in different paths, the participant's hand like an eye scans the contact zone and generates various stimuli during this exploration. The stimuli felt by both touching and being touched are fed back to the participants' brains at the same time and are interwoven into the next moment's choices and feelings. In the self-touch of the participants, they have new discoveries and deeper feelings about the physical states and inner feelings of their own bodies.

Another kind of touch practice is also used for purpose of sensitization. By blocking the vision temporary, the participants are engaging in "blind movement" that can concentrate on feeling the movement (Brandstetter et al., 2013, p. 7). While most people's lives depend heavily on visual feedback, other senses are less likely to be perceived and applied. Covering the eyes briefly during self-touch allows the participants to carefully experience the tactile sensation from the skin. With previous discussions about the psychological needs of affective touch for the elderly, the gentle self-touch with concentration on their own bodies and minds provide the participants emotional feedback to comfort their loneliness and isolation during COVID-19 protocols.

The dance lesson designed for the elderly and those with dementia

Analysis of the quality and motion of the silk scarf

There were several major considerations for choosing the silk scarf as the medium to awaken the sense of touch in the dance activities for the elderly. First, the material of the silk scarf is light and delicate with light transmittance. Compared to a towel that is often used in daily life and physical fitness exercise, the silk scarf provides and strengthens the sensitive feeling in the touch between the material and skin. Also, the silk scarf has a flexible role as a well-used medium in both inner and outer explorations of sensations and space throughout the whole class. Finally, for older adults, the silk scarf is a well-acquainted item often used in Chinese traditional culture. Compared to the props from foreign countries that are often used in physical fitness activities, such as yoga balls, the silk scarf is widely used in folk dance and temple festivals. Its variety of dazzling and bright colors also enhances the attention and enjoyment of participants when dancing with it.

To discuss the possible variety of dynamic motions of the silk scarf, we analyze it from the aspect of Effort in LMA. The silk scarf is light in weight and either Direct or Indirect in Space. It is also either Quick or Sustained in Time. Its tendency to flow is free because it is difficult to fully control its movements.

From the previous analyses in Effort, we continuously discussed the possible ways to feel the touch of the silk scarf. Considering the perspective of Effort Action Drive, the possible combinations to feel touch are Glide (Light-Sustain-Direct), Flick (Light-Sudden-Indirect), and Float (Light-Sustain-Indirect).

Considering the participants' habits of body movements and the interaction with the prop, we decided to let the silk scarf Glide on the skin of different body parts as the major motion to awaken and experience the gentle sensation of touch. We also included the movement of "lightly rub" (Light-Sustain) to prepare the participants to be aware of the material of the silk scarf and to feel its detail.

Introduction of the lesson plan "Uncovering your Veil"

The content of this class adopted the title and the music of a Chinese folk song "Uncovering your Veil" and the meanings of the lyrics "uncovering your veil, so I can see your face." The target participants include sub-healthy seniors and those who are mildly disabled and mildly living with dementia, but could also be extended to seniors in general. For the safety of participants, most of the dance movements are practiced on a chair. The latter parts of this class encouraged the participants to dance while standing and include simple locomotion, such as one step to the right and one to the left. The content is described as follows. The instructions are written in the style of verbal prompts.

1   *Warming up*
    Massage with hands. After rubbing both hands together to warm them, gently massage and rub all body parts. Guide the participants to gently rub in the order from the face, neck, arms, torso, legs, etc. The process of this warm-up activity is about five minutes.

2   *Throwing the scarf to welcome the healing I: the sensation of touch*
    Following the warm-up, this activity focuses on the feeling of the inner self and the awareness of touch. First, with guidance on breathing, rub your veil gently to feel the soft texture of the veil. Then, let us spread the veil over our heads and pull it down gently to feel the veil brush across our faces lightly. Later, hold the veil with the right hand and slowly move up from the left foot, through the left calf, through the knee to the thigh, and then from the fingers, wrist, arm, to the shoulder, to the air above our heads. Let us repeat from the other side.

3   *Throwing the scarf to welcome the healing II: the interaction with space*
    Following the practices of touching, this activity focuses on the feeling of the Outer Space and the awareness of interaction with the air and with others. First, spread out the silk scarf and hold one corner with your right hand. Throw it into different directions in your personal space. Like setting off fireworks, throw the scarf straight up, right, left, and also diagonally. Then, with the throwing into space on our upper body, we incorporate the stepping of the lower body. With each throw in one direction, we then take two strong steps. Later, imagining the scarf is our pen and the space is our paper, let us draw patterns in the air, drawing one and then another circle on your right side and repeating it on the left side. Let us draw several "S" shapes in the air, then weave the scarf above our heads like saying "Hi."

4   *Dance with the folk song "Uncovering your Veil"*

Matching the meaning of the lyrics, the teacher uses the movements that have been practiced in the class and choreographed into a short repertoire. Leading the participants, all the movements are made while standing. The first part of the dance is weaving and throwing the silk scarf. The second half is a duet, dancing with a partner face to face. The two connect by holding each other's silk scarves in their hands and weaving them up and down together. The whole dance ends in interesting interactions with the partners.

The analyses of movement elements and teaching implementation

Warming up awakens the body

Gently rubbing the skin with the palm of both hands awakens the body's awareness of the stimulation of touching. Sparking touch as the tinder, the participants can feel their own body and body parts inwardly through their own skin, the largest receiver in the human body. From observations, under the introduction of gentle music and breathing, most participants were in a situation of inner awareness and maintained the status of Shape Flow. They sensed their own bodies and revealed the inner feeling of each of their body parts. They also inspected their hands, making a connection with their skin and body parts by which the sensations of the body started to materialize gradually.

Occasionally, there was a period when the participants departed from their inner sensations. It was when the participants looked at the teachers' movements and tried to imitate the routes of the hands moving on and touching their skin. Because of the intention of touching different body parts, the participants performed the hand functionally with the task of moving in particular ways. Therefore, the participants may show Arc-Like Directional in Shape and reveal the outer relationship between themselves and their bodies. However, the intention of designing this warming-up activity is to emphasize the inner touching and its following sense of connection with the self, without putting too much attention on the Outer Space.

Body	Effort	Shape	Space
Upper body Hand-Initiated	Light Indirect/Direct Sustain	Shape Flow/ Shortening and Hallowing Arc-like Directional Shape+ /Spoke-like Directional Shape	Sagittal Plane

FIGURE 5.3A   BODY, EFFORT, SHAPE, SPACE chart

Introducing healing with touch

Lightly rubbing the silk scarf with the hands, the tactile sensations are concentrated on the palms and fingers. Initiating the feeling of the texture of the scarf more intimately, we carefully sense the soft flowing material without a fixed shape and the feeling of it sliding over the skin of the hands. The action of covering the head with the silk scarf allows the whole head and face to feel the touch of the silk scarf, which brings fresh insight. When slowly pulling down the scarf and letting it slowly slide down the skin of the face, the dynamic motions of the scarf intensify the tactile perception of brushing across the face.

Covering the head with a silk scarf, similar to a hide-and-seek game, is a process from unseen to seen. This experience caused the participants to feel anticipation and interest. The instructor, Tsai, points out that, "It may be because that when the head is covered, the light is dark. Then it suddenly brightens when the scarf is pulled down, which makes the participants surprised" (Tsai, personal interview, 2022). As a result, the covering and uncovering of the face motivated the sensations of visual side-by-side when feeling the touch of the silk scarf.

The gliding of the silk scarf on different body parts enables realizing the different feelings of the skin on certain body parts. The sensations of touch differ from one body part to the other – and the practices of distinguishment are important.

However, in the actual teaching implementation, it was found that the participants with moderate to severe dementia encountered difficult challenges when they tried to control the routes of the silk scarf with one hand. As Tsai observed,

> The hand, without touching the skin directly, was supposed to hold the silk scarf and only the silk scarf touch and flick the body part. But those participants who cannot control the movements well had difficulty, so their silk [scarves] were completely suspended without touching the skin.
>
> *(Tsai, personal interview, 2022)*

Therefore, Tsai changed her instruction so that these participants could really touch their body parts with their hands, similar to the warm-up activity but with the silk scarf. The silk scarf is located between the hand and the body, and it becomes a towel-like wiping touch, which slightly increases the frictional force compared to the original flicking action. Thus, although the content of this part still maintained a more introverted Shape-Flow state, like in the warm-up activities, there were also some Direct and Indirect effects on the quality of their touch, from the perspective of Effort.

Regarding the aspect of Space, the Sagittal Plane was widely used when the silk scarf flicked the lower body, in the order of the feet to the calves and thighs to the waist, abdomen, chest, and other parts of the torso. The participants have to bend their upper body forward and then gradually strengthen upward. Besides the purpose of the successive glides through the adjacent body parts from the lower body to the upper body, which is to awaken the sensation of touching, it is also intended to increase the connectivity of these body parts, which is emphasized as an important connection for people to rebuild the sense of subjectivity in the theory of LMA.

Body	Effort	Shape	Space
Upper body Hand-Initiated Arms	Light Direct Quick	Spoke-like Directional Shape	Sagittal Plane/Vertical Plane Central spatial Pathway

FIGURE 5.3B   BODY, EFFORT, SHAPE, SPACE chart

Throwing out the scarf and feeling the surrounding air

The throwing of the silk scarf straight from the center of the body to its surroundings is a breakthrough in Space and a more positive outward energy. The force of the silk scarf's motions creates frictional contact between the hands as well as the arms and the space surrounding the body. The arm feels the resistance and pressure of the air and generates the strength to actively break through the resistance. Because of the variety of the participants' movement abilities and the texture of the silk scarf, the motions of throwing the scarf may show Light or Strong in Weight, from the perspective of Effort. Thus, the different levels of Weight, combined with Direct in Space and Quick in Time, contribute to the Effort Action Drive "Flick" and "Slash," both of which are qualities of movements that the elderly with dementia often use in their daily lives.

The operations and combinations of limbs and silk scarves in Space, including direction, routes, and levels, from spatial visual images, arouse the interest of the participants. The first part of throwing the silk scarf uses the Central-Spatial Pathway and the Spoke-like Directional Shape to allow the participants to practice within the safe range from the center of the body to near-reach distance. Later, through the extensive weaving of the silk scarf, the participants are encouraged to reach out to the Middle-Reach distance in Space. Due to the great differences in the physical state of the participants, it can be seen that those spatial paths offered opportunities for challenges and repeated practice. Tsai noticed that "Some participants have weak muscles on their arms. They only raised their hands and cannot throw the [scarves] out" (Tsai, personal interview, 2022). The instructor changed her pedagogy immediately so that the participants can adapt the High-Low level difference to achieve the action. For those participants who were unable to throw the scarf, the instructor encouraged them to wave it from a low level to a high level repeatedly. After mastering the feeling of throwing the scarf, they further use the bending and straightening of their elbows and wrists to gradually perform the pattern of throwing the silk scarf.

From the perspective of space, the Sagittal Plane (upper front, front, lower front) and the Vertical Plane (upper right, upper left, lower right, lower left) were selected because they are easier for those sitting on chairs with backrests to move. The outward directions of throwing, which move from the center of the body to the multiple directions in the Space with lively and rhythmic folk songs, correspond to the

Body	Effort	Shape		Space
Upper body Hand-Initiated	Light Indirect Sustain	Shape Flow/ Shortening and Hallowing Arc-like Directional Shape		N/A

FIGURE 5.3C   BODY, EFFORT, SHAPE, SPACE chart

projecting of their emotions from the inside outward, and therefore produce the enjoyment of expressing their inner feelings. However, just as the diagonal line is the last mature development of the human developmental model when aging, the direction of the diagonal crossing also tends to become difficult to achieve at first. "They experience more difficulty in executing this when they use the right hand to throw to the left, or vice versa." (Tsai, personal interview, 2022). As a result, the instructor encouraged them to spend more time practicing these diagonal movements.

Discussion and conclusion

Results from observations and analyses

The practices of touching for participants with dementia

According to observation and analysis, the perception of touch on the skin was aware of and perceived by the participants. Through the warm-up to the main activity, the awareness of touch is magnified and practiced multiple times. After being given time and certain movements to experience the sensation of touch, the participants seemed to have a new understanding and discovery of their own body and skin. However, among the practices of these different types of touch, it can be clearly seen that the participants have different reactions to active touch, passive touch, and being touched by others. The participants seemed to feel a little hesitant and doubtful when guided to intently experience their self-touching. It may be that because the participants need to focus on the inner feeling of their own initiative to touch themselves, they may feel relatively unfamiliar with the set of relationships that occur at the same time as touching and being touched. They are more surprised or amused by being touched accidently by someone else or someone else's scarf. In the context of dance and games, this feeling of being unexpectedly touched may bring more excitement and fun to the elderly, especially in situations when they are familiar with each other.

Other aspects of interactivity and connectedness were also observed in the process of practicing touch. The senses of adjacent parts of the participant's body seemed to be connected as the silk scarf was flicked across these parts, one by one. Participants often performed separate repetitive actions one by one in past physical activities, but in this activity, the touch track of the silk scarf made the entire movement a continuous action journey. The hand with the silk scarf not only visited carefully but also interacted with different body parts that altogether composed their own body. Similarly, participants waved their scarves into their personal space, allowing their bodies to engage in a contact improvisation with their surroundings. Body parts and the surrounding air both contributed to a dynamic motion that connects and interacts with each other at the same time. Because throwing the scarf requires traveling through personal space, the air exerts a weighty pressure on the skin of the hand to make the resistive contact between them more apparent and perceptible. This kind of touch requires both piercing and resistance, and the resulting interactivity makes the participants find the activity more engaging, fun, and fulfilling. Silk scarf played an important role as tactile mediators and visual assistive device in the practices of touch.

The dance pedagogy for guiding the practicing of touch

The way that the dance instructor incorporated dance professional knowledge into dance pedagogy is shown in detailed movement disassembly, sequential guidance, and repetitive movements. She performed good demonstrations and patiently allowed sufficient time to repeat movements that allowed the participants to understand the pattern without feeling frustrated. She also paid "mindful attention" to encourage the individuals and responded quickly with adjusting her teaching methods and the movements taught. Also, it is important that the major instructor, the assistant instructor, and social workers, as well as volunteers, all worked almost one-on-one with the participants with dementia interactively. Adequate and complete attention and concern are the main keys to working with people with dementia.

Last but not least, the established reliance and friendship between dance instructors and the participants is essential for guiding the activities on the practices of touching and being touched. Although in the pandemic situation, the dance instructor did not actually touch the participants with dementia, a large number of active self-touching and being touched guided by the silk scarf still requires the participants' trust and willingness to follow the actions. Therefore, in addition to compiling the teaching content with professional dance knowledge, establishing a reliant relationship in advance, understanding the physical and emotional conditions and characteristics of the elderly with dementia, responding flexibly and instantly during the activity are all keys to a successful dance pedagogy on the theme of touch.

Reflection and feedback

The introduction of breath and Shape Flow in the practice of touch

In the process of implementation, it was found that the instructor's guidance on breathing was relatively simple and short, and the participants in general were less able to enter a stage of gentle breathing applied with movements of touch by listening to the oral guidance. From the perspective of LMA, breath is the first stage and also the most important development for human beings, and it therefore is important to be aware of this and practice breathing in order to bring the body into a whole. The participants may concentrate more on their inner feelings and sense more details from the touching and being touched in deeper breathing. With careful breathing, they may also explore their feelings on the skin more and be aware of the subtle changes on every inch of skin while the scarf is moving. The incorporation of breath into the practices of touch could also bring Shape Flow of the body. When Shape Flow is integrated, this is the time for them to work deeply with their inner feeling to express through their bodies. In other words, Shape Flow could be the connection to bridge the inner feeling and outer expression and move their practices of touch forward, from physical touch to emotional touching and being touched.

The exploration of and discussion about the sense of touching

Due to the limited time of the course, the guidance and reminder on tactile perception are still not sufficient in this class plan. The time to practice touching can be extended and the movements designed can be more varied. Especially for different types of touch – such as active touch, being touched, and being touched by others – each of them can have different movements and exercises developed. The observations from the dance instructor Tsai shows that the participants with dementia have different reactions to and perceptions of different kinds of touch, which should be explored more. The further study of different types of touch and exploration in transforming them into dance activities require further development.

Suggestions for future development

From class to course: developing connectivity between inner and outer

The time and content of a single class are too short to properly guide the perception and exploration on the theme of touch. Such a brief lesson also has insufficient time and depth to bring out participants' attention to their inner and outer connections, which is an ultimate purpose of practicing touch in these dance activities.

Especially with activities designed for the elderly with dementia, it is often necessary to deconstruct and simplify the steps of practice and then give sufficient time to repeat the short dance sequences. From one class to at least three classes, the future design of the course on the theme of touch could focus on different kinds of tactile sensations; each should be guided to explore and practice separately, and appropriate dance activities or physical games should be developed from them. Further discussions and expressions should be integrated into activities to allow the participants to share their feelings and thoughts. These feedback sessions could be in other forms that these participants are good at, such as oral expressions, movement creation, drawing, or singing. Moreover, with the focus on the connectivity between the theme of Inner and of Outer through the practices of touching and being touched, the designed curriculum should focus and notice the sequence and coherence among these dance activities in articulating and arranging the orders. The step-by-step explorations of touch may gradually touch the inner emotions of the participants, and the accumulated sense of trust in this process may also enhance their willingness to share with others.

Improvement of teaching strategies and guidance

Because the teaching experience and methods of the student-teachers who implemented the course are still relatively unskilled and immature, there is still a lack of teaching strategies for establishing interactive relationships in the guidance process, even though the participants were already familiar with them. For the elderly with dementia, gradually deteriorating memory often makes them feel uneasy and unable to cope with changes in their surroundings. Therefore, interpersonal interactions and relationship building applied in dance activities are the important teaching methods to erase their anxiety and enhance their willingness to respond, which should be pretrained and practiced in advance by the dance instructors.

Just as touch is the most indispensable interaction between dancers and themselves and among dancers, the dance instructors should be able to make the participants feel moving and moved during the dance teaching process on the theme of touch. Dance instructors should sincerely teach and pay attention to the diversity of each participant, just as the movers need to carefully feel the various information of every inch of skin in the process of touching and being touched. When professional dance artists transform dance knowledge into a dance course for the elderly with dementia, in the practicing of the physical and mental touching and being touched, we are feeling, experiencing, and bringing in "the world" altogether.

Notes

1 In a lecture, Yunyu Wang and Ruyuan Tseng once shared that they led students to offer elderly peoples' dance activity in the nursing center of Guandu Hospital. They would start the warm-up activity by physically hugging their participants.
2 This study was developed from the researcher assisting the University Social Responsibility (USR) project in dance department in 2020–2021. This project, titled "Accompanying

Love and Art: Dancing the Vitality of the Weak and Bringing Up the Care for Dementia," hosted by Chan Chia-Hui and co-hosted by Szu-Ching Chang, is to provide dance for the underprivileged groups and the elderly with dementia. I led the students to participate in the observation of the demented elderly group, to enter the day care as the site, and to develop relevant teaching materials as a brief result of this project. This project is meant to test the diverse possibilities of dance as a physical and mental health activity for the elderly.

References

Amans, D. (2017). Community dance – What's that? In D. Amans (Ed.), *An introduction to community dance practice* (2nd ed., pp. 3–10). London: Palgrave.

Andersson, N., & Almqvist, C. F. (2020). Dance as democracy among people 65+. *Research in Dance Education, 21*(3), 262–279. doi:10.1080/14647893.2020.1766007

Brandstetter, G., Egert, G., & Zubarik, S. (2013). Introduction: Motion, emotion and modes of contact, In G. Brandstetter, G. Egert, & S. Zubarik (Eds.), *Touching and being touched: Kinesthesia and empathy in dance and movement* (pp. 3–10). Berlin; Boston, MA: De Gruyter. doi:10.1515/9783110292046

Gibson, J. J. (1962). Observations on active touch. *Psychological Review, 69*(6), 477–491. doi:10.1037/h0046962

Lehikoinen, K. (2019). Dance in elderly care. *Journal of Dance Education, 19*(3), 108–116. doi :10.1080/15290824.2018.1453612

McIntyre, S., Nagi, S. S., McGlone, F., & Olausson, H. (2021). The effects of ageing on tactile function in humans. *Neuroscience, 464*, 53–58. doi:10.1016/j.neuroscience.2021.02.015

Tammi, T., & Hohti, R. (2020). Touching is worlding: From caring hands to world-making dances in multispecies childhoods. *Journal of Childhood Studies, 45*(2), 14–26. doi:10.18357/jcs452202019736

Wickremaratchi, M. M., & Llewelyn, J. G. (2006). Effects of ageing on touch. *Postgraduate Medical Journal, 82*(967), 301–304. https://doi.org/10.1136/pgmj.2005.039651.

5.4

EVERYDAY WALTZES FOR ACTIVE AGEING

A creative intervention for seniors and training programme for eldercare staff

Angela Liong

Dancing the everyday

Everyday Waltzes for Active Ageing® (*Everyday Waltzes* for short) is a senior wellness programme conceived and initiated in 2009 by choreographer Angela Liong. The senior wellness programme is supported and delivered by professional dance group THE ARTS FISSION COMPANY ('ARTS FISSION' Singapore) under the direction of Angela, who is also the artistic director of the company.

What distinguishes the approach of *Everyday Waltzes* from clinical dance therapy or physiotherapy is the creative impetus of the programme delivery. As the programme is conceived and developed by a dance artist, the technical curriculum takes on the perspective of dynamic movement designed to empower kinaesthetic imagination.

The programme helps seniors to reimagine the everyday and enable them to connect to people and places around them. This is especially important for infirm elderly in assisted living often under highly regimental and organised systems in senior care facilities. The curriculum turns everyday mundane routines into fun little dance expressions. For example, the simple act of peeling a mandarin orange is not just a drill of fine motor skills of the hands. The action of peeling the orange rind also conjures up kinetic memory of serving guests the citrusy fruit as part of traditional customs in celebrating Chinese New Year.

The *Everyday Waltzes* programme aims to stimulate the cognitive and physical capabilities of the senior participants. The curriculum motivates the seniors to rediscover the spontaneous moments and simple joy in daily life. Seating in a circle, the senior participants perform the interactive creative dances to specially composed scores with lively music tempos. The objective is to improve the seniors' mood and reinforce their sense of wellbeing in group activities.

DOI: 10.4324/9781003307624-34

Target senior beneficiaries

The wellness programme has since diversified specific curriculum to adapt to the needs of ambulant as well as frail seniors. A facilitation guide is also developed to enable eldercare staff to learn and deliver the *Everyday Waltzes* curriculum at their respective senior facilities.

Since its inception, the *Everyday Waltzes* programme has been actively involved with the community through partnerships with healthcare professionals and social service organisations and hospitals. Some of the early research works have involved collaborations with neuroscientists from the hospitals. For example, pilot research work was conducted with neurologists from the Singapore General Hospital and the Changi General Hospital on applying creative movement as intervention for people with early dementia condition back in 2011 and 2012.

Facilitating training for care staff

In 2014, ARTS FISSION was commissioned by the Agency for Integrated Care (AIC) to develop a viable facilitating and training programme for eldercare staff to engage frail elderly with meaningful activities. A printed facilitation guide and learning kit were produced for the care staff to undergo intensive workshops conducted by ARTS FISSION. To date, the *Everyday Waltzes* training programme continues to provide four regular runs throughout the year in partnership with AIC.

FIGURE 5.4A *Everyday Waltzes for Active Ageing®*, THE ARTS FISSION COMPANY, Singapore

Source: Photograph by THE ARTS FISSION COMPANY

More recently in 2020, ARTS FISSION received a movement research commission by Yishun Health – a network of medical institutions and health facilities under the National Healthcare Group located in the north zone of Singapore. The objective comprises the outcome of designing a series of exercises and creative dances to enable seniors to improve balance and prevent fall mishaps in their daily activities.

But the commission specified the condition of making the prevention of fall curriculum a grassroots (community)-run project. It includes selected community members to be trained by the professional dance facilitators of ARTS FISSION. They are to form a core group of community dance leaders and to deliver the curriculum to other community members. The idea is to disseminate and expand the prevention of fall curriculum in the north zone communities through peer mentorships and community training.

Artistry beyond intervention: intergenerational performances

As the creative brainchild of the dance artists, one of the facets of the *Everyday Waltzes* programme is realised through theatre productions presented as intergenerational performance with support from professional dancers and musicians and even a full orchestra. Since 2013, bi-annual intergenerational productions spearheaded by ARTS FISSION in collaboration with maestro Lim Yau and The Philharmonic Orchestra have make their public presentations.

FIGURE 5.4B   *The Rite of Spring: A People's Stravinsky*, THE ARTS FISSION COMPANY, Singapore

Source: Photograph by THE ARTS FISSION COMPANY

The gathering of intergenerational performers becomes the hallmark of these large-scale dance and music productions. Elderly participants from different senior activity centres and care homes spread across the island of Singapore have the opportunity to come together with dance students from tertiary training institutions. They rehearsed intensively for a dance-theatre performance under the artistic direction of ARTS FISSION. A truly community-based creation is thus manifested.

The intergenerational productions yielded moving performances in 2013 with seniors playing the Elders presiding over the sacrificial ritual in the form of child-marriage in *The Rite of Spring – a People's Stravinsky*; in 2015 with former retired seafarers and traders who played themselves in *The Mazu Chronicle*, a homage to the Chinese sea goddess and protector; and in 2018 when seniors performed as nature's guardians in the production, garden•uprooted. All these productions were staged either at the grand Esplanade Theatre or the Concert Hall in the form of a ticketed public performance.

Artists of care

Throughout the rehearsal process of these intergenerational productions, the camaraderie and friendship bonded between young and old often continued even after the production is over. For the professional dancers of ARTS FISSION, the *Everyday Waltzes* has empowered them through a mutually beneficiary relationship with their senior charges.

In their regular process of working with the seniors, the company dancers not only help to light up the days of the seniors, but the seniors also in turn enrich the professional dancers' practice. This synergy between the elderly and the dancers lends validation and augments the dimension of professional dance practice. Their creative craft has the capacity to illuminate the act of care and lift the human spirit with what they do best. They can call themselves 'Artists of Care'.

5.5

WINGSPAN

A seated dance performance

Paige Gordon

Dance can be a key to many physical health benefits. This may include increased physical confidence, balance, improved body awareness, bone strength and being a highly social physical activity, it has the potential to increase body awareness, wellbeing and movement control through the use of cueing, cognitive strategies, creativity and music (Aguiar et al., 2016).

Seated dance based on the Dance for Parkinson's Disease (DPD. RSS, 2001) methodology has been a source of joy for many participants across the world. This genre of dance – seated dance – is also a source of inspiration for choreographic expression.

Lifespan Dance seated dance classes are endorsed by Dance for Parkinson's Australia. The classes are taught by qualified dance artists who have completed the DP Training and have empathy and communication skills. The classes utilise the framework of the DPD methodology to suit a variety of people who are affected by limited mobility factors. The classes at times can be made up of people living with Parkinson's, multiple sclerosis, chronic pain and other conditions that affect confidence in mobility (hip replacements, weakened knees, arthritis, post-cancer treatments, etc.). And once they begin to attend the Lifespan classes, the participants are referred to and considered as 'dancers'.

Seated dance classes have a clear structure. The classes begin 'seated' on chairs and work on alignment, warming up the torso, moving the spine then gently opening the front of the body, the shoulders, articulating the arms and feet through choreographed sequences. The class progresses to standing options for those who wish/can, using the chair for balance for plié exercises, stretches and locomotion sequences. The movement sequences are choreographed to music, utilising rhythm, timing, accent and other qualities of movement which together become dance. There is comprehensive use of dance language throughout the class,

DOI: 10.4324/9781003307624-35

including references to kinesiology, movement dynamics, imagery and history of dance. There is an immediate shift in purpose and curiosity when the class begins and as the dancers learn and become more aware of their bodies, their form and their capabilities. The dancers begin to enjoy moving in different ways with different movement qualities engaging with dance language, much like professional dance artists grow and evolve in their own techniques and language. Choreographic devices such as repetition, embellishment and retrograde are part of the classes over time.

A part of engaging with any dance genre is extending the dance experience from a 'technique' class to a performative mode. This can be done through opportunities to share the dance, which may be for each other or in a studio-sharing, theatre or public performance. In considering making a work for the seated dancers to perform, ruminations are necessary about the length of the performance and its topic, choreographic content, inclusiveness and essential connection to community and place.

The *WINGSPAN* project

WINGSPAN was a 'seated dance' performance event which premiered at the Mandurah Arts Festival 2021. Inspired by the shore and water birds of the Peel-Harvey Estuary, the original movement choreographed was created alongside an original score composed by Claire Pannell. *WINGSPAN* was performed in the outdoor, public space of the Mandjar Square, Mandurah, which is adjacent to the Peel-Harvey estuary – an internationally recognised Australian sanctuary for estuarine migratory birds in south-western Australia (Admin, 2020, May 29). There are over 100 different species of native and migratory birds that nest, breed and feed in this estuarine environment. Pannell was able to record bird sounds from the area, including seagulls, terns, pelicans and magpies, as well as the sounds of the waves, wind and water to use in the score. The recordings of local bird sounds became layered with real life bird calls at the beginning and end of the score, connecting to place and embedding the performance into its environment. The movement connected to imagery of birdlife through moments of flying, soaring like pelicans in the updrafts – birds on the wing, together.

> I love the choreography. I like that it bookends and we return to the beginning. I like the familiar feeling this creates. There are sections in the middle that are quite striking – the framing of the face with the wings. It reminds me of borrowed views through a window. The sharp movements with the hands surprised me and were very beautiful.
>
> *(Karin, WINGSPAN participant)*

FIGURE 5.5 *WINGSPAN* project performers

Source: Photograph by Michael Bond

WINGSPAN provided a platform for the community to perform in a cohesive and connected dance. The performers in the project were regular participants in weekly Lifespan seated dance classes, as well as interested community dancers and professional dance artists. *WINGSPAN* provided an opportunity for dancers in our community to build on their skills in classes, engage in a creative process – rehearsing, performing and connecting to each other and to place, visibly. Connecting to each other through the shared movement and performance experience. Extending our own individual 'wingspans' together.

Given the pandemic and ensuing lockdowns and restrictions, the process of coming together into a dance studio was not feasible. Communicating the concept and creating the movement required consideration and innovation. The *WING-SPAN* creative process had to engage with and utilise online technology to facilitate the easy uptake of the 'choreography', so the participants could learn the movement in a COVID-19–safe environment. An 'instructional film' was made, in order to communicate the concept and choreography. In order for the choreography to be filmed, it first had to be created together collaboratively with the composer and the score. The instructional video introduces the creative team, the concept and the score, and then unfolds the movement in easy-to-learn sections. Details of the movement, counts, sections, and the names of each section are unpacked. The final section is a 'full run' of the choreography with two dancer-guides in place.

Once a participant registered to be part of the performance, they were sent the Vimeo link. The participants were able to access the choreography in their own space at their own time, as many times as they wanted. Family members, support workers and carers who would support class participants were invited to be involved in the process of learning the movement. This engagement and investment of time learning the movement began the shared responsibility of understanding and becoming familiar with the movement.

The engagement of the performers to learn the choreography was phenomenal. It was liberating. This was not an in-studio collaborative dance-making process and yet the endpoint of all the performers learning and understanding the movement and being willing to perform the work was achieved and surpassed.

> the process to be able to take part was so easy, so accessible, and yet the quality and integrity of the work was also incredible.
> *(Serina, WINGSPAN Performer)*

After five weeks of at-home learning, the in-studio community rehearsal was scheduled. This allowed the performing group to come together in-person and meet the Creative team and work through the choreography together, in place and with the dancer-guides. The dancer-guides were professional dance artists placed in the centre of the circle, who become reference points of movement and timing, in the case that a performer forgot the movement or needed movement prompt assistance within the performance.

> What a triumph. The true epitome of community performance.
> *(Mark Le Brow, community engagement coordinator,*
> *Mandurah Performing Arts Centre)*

The premier of *WINGSPAN* performance featured a stunning debut performance by 95-year-old Ann Cornish. Ann was magnificent and a valued part of the performance ensemble. Assisted by her daughter, Liz Cornish, a professional dance artist and *WINGSPAN* dancer-guide, Ann was able to access this inclusive dance opportunity and was able to engage with the creative process and perform in the most spectacular way.

> I watched a frail 95-year-old transform into an exuberant and delicate mover. I was constantly surprised by the difficulty of the moves she was capable of embodying. She picked up on the nuances in the choreography, the changing dynamics and quality of the movement vocabulary. She began to glow from within as her latent performer emerged, and she realised she could achieve the movements. It was fantastic to be able to perform with my mum and witness the transformative power of dance.
> *(Liz Cornish, daughter of Ann, dance artist and WINGSPAN dancer-guide)*

Ann's success in the performance was celebrated by the cast and more widely by the audience. By becoming involved in this dance performance, Ann instantly dispelled myths about ageing commenting: "I felt young, younger than springtime".

Scenically, the concept was assisted by designer Noel Howell, who created 'feather-wear' for each of the performers to wear (their own choice of) black or white clothing as "a reminder of the soft moments in life, like a feather dancing in the wind. It's important to catch those moments and hold space for them". The feather-wear was an estuarine green with a small play of feathers attached, which moved in the wind. The feather-wear united the ensemble, connecting us to each other and connecting us to the environment and thematically.

The *WINGSPAN* Seated Dance Performance project was a visible celebration of seated dance and its physical and social benefits. The recognition of locality and significance connected place and community, extending the impact of dance that little bit further.

Note

A new iteration, *WINGSPAN II*, was performed in 2022.

References

Admin, H. E. (2020, May 29). Peel-Harvey estuary. *Healthy Estuaries*. Retrieved June 30, 2022, from https://estuaries.dwer.wa.gov.au/estuary/peel-harvey-estuary/

Aguiar, L. P., da Rocha, P. A., & Morris, M. (2016). Therapeutic dancing for Parkinson's disease. *International Journal of Gerontology*, *10*(2), 64–70. Retrieved from https://doi.org/10.1016/j.ijge.2016.02.002

Dance for PD. RSS. (2001). Retrieved June 30, 2022, from www.danceforparkinsons.com/

INDEX